PRAISE FO
BEHIND CLOSED DOORS

"Teenagers today face a minefield of challenges to traverse—Dr. Peck isn't afraid to tackle them. She pulls from decades of experience and research to offer valuable tips and reflections for parents on even the most sensitive and unfamiliar topics. Dr. Peck restores hope that, by God's grace, parents can raise resilient teenagers who are equipped to navigate the world we live in."

Linda A. Livingstone Ph.D., Baylor University President

"This book is a gift for learning how to live with and love your children and yourself. The secrets behind closed doors are illuminated and revealed as case studies show actual work and healing can occur in a family system. Listening, music, prayer, faith, and legacy letters are tools of regeneration for the teens and family. This book is a lifeline to those who may not even know they are drowning."

Beverly Malone PhD, RN, FAAN, President
and CEO, National League for Nursing

"*Behind Closed Doors* is a must read for everyone preparing for or currently navigating parenting teenagers. Jessica brings the knowledge and experience of a Pediatric Nurse Practitioner and the heart of a parent to real issues every 21st century family faces. As both a parent and a pastor, I recommend this book to you highly."

Brian Haynes, Lead Pastor, Bay Area
Church and Christian School

"Dr. Peck's gracious authenticity and her medical credentials come through in every letter, every word, every topic, every practical suggestion, and every role play opportunity provided in this very practical book. As one who has served broken-hearted parents as well as young people who doubted that any adult was on their side, I see the potential of this book to prevent mistakes with vulnerable, yet courageous parenting. Each one of my adult children will receive this in their Christmas stocking as well as many other friends and family I love who are in the throes of raising their children. It is essential and well-timed for a generation growing up in an era so very different from the one even very young parents experienced as adolescents."

Kerri Taylor, Executive Director, Unbound Now Houston

"With the rising numbers of mental health struggles among kids and teens, *Behind Closed Doors* equips parents to understand their child's culture and gives them words to begin significant conversations along with providing encouragement and hope. As a professional counselor of twenty-five years and previous school counselor, I'm excited to recommend this faith-based resource to clients at our counseling center."

Michelle Nietert, M.A., LPC-S, Author of *Loved and Cherished* and *Make Up Your Mind*, Host of the *Raising Mentally Healthy Kids* podcast

"Jessica's heart for teens shines through in her gentle, direct approach. *Behind Closed Doors* offers the necessary language, steps, and understanding to the challenges teens face every day and how we as adults can provide guidance and support that will lead to a healthier lifestyle—mentally, physically, and relationally."

Torrie Sorgie, Motivational Speaker, Writer

"*Behind Closed Doors* is a priceless guide. Dr. Peck illuminates the critical challenges youth today are facing and provides a comprehensive how-to-guide for meeting our children where they are on topics ranging from pornography to social justice. This book is an investment you will not regret, and its impact will echo.

Michelle Scotton Franklin, PhD, APRN, Assistant Professor, Duke University School of Medicine

BEHIND
Closed
DOORS

BEHIND
Closed
DOORS

A GUIDE TO HELP PARENTS
AND TEENS NAVIGATE THROUGH
LIFE'S TOUGHEST ISSUES

Jessica L. Peck
DNP, APRN

W PUBLISHING GROUP

AN IMPRINT OF THOMAS NELSON

Published in Nashville, Tennessee, by W Publishing, an imprint of Thomas Nelson.

Thomas Nelson titles may be purchased in bulk for educational, business, fundraising, or sales promotional use. For information, please email SpecialMarkets@ThomasNelson.com.

ISBN 978-0-7852-9200-5 (audiobook)
ISBN 978-0-7852-9199-2 (eBook)
ISBN 978-0-7852-9198-5 (TP)

Library of Congress Cataloging-in-Publication Data

Library of Congress Control Number: 2022932758

Printed in the United States of America

22 23 24 25 26 LSC 10 9 8 7 6 5 4 3 2 1

With great admiration, appreciation, and affection I dedicate this book to my four children. They embrace our family mantra of "to whom much is given, much is required." They are an integral supportive force in this book journey. They make hospital rounds with me on Christmas Eve. They wait in hospitals and clinics for me to finish seeing patients with my pleading "five more minutes." Every summer when I was a camp nurse, they brought me lonely or hurting kids, saying confidently, "My mom will help you." They wait patiently and quietly through hundreds of hours of phone calls and meetings—at home, in the car, at the ballpark. They are examined by countless students as pretend patients for practice. They let students give them shots. They travel with me, joining me for dinner to share their adventures of the day. They are a practice audience for speeches. They see the recording sign in my office and tiptoe around like church mice until given the all clear. They hear more lectures on pediatric health than any kid should ever endure. They sit through painfully boring ceremonies. They edit the stories I write. They educate me on the latest teen trends. They serve as photographers and social media managers. They clap and cheer when I speak at their school or in our community. They accept my talking about embarrassing subjects in public forums and even thank me for having the courage to do it. Because of my work, they know the world is a scary place. But they also know there is hope and light in the world and how to share it. They know God's mercies are new every morning. They are the inspiration behind everything I have done or will ever do. You are loved beyond measure and have filled my heart with greater joy.

To my dearest husband, most faithful companion, most dedicated supporter, most fervent champion, and most cherished friend, thank you for bearing all things, believing all things, hoping all things, and enduring all things. You are a treasure. May our family's journey reflect the love, healing, restoration, and freedom found in the love of God.

CONTENTS

CONTENTS

INTRODUCTION

*How to Unlock the Door to a New
Relationship with Your Teen*

I was in the driver's seat of my car having a recurrent and heated argument with my then thirteen-year-old daughter who was in the back seat . . . when it happened.

Something heavy whooshed past my shoulder, centimeters from my face. To my utter amazement, in anger, she had thrown the book she was reading right at my face while I was driving! My mind raced a million miles an hour in shock as I frantically pulled over.

What in the world?!

Surely my adored and angelic daughter did not just hurl a book at my head!

How could more than a decade of painstaking parenting effort with my expertise as a pediatric nurse practitioner arrive at this rude awakening?

Days before, she had left a handwritten manifesto on my pillow, outlining my many shortcomings in painstaking detail. I didn't give her enough freedom to choose her clothes or friends. I was strict, mean, and uncaring. I didn't trust her. I embarrassed her. But most of all, I didn't understand the challenges she was facing in "modern times" as I was raised in "literally the previous century" she said.

My thoughts returned to the present as I tearfully put the car in Park.

Am I a fraud? A failure?

Am I crossing over into the much-discussed miserable abyss of parenting a teen?

Will I pass on generational trauma and lose my carefully cultivated relationship with my daughter, which was my single greatest fear?

I pulled over. I took deep breaths, and I did the most important thing by far I had learned to do as a mom. I prayed . . . tearfully . . . loudly.

And I made a life-altering decision.

In that moment I committed to do everything humanly possible to reverse my family trend and beat the odds. My relationship with my mother became strained in my teen years before completely crumbling in early adult years with no recovery.

Although I had advanced professional knowledge of pediatrics, I certainly had no personal role model for parenting a teen, no wisdom to gain from my relationship with my parents, no parental support on which to rely.

But God . . .

My favorite phrase in the history of ever.

I was raised in a world that revolved around family and church, and I'm grateful for my heritage of faith. I grew up in the era of modesty culture, purity rings and abstinence pledges, youth camp, trust falls, WWJD bracelets, sword drills, kissing dating goodbye, and edgy modern songs like "Our God Is an Awesome God." (Some of you are having flash-backs.) Although conversation about faith was frequent, conversation about personal matters was *unthinkable*. Whispered conversations with my *church* friends found me listening wide-eyed as they shared sketchy details of sexual escapades and drinking experiments. Their parents didn't know or, if they did, they never said a word. Without the inter-net, we relied on peer-to-peer information sharing with gems such as you can't get pregnant your first time or jumping jacks after sex pre-vents infections. I would have rather died than ask my mother about something like the missionary position, which, by the way, was nothing like any missionaries I'd ever heard about in church!

So how did I officially learn about the birds and the bees? One fateful day at the age of ten, my mother handed me a book on puberty to peruse and left me to figure out the mysteries of reproduction before watching a video at school where all I remember is a mother making pancakes in the shape of a uterus. The next official conversation I had on the matter occurred in my women's health course in nursing school at the age of eighteen. I listened to a lecture on sex, scribbling notes furiously in absolute shock. I peeked around carefully as the classroom seemed quiet, and to my utter amazement, people were sleeping! They knew this stuff? I took a late-night stealthy trip to Walmart, where I sneaked down "that aisle" to see if the products they told me about in class were, in fact, real. (Um, they were.) Imagine my humiliation as I encountered the word "spermicide" and an overwhelming variety of condoms in front of God and everybody. I tried to reconcile in my mind this was not some seedy store with neon lights on the freeway but the place where people bought dental floss and bath towels. I realized in that moment that for the first time I thought sex was bad and I didn't know why.

In fact, everything in my life at that time seemed categorized into good and bad. I felt an inescapable pressure in the absence of authentic parental relationships to hold an unattainable standard of a perfect public image. I experienced a crippling yet inexplicable guilt complex. This crushing sense of inadequacy fed a perpetual shame of hypocrisy. It was quietly debilitating, with no path to relationship restoration outside of immediate and unquestioning compliance. I increasingly chased a brutal and unrelenting standard of perfection trying to be the "good" girl as if somehow I could earn the approval of my parents (an elusive pursuit). My legalistic approach to remain above reproach left me perceived as unrelatable, unapproachable, and just plain unlikable. I lost myself trying to be what my parents wanted me to be, namely, submissive and subservient. My deepest desire was to be known and loved and to have a parental relationship filled with acceptance, affection, and understanding. Instead, I encountered rejection, isolation, and disapproval of any hesitation to accept my predetermined life's calling to be a ministry wife and mother immediately after high school graduation. I longed for the freedom to pursue an education. I was bright but had no accessible university path, and in my wildest dreams I could only imagine myself, as a woman, being a nurse or a teacher. Conflict over my choice to go to community college for nursing escalated until, one day, I found myself at my grandmother's house, desperate and silently begging . . . for what I didn't even know. I was then accustomed to living in my parents' garage with few creature comforts and working three jobs to pay for school, rent, transportation, and food, all of which made my granny's extra bedroom, private bath, and encouraging words seem like an oasis. In the morning, she made a lavish breakfast with a formal table setting using real plates and real silverware. I couldn't even bring myself to entertain the hope that I could stay, and I found myself simply grateful for the momentary reprieve. As I solemnly picked up the blue-checkered cloth napkin to place in my lap, my eyes began to comprehend the image of a key on the table next to my plate. My face lifted to Granny's with the audacity of a single spark of fragile hope. With no words, she nodded affirmation of her offer to support my purported rebellion with a place to stay and emotional support when I had neither, even as we both knew it would cost her dearly. That key unlocked more than the door to my new home. It opened the door to a new future I couldn't have ever dared to imagine.

As I grew in my professional role as a pediatric nurse, I eagerly anticipated being a mother. But my early years as a parent were marked by deep insecurities, desperate to spare my children from the pain of separation and disapproval I had endured. One day as I sat on a recliner weeping over broken relationships, my husband took a photo of me. I felt so betrayed in that moment of vulnerability, but he lovingly told me this was what my young children saw every day: my mournfully watching real life passing by while I wept for the life I'd never have. Something shifted in me and I vowed to be present. That day I came to the crushing revelation that perfection is not attainable, real love is not earned, and it was no longer my job in life to protect others from the consequences of their own destructive actions. My relationship with my parents has been mostly absent for more than a decade. Being estranged from the people who gave me life created a lonely, deep abyss that often felt insurmountable. The grief that accompanies this type of relationship loss is soul-wrenching. There were so many times I wanted to be able to speak freely, to be held, comforted, reassured, and understood, but the gap has not been mended. It is because of these deep hurts and the still, small voice of loneliness that sometimes rages like the sea in my soul that I want to ensure my teenagers will never feel the wretchedness of that kind of aloneness. It is also the reason I want to support and encourage other parents of teens who may also be exploring these tough teen issues alone, but without ever having the opportunity to learn how to have meaningful conversations in a parent-child relationship.

That day, in the car with my daughter, I knew there were challenges ahead, but I had no clue of the enormous and unprecedented struggles waiting for us around the bend. I didn't know a thing about social media, vaping, sexting, cyberbullying, social justice, or COVID-19. What I did know is that I would be prepared to help my teens navigate whatever came their way.

What started as a book thrown at me became a new story of building healthy relationships with my teens. It wasn't the end of the road for us but the start of a new and beautiful adventure. We have navigated together some of the toughest challenges facing teens today. Now God has laid it on my heart to share lessons from this journey with you: personal and professional, good and humiliatingly bad, utterly mundane and truly miraculous.

Welcome to your personal journey to invest in
strengthening your relationship with your teen
so you can navigate in a healthy way through
life's toughest challenges together!

The fact you picked up this book tells me your heart aches for soul-deep conversations with your teen. You want to share their fears, hopes, and dreams. You desperately want to be a good parent, but like me, you fear your failures will scar them for life. When we were growing up, our parents basically just had to keep us alive, right? "Be back before dark," they said, and we were, after spending the day looking for coins and riding miles alone on our bikes to buy candy cigarettes at the corner drug store to gleefully shock our elderly neighbors before coming home and drinking from the hose. And our parents didn't even raise an eyebrow. Or make us wear seat belts.

Today, parent pressure starts even before birth, with expectations for the perfect Facebook-live gender reveal party, Pinterest-worthy baby shower, and Instagram-worthy delivery. New moms post every milestone on social media and obsess about other babies excelling over theirs. They buy the latest designer babywear gear and a stroller that closes with the touch of a finger, choose outfits for ridiculously expensive photo shoots and transform said photo shoots into magazine-worthy holiday cards, interview babysitters like FBI agents, monitor nanny cams, invest in developmentally stimulating toys, buy and prepare organic meals in Bento boxes, spend every spare dollar and minute on select sports, work to pay for select sports and a sports utility vehicle to tote the sports equipment, make sure their kids take every advanced placement class—all while meeting every emotional need. If you relate, consider yourself blessed *and* deeply convicted. Many parents are struggling just to put food on the table and keep a roof over their heads.

Media portrayals of teens from all walks of life have a singular commonality as notoriously tumultuous. Movies, television shows, novels, and plays are dedicated to their portrayal. Think *Rebel Without a Cause* of yesteryear or *Dear Evan Hansen* of today. Teens in this modern world are facing extraordinary challenges of a different sort than we as their parents ever faced.

We need new social skills to parent effectively in a social media, social distancing, and social justice world.

Society is changing dramatically at a critical point in teen development that will permanently shape them. Anxiety and depression increase at an alarming rate as public health officials try to balance caution with care in a post-pandemic world. During this time of uncertainty, what teens want more than anything is our time. You might be thinking, "I can't get my teen to get their face out of their phone, and I'm the last person on earth they want to spend time with!" Research tells us otherwise. The stereotypical notion of spending more time with peers is balanced by the desire to maintain close parental relationships. Parents who invest more time have teens with better social skills.[1] Working to develop better social skills as a parent will help you create inviting conversations and environments for your teens.

In a world of instant fixes and instant gratification, there are no instant relationships. Relationship building takes time.

Parents, with so many things competing for our most valuable resource, we must carefully consider where we invest that precious commodity. This book will help you to start investing in the journey and prepare you to turn tragic moments navigating life's challenges into triumphs.

Let's back up and start with an introduction. First and foremost, I am a Christ follower. I will share how faith informs and influences my nursing practice and worldview. My life's ambition is to know God's voice and follow it. My own dreams are pitiful substitutes to the plans God has for me. If you told me back on the day of the book throwing I would be an international nurse leader and writing a book for parents, I likely would have referred you for mental health care. So there's that.

From a personal perspective, I am a wife and a mother. I've been married for a quarter of a century to a rocket scientist who is the absolute love of my life and greatest supporter. He cooks, cleans, and carpools, and he is my greatest champion. The day I told him I had a dream to write a book (with a big cringe because I knew he knew it would require an investment of my most valuable commodity—my time), he went out and had a charm engraved with the title of this book so I would have tangible evidence of his belief and conviction it would be so. We are a team. I have four teenagers. Yes, at one time! Two girls and two boys. Two sets of best friends—some days more than others. The biggest compliment they give me is saying to their friends, "You need to talk to my mom about that." They are my greatest inspiration for world changing. I adore my family and love spending time together, especially on new travel adventures.

From a professional perspective, I am a nurse. I have an associate's and a bachelor's degree in nursing, a master's degree as a pediatric nurse practitioner, and a post master certificate as a nurse educator, all from the University of Texas Medical Branch. I have a doctor of nursing practice (DNP) degree from the University of Alabama. I am now a professor at Baylor University (which I absolutely love—and Sic 'Em Bears!). This opened a door to uniquely speak from my faith-based perspective. My nursing career is blessed with success and gives me valuable knowledge and practical tools to equip parents to talk about uncomfortable things in a comfortable way that builds relationships. I practiced in pediatric primary care for more than twenty years. Accordingly, I've facilitated thousands of conversations between parents and teens, which I love to do.

PLEASE READ THIS CAREFULLY: The information in this book is meant to be a general guide and should not be considered personal medical advice. Each family and teen are wonderfully unique, and it isn't possible to address each individual circumstance. It's essential for you to have a strong connection to your teen's primary health-care provider. Find someone you trust and, of equal importance, someone you *like*. Primary health care is *critical* for your teen. You should be going at least annually for physicals and immunization updates. Primary care can also help you more than you probably think. This advice should not take the place of that relationship in any way. I'll be guiding you along the way with tips on when to schedule a visit.

HOW TO USE THIS BOOK

This book is titled *Behind Closed Doors* because I know, from firsthand experience, things are not always what they appear. In my clinic the cheerful teen in a softball uniform with her mother is actually suicidal. The teen boy limping into the exam room and wincing in pain is not actually injured but coming in secret because he applied hair removal gel to his nether regions in anticipation of certain amorous activities and now has a painful chemical burn he doesn't know how to tell his mother about. The perfect family admired on social media and stirring jealousy in the hearts of onlookers is actually in the middle of a divorce. The minister's son is in church every Sunday but ordering drugs on Snapchat. The girl who seems as if she has it all together is heavily engaged in sexting. These are all real stories. I want to give you a glimpse into the real conversations I'm having with teens. Just as my grandmother gave me a key to a new future, I want to give you some keys to unlock closed doors so you can meet your teen where they are with compassion and help them walk through life's toughest challenges with strength, grace, and dignity.

EACH CHAPTER IS DIVIDED INTO THREE SECTIONS:

Behind the Clinic Door

Case Study	Peek behind the exam room door in my clinic to see a case study from my clinical practice. These are inspired by true stories, but I changed details to protect privacy, and some cases are composites of multiple patients. I assure you that each case accurately represents teens in primary care today.
Health Impacts	Learn how each issue impacts teen health emotionally, spiritually, mentally, physically, academically, and sexually. The purpose is not to invest your time feverishly in studying *health issues* in an *attempt* to connect, but to study your *teen* with the *intent* to connect.
Parenting Pro Tips	Receive valuable guidance on preventing health problems and responding supportively when issues arise.

Behind the Home Door

Conversation Doors and Conversation Keys	Be equipped to initiate authentic conversations with specific settings and strategies (Conversation Keys) to facilitate open dialogue and build relationships. There are many suggestions from which to choose. Not all media and activity suggestions will be to everyone's taste and preference. Screen carefully and decide what's best for your family. My goal is to provide relatable options.

Behind the Heart Door

Devotional for Parents	Explore the complex feelings emerging from your conversations. As a parent, you will receive devotional readings, prayer guides, Scripture readings, and music playlists just for you. I'm not a pastor or a theologian, but I will share simple integrations of faith into health from a Christian nursing perspective. I encourage you to connect with a church where you feel at home seeking spiritual instruction and guidance.

Application	Commit to follow through by writing a Legacy Letter to your teen. Specific instructions are given at the end of each chapter, with creative options for all personality types and parenting styles. At the end of this journey, your teen will have twelve incredibly special Legacy Letters to cherish forever. I recommend selecting a special keepsake box or album.

TEN TIPS FOR SUCCESS IN THIS JOURNEY

1. **SHARE OPENLY.** These conversations and activities are designed for all parents of all teens: single parents, divorced parents, married parents, grandparents, stepparents, godparents, bonus parents, adopted parents, and anyone serving a parental role in any teen's life. Share your journey with other parents. We need to encourage each other and share openly to break down the barriers of stigma and shame. No one's family is perfect, mine included.

2. **PLAN CREATIVELY.** This is a 100 percent customizable, personalized journey with create-your-own endings. Every family is different. Your hobbies, preferences, and personalities vary tremendously. Feel free to choose something that's suggested or be inspired to come up with your own.

3. **COMMIT INTENTIONALLY.** This book is designed as a milestone journey. There are twelve chapters you can cover in a year, giving you time to read, pray, and plan each topic. You can go out of order, faster or slower. If something relevant comes up at school or in your teen's social circle, feel free to jump around. You can read the whole book first and then plan your activities. You can have several conversations in the summer and fewer during the school year. Do what works for you.

Having said that, I want to gently prepare you for what's ahead. Our conversations will not be easy. These topics are difficult, deep realities we face as parents today. Navigate carefully and seek support. Go at a comfortable pace.

4. **GIVE FREELY.** When you have a conversation or gift a Legacy Letter, commit to not expecting any response from your teen. You might have a beautiful, emotional experience writing something, and you just can't wait to see their reaction. Don't let an unexpected or negative reaction or no reaction disappoint you. Commit now to give as a free gift with no strings attached. These letters will be a treasure, even if you don't get that validation now. You can give them one at a time, together at the journey completion, or later at a special milestone of your choosing.

5. **LISTEN PATIENTLY.** Your teen desperately wants to talk with you. They care tremendously what you have to say. I know it doesn't seem that way, but teens with strong parental connections are far more influenced by their family than their friends. Your best bet is to commit to these conversations no matter the response. You might spend a lot of time and energy planning something, and your teen will give you a shoulder shrug and say, "Meh." They might complain the whole way. They might roll their eyes and tell you how stupid this is. They might tell you they hate it. But remember: this is a journey to an unknown destination. It's not about where you're going, it's about how you choose to lead the conversation along the way. This journey will plant seeds to be harvested in another season. This isn't chia-pet parenting with immediate, dramatic growth. In an age of instant gratification, purposefully determine in your heart to dedicate the outcome to the Lord. Don't put any expectations of response on your teenager. Offer yourself with

open hands. Give your heart confidently and vulnerably with unconditional love, no matter the response. Specific questions and conversation prompts will be given to you as tools, but in the words from *Hamilton*, "Talk less, smile more." You have two ears and one mouth. Commit to *listen* twice as much as you speak. Be brave. Step out of your comfort zone.

6. **COMMUNICATE THERAPEUTICALLY.** Your child's adolescence is the time for you as a parent to transition to the role of coach. If it's safe, let your teen fail. Let them try. Inspire. Motivate. Cheer success. Speak hard truths when needed. Tell them when they get it wrong. Tell them when they get it right. Tell them when they're ready to move on to the next skill. Make mutual goals and strive to achieve them! You'll experience exhilarating victories and crushing defeats. You'll have plateaus and mountaintop training days. Collaborative communication is key. Don't be a kindergarten teacher, babying them through every step. Don't be a helicopter parent, hovering over their every move. Don't be a lawnmower parent, clearing every obstacle ahead of them. Be a good coach, tough but fair. Throughout this book we will be exploring Conversation Keys using the LOVE Your Teen model I developed for you. Familiarize yourself with it now, because you'll see it in every chapter. It requires practice.

| L | Listen with your face | Too often we try to listen with our face in our phones or looking around, distracted. If you find yourself having to say, "I *am* listening," that's a clue your teen does not *feel* heard. Resist the urge to parrot back everything they just told you to prove yourself right. Commit to listening intently, giving your teen your whole face. Make eye contact. Put your phone *down*. Hold nothing in your hands. Don't |

interrupt. Don't roll your eyes and sigh (you don't like it when they do that). Try to keep a neutral expression, no matter what they share. Reflect back what you hear, starting with, "What I'm hearing you say is _____." This is validating and helps clarify if you really do understand what your teen is trying to say.

O	Offer open-ended questions	When we hear things we don't like or with which we disagree, our tendency is to get angry or lecture. *Resist the urge!* Ask open-ended questions instead. Seek understanding. Gain trust. Specific questions are suggested in each chapter. Don't ask yes, no, or rhetorical questions (like the infamous, "What were you thinking?!"). There is no safe answer there.
V	Validate their feelings	Your teen might be wrong in their thought process, but their feelings themselves are not wrong. As a parent, your nonverbal behavior is more meaningful than words. Don't sigh heavily, fold your arms, tilt your head with a look that says "Really?" or walk away. Maintain a neutral posture with open hands, open eyes, and an open heart.
		Remember, Jesus had emotions. He got angry. He also got sad, scared, tired, and frustrated. Emotions are human feelings that need to be named and claimed! This approach enables you to address behaviors in a way your teen can better receive. For example, if your teen didn't study and comes home visibly upset with a poor grade, it's not the time to say, "See! I told you so." Saying something like, "I can see this is very upsetting to you," acknowledges feelings without validating lack of studying. After a measure of sympathy, teens are more likely to be open to a discussion of natural consequences (usually better than anything you can dream up).

E	Explore next steps together	When issues arise during conversation, decide the next steps together. The more investment they have, the more they'll engage. Having your teen be an active partner in creating an action plan will strengthen your relationship.
		Decide who you need on your team to make the best decisions. It could be family, friends, mentors, ministers, teachers, counselors, coaches, or other positive influences. In some cases your teen could express actions that endanger themselves or others. You might need to act against their will for safety. You'll need help to do so.

7. **PLAY MUSIC THOUGHTFULLY.** In the appendix you'll find carefully curated playlists themed for each topic we cover with widely varied music genres. If you don't regularly listen to Christian music, challenge yourself to do so. Music has a powerful emotional connection to our spirits. It influences or reinforces our mood. Music also gives us earworms, a (gross and squirmy) term coined in Germany more than a century ago to describe the phenomenon of a song being stuck in your head. Scientists found the auditory complex in your ear is activated when it hears music, but it is also *reactivated* when you just *imagine* hearing a song. Music memory is a powerful and mysterious thing. Think of a song from your childhood or one you haven't heard in years but to which you still know all the words. "Twinkle Twinkle Little Star." "Livin' on a Prayer." "Call Me Maybe." "It's a Small World" (my husband's particular favorite). Oops, did I just give you an earworm? Really, though, song messages play in your teen's head and heart (and yours too). I've always made a practice of playing Christian music in my

home. To hear my children subconsciously singing lyrics such as "My fear doesn't stand a chance when I stand in Your love," "I am chosen, not forsaken, I am who You say I am," "You are for me, not against me," and "I'm resting in the shadows of Your redeeming love" is hands down one of the most heartwarming experiences I've ever had as a parent. Contrast that with the lyrics of current popular songs. If you haven't seriously considered the lyrics in your teen's playlist, I challenge you to put this book down—right now—and go have a look. Do it. These lyrics whispering in your teen's heart and mind are your competing messages. Now, don't get me wrong. This is not at all about the evils of secular music. I'm a Texas girl, born and raised. When you find me at the rodeo (yes, that's a real thing, and yes, I wear boots), it's 100 percent likely I'll be singing a country song *loudly*. My husband can school you in 1980s music trivia. My girls can sing every Taylor Swift lyric and frequently gift my husband with six hours of karaoke on college car trips. What I'm saying is this: music sets the tone in our hearts and homes. I even play worship music when I'm not home, because I want God's spirit to rest there in the atmosphere, greeting me with messages of hope as I walk in the door after a discouraging day.

8. **MEMORIZE SCRIPTURE.** If you're like me (be honest), when we read Christian help books, our eyes fly quickly past the Scripture quotations, thinking we'll read those later. Confession: we don't read them later. So much of my parenting is using God's words of wisdom instead of my own. Memorizing Scripture was a game changer for me. For example, when my son tells me he's feeling afraid, the nurse/mom in me will say, "I'm here, you're safe." A powerful follow-up is, "For the Spirit God gave us does not make us timid, but gives us power, love and self-discipline."

You might feel a little awkward at first, but be sincere and be bold. Scripture memory is one of the best investments in spiritual discipline you can make as a parent. You'll find Scripture references in the appendix at the end of this book.

9. **SEEK COUNSEL.** These issues are too heavy to bear alone. You need support for this journey. Do you have a friend you can call and safely express your fears and frustrations? Do you have a trusted spiritual leader to guide you through difficult theological issues? Do you have health-care providers you trust? Who can help bear your burdens?

10. **PRAY.** *This is the single most important thing you can do for your teen.* Keep a prayer journal to accompany this journey and praise God for prayers answered! Be faithful in the waiting. When you feel least like praying, pray the most. Pray often, pray boldly, and pray loudly. No fancy words are needed. Pour out your heart before the Lord. He knows, He sees, and He cares.

This journey will require your most significant commodity: your time. It's not something you can buy or borrow. It's begotten through blood, sweat, and tears. There's no easy way. Deuteronomy 6:7 instructs parents to have conversations diligently as we sit in our house, walk on the way, lie down, and rise. That requires time dedicated every day to intentional conversation.

This is a significant moment for you right here, right now, to answer the following simple question.

Will you decide to intentionally invest in a living legacy of healthy relationships for your family?

The work will be hard, the tears will be many, and the frustrations will be frequent, but in taking this legacy journey, the rewards will be immeasurable as you invest in generations to come, right down to impacting the literal reading and transcription of the DNA of your great-grandchildren. (Read on and I'll explain.)

I'll be praying for you and your family as you begin this journey.

The Lord bless you and keep you; the Lord make his face shine on you and be gracious to you; the Lord turn his face toward you and give you peace. (Num. 6:24–26)

one

MENTAL HEALTH

How to Break Free from Stigma and Silence

Worry clouded a mother's eyes in an exam room with her eight-year-old daughter. Noticeably small in stature, this frail girl with wide blue eyes climbed quietly onto her mother's lap. Her oversized, cheerfully perched hair bow created a stark contrast to her somber expression. The family experienced a significant health scare when this cherub was diagnosed with a severe immune disorder before her first birthday. A long procession of specialist visits, hospital stays, painful tests, scary nights of high fevers, and many tears overshadowed her first seven years of life before getting the good news that she was one of the few who were fortunate to outgrow her condition. Her family was guardedly optimistic about reentry into a seminormal life after living through years of restrictions.

That's why, this Christmas, the little girl was beyond excited to go to a birthday party at an American Girl store. With eager anticipation, she wore a festive party dress, shiny patent leather shoes, and her trademark impossibly large hair bow. In the middle of the party, as the little girl presented her gift, she started having trouble breathing and it rapidly worsened. Her mother panicked and gave her an asthma rescue inhaler. It helped a little but not enough. A devastated little girl and a horrified mother abruptly left the party to speed to their pediatrician. When they got there, she looked fine. They scratched their heads, worrying about any sign that the immune deficiency was returning. It took years to diagnose. It was . . . anxiety?

BEHIND THE CLINIC DOOR

The thing you don't know is this serious little girl is *my* little girl, and the worried mother is me. Yes, I'm an expert and seasoned pediatric nurse practitioner. But parents, can we agree it's difficult to be objective with our own kids? Our emotional investment clouds rational thought and we fall into the "you don't understand, this is my baby" mentality. We intensely fear fatal injuries or debilitating diseases such as cancer. We don't fear things like depression or anxiety because those seem less scary and, frankly, something we think we can control.

It took me two years to realize my daughter was having panic attacks. When we find out it's not something "serious," our natural reaction is to feel relieved. When we hear "anxiety," we think, "Oh, is that all?" There's often a mixture of doubt and, if we're honest, annoyance. Our secret inner monologue says, "Is this real? For attention?" We want a rapid anxiety test like a rapid strep test. Then we want a quick fix, like the "pink stuff"!

As parents we treat issues of mental health much differently than physical health. Imagine your teen says they're having trouble seeing the board at school. It's blurry and gives them a headache. Your likely instinct is to call an optometrist to promptly schedule an appointment. If you're told your teen is nearsighted and needs glasses, you excitedly choose flattering frames. You affirm their choice and compliment their appearance with words of encouragement and a social media showcase, right? You follow up to make sure they can now see the board at school. You may be wondering where this is going.

Think with me about a different ending. Say this story starts the same way, but instead of calling an optometrist, you tell your teen they're probably not getting enough sleep and advise a wait-and-see approach. It gets worse. You decide maybe it's diet related and go gluten-free everything. This doesn't help, so you buy some vitamin supplements and do some internet searching. You argue with your spouse or your mother about it. It's been six months. Now the teacher is calling. Grades are dropping. You finally go to the optometrist, and they tell you your teen is nearsighted and needs glasses. You respectfully say thank you, but you're not ready to do something that extreme and would like another opinion before purchasing glasses. You start to wonder if your faith is strong enough and why you can't just pull yourself together and be a better parent with more faith so your child can see clearly. This may seem ridiculous, but here's the kicker: *this is exactly what we do with mental health.*

Health Impacts

Today's teens are experiencing the compounding mental health effects of social isolation, social media, social justice, and social stigma.[1] Even before COVID-19, eight million children had a recognized mental health disorder. One in three high school students felt sad and hopeless most of the time, a 40 percent increase from the previous decade.[2] Only about half of children diagnosed with a mental health condition actually receive treatment.[3] Mental health crises

3

among teens are skyrocketing with increasing emergency room visits for self-harm and suicidal behaviors, prompting an advisory from the US surgeon general.[4] Teens with untreated mental health conditions are more likely to engage in risk-taking behaviors including unhealthy sexual activity, alcohol consumption, drug use, and acts of violence.[5] Two of the most common mental health conditions faced by teens are depression and anxiety.

Depression is a serious mental health concern and a leading cause of disability among teens aged fifteen to nineteen years,[6] impacting approximately 17 percent of adolescents.[7] Depression can be caused by alterations in brain chemistry, hormone imbalance, inherited genetic traits (running in families), early childhood trauma, or learned patterns of harmful thinking. Teens with depression often initially show irritability. They are self-critical and feel genuinely unworthy of joy in life and love from others. They avoid situations that require energy to pretend things are normal. They hide but only feel worse. Depression easily mimics a physical illness. Teens come to me with mothers who are sure they have mononucleosis because they lack energy or appetite and have altered sleep patterns or weight changes. Other common physical complaints include headaches, stomachaches, vomiting or diarrhea, and back pain. Affected teens experience loss of interest in the activities they once loved, lower grades at school, avoidance of others, and self-harming behaviors. Depression is not a choice, and physical pain occurring with depression is very real.

Anxiety is something everyone experiences at some point and is an effective temporary coping tool. It alerts our bodies that something is wrong so we can take protective actions. It helps us identify danger and mount a fight-or-flight response. In healthy circumstances, anxiety can motivate us to perform tasks better (get pumped up for the big game) or stimulate creativity (work on a project with a deadline).

When you feel anxious, your body naturally responds by increasing your heart rate and blood pressure, dilating your pupils, and shaking or trembling. We've all been there at some time, right? Public speaking? Skydiving? Small dogs barking? (Or is that just me?) Usually this on-edge feeling goes away quickly. However, teens with anxiety disorders experience these symptoms in extreme or prolonged fashion. It can be uncomfortable and downright scary.

There are five major types of anxiety disorders:[8]

1. **GENERALIZED ANXIETY DISORDER**: chronic exaggerated worry or feeling overwhelmed, often with no obvious external stressors (you genuinely don't know why you feel worried)
2. **OBSESSIVE-COMPULSIVE DISORDER**: repetitive, unwanted thoughts with ritualistic behaviors such as handwashing, counting, or cleaning
3. **PANIC DISORDERS**: sudden, severe, unanticipated episodes of intense worry or fear with physical symptoms such as chest pain, shortness of breath, dizziness, heart racing, and stomach pain (these look like very scary health crises)
4. **POST-TRAUMATIC STRESS DISORDER**: triggered episodes of anxiety following a traumatic event that caused threats of or actual physical harm
5. **SOCIAL PHOBIAS**: overwhelming self-consciousness in everyday social settings, including fear of speaking, eating, or drinking in front of others

Recently, a sixth emerging concern is post-pandemic separation anxiety.

If your teen feels anxious but cannot identify a reason for it or experiences prolonged anxious symptoms or fears not matching the situation, you should pursue evaluation for an anxiety disorder. Sometimes your body simply gets depleted from being in a constant state of fight or flight and depression follows.

Now think back to the optometrist analogy and how symptoms of blurry vision were overlooked or denied and compare it to how we react to symptoms of anxiety and depression. It doesn't seem so far-fetched. Many mental health conditions are biologic, meaning our brains or bodies act in a way we cannot control. If your health-care provider recommends therapy for depression, we often adopt the mind-set in the optometrist scenario and resist. Why do we treat our eyes differently than our brains?

Why Is It So Hard for Parents to Accept a Mental Health Diagnosis?

Stigma and bias with mental health is real. We'll revisit this when we delve into the heartbreaking tragedy of suicide. Even as parents, we sometimes unintentionally let our own bias and fear of social stigma cloud our ability to see and accept a mental health diagnosis. We're human. As I told you, it took me almost two years to realize my daughter was struggling. I was so worried about her physical condition, I just couldn't see past that bias. She had frequent stomachaches and intermittent asthma attacks, which in hindsight were obviously panic attacks. Her trigger happened around Christmastime when she was five years old and developed a severe medication reaction. Within two hours of showing symptoms, she was critically ill. At our pediatrician's office, she deteriorated so quickly we called 911. The ambulance couldn't find us, so we jumped in my pediatrician's car with a nurse squeezing IV fluids. We drove five minutes to the hospital, and this dear physician friend carried her in his arms, running to the pediatric ICU. Praise the Lord, she recovered.

But at the American Girl store three Christmases later, what I realize now is she was experiencing post-traumatic stress, which was triggered by the Christmas decorations and the hustle and bustle. At first, my daughter didn't know how to talk about it with her peers or support people in her life. She instinctively feared stigma, even when she didn't really know what that was. One day at her camp, where I was serving as the nurse, she came running into the clinic in a full-blown panic attack. She raced through the building, ran to my bedroom, locked the door, and hid on the floor behind the bed. Her friends came running after her, wide-eyed and afraid. They had no idea what happened and told me she just ran off, thinking they somehow hurt her feelings. She begged me not to tell them. I saw her in desperate need—lonely, terrified, and crying. On the other side of the door was grace, love, understanding, and support, but she locked herself away and suffered alone. I invited her friends in and simply explained their friend has anxiety. I told them sometimes she feels scared for no reason, and when that happens, she needs to know she will be okay. I explained it helps if they give her some physical space but to stay with her, speak calmly, reassure her, and get a trusted adult. That worked wonders. These friends now had a serious mission. They were educated and empowered. They knew what was happening, what to do about it, and when to get help. I share this experience not only with my daughter's permission but with her blessing. I admire her greatly as it has encouraged and empowered many.

Parenting Pro Tips

First and foremost is safety. Life-threatening emergencies warranting a call to 911 include suicide intent, threats or acts of violence, and any other life-threatening safety risks. *Any* reports of physical or sexual abuse should be reported *immediately* to a licensed health-care provider, child protective services, and local law enforcement. Abuse experiences can prompt mental health crises.

When Should I Be Concerned and What Should I Do?

This is a long road with no easy fix. Give yourself grace and space to take the journey. When considering your teen's mental health, it's important to have an open mind. If your teen voices feelings of anxiety or depression, *stop* what you're doing. Listen carefully and respectfully. Resist the urge to be dismissive. Normalize these feelings as indications to see a health-care provider just as you would if your teen reported a sore throat or fever. Some parents are resistant the moment a provider suggests the issue might be related to mental health. They're even offended. I've seen this more times than I can count. Many symptoms of anxiety and depression masquerade as tummy troubles. Families sometimes go down an avoidable road of expensive and invasive testing when a balanced perspective also considers mental health. If your provider suggests this possibility, be open.

The next critical step is finding a primary health-care provider both you and your teen trust. Remember baby immunizations and ear infections? Those same providers see teens with mental health issues. Pediatric providers generally see children through age twenty-one. Your teen may feel more comfortable at some point with an adult provider. For older teen girls, gynecologic providers can often provide primary care services as well.

If your teen's ability to daily function and engage in activities they normally love is impaired, you should be concerned. Schedule an appointment with your health-care provider to discuss further assessment and interventions. In this age of internet searches and information superhighways, it's tempting to self-diagnose or arm-chair quarterback treatment. Frankly, it's dangerous. If you identify concerns, seek consultation from a trained mental health-care professional. Your teen needs to know you're their advocate working to connect them to the help they need.

What Should I Expect During a Health-Care Visit?

For concerns about depression, you can expect a behavior rating scale (questionnaire) like the Patient Health Questionnaire-9 (PHQ-9).[9] This is a simple nine-question screening tool about things such as sleeping, eating, or feeling down or hopeless. Scores are ranked from minimal to severe and guide your teen's care. The General Anxiety Disorder-7 (GAD-7)[10] helps gauge the presence and severity of anxiety symptoms. It asks questions about how often your teen feels restless or irritable. These tools are easily found with an internet search. Taking them at home, however, should *never* substitute for a professional medical evaluation, but it can help you to know what to expect.

Martin Luther King Jr. said, "You don't have to see the whole staircase, just take the first step."[11] Many parents have an intense fear of voicing any symptoms of mental health concerns, thinking such a diagnosis will lead to immediate pressure to take medication. That's not how this should happen. Evaluation should take a stepwise approach. If your teen has symptoms, your provider will do the following:

- Ensure there is no safety threat to self or others
- Carefully rule out physical problems
- Consider questionnaires to identify mental health concerns
- Determine if labs or other tests should be ordered
- Decide if the issue can be handled in primary care or if a specialist is needed
- Discuss treatment options

What Kinds of Therapies Are Recommended?

Mental health therapies such as counseling, cognitive behavioral therapy (CBT), and behavioral management are ideal for mild symptoms of anxiety and depression. CBT is a way of retraining your brain to change behavior patterns. It's safe, effective, and doesn't involve medications, but it's time intensive, challenging to find qualified providers, potentially expensive, and requires dedication to regular visits usually necessitating time off from school or work. If you're waiting to see a mental health-care provider, but there is no appointment available for several weeks, talk with your primary health-care provider about using CBT tools at home. This may be helpful in the interim with professional consultation while awaiting specialist appointments (see nami.org under the "Support & Education" section).

If medications are recommended, be reassured there are safe and effective therapies to treat anxiety and depression to help restore chemical imbalances beyond your control. Clearly communicate to your health-care provider your concerns, questions, and hesitations surrounding prescriptions. Potential long- and short-term side effects should be discussed. Mental health medicines generally have to be taken every day to maximize therapy and minimize side effects. These may not be forever but just for a season. The dosing schedule should be considered. If four times a day will not work for your family, be honest about it up front. If a medication is too expensive, say so. There is a wide variation in clinician comfort treating anxiety and depression. If your primary health-care provider is uncomfortable initiating treatment for your teen, they can refer you to a qualified mental health specialist.

Let me address complementary and alternative therapies briefly. Common options such as meditation, yoga, and equine or pet therapy have evidence as supportive for anxiety and depression treatment. Diet changes, vitamin supplements, acupuncture, herbal remedies, homeopathy, massage, aromatherapy, and energy healing are far less studied, limiting confident recommendations. Each family should address this with the clinician you trust for individual consultations. Be open in disclosing which therapies you have pursued or are interested in pursuing for an honest discussion of risks and benefits.

What Are the Best Steps for Prevention?

Let's close this section by talking about prevention. These may sound overly simplistic but are so often neglected by busy families trying to plan dinner and keep life together (guilty mom here). Unpredictability increases stress, so do your best to keep a routine schedule. This looks different for each family. For mine, routine means family dinner most nights, even if it's peanut butter sandwiches while standing around the kitchen island. Bedtime should have a rhythm. I still read out loud to my kids. Yes, even my teens. Don't get me wrong, they don't jump up and down with excitement but instead appear ambivalent with a casual request of "Are you reading tonight?" One of the most important parenting lessons I've learned is to give without expectation of response. I invest what I think is wise, recognizing that all harvests are not instant. If they don't jump up and down and hug me every night and brag to their friends how much they love to hear me read but instead leave home with memories of me in their room during cozy bedtime hours and telling stories, I'm okay with that.

We can't expect instant gratification from our teens. It's not their purpose in life to validate our parenting choices.

The importance of sleep cannot be overemphasized. Teens need a comfy, safe, peaceful place to sleep, and almost always they need more than they're getting. This is called sleep hygiene. Teens often eat, sleep, study, and have screen time in their rumpled bed filled with chip crumbs and dirty clothes. Their bodies don't experience physical fatigue and this leads to mindless phone scrolling at night with sleep cycle disruption. Exercising at least sixty minutes a day promotes a healthy sleep cycle and positively impacts mental, emotional, and physical health. Spending time together as a family having an adventure, learning something new, or doing something silly is powerful. Adopting random acts of kindness and practicing intentional gratitude are also documented in their ability to improve mental outlook.

Take every opportunity to increase your comfort in talking about mental health. Conveying to a teen their struggle is a secret implies shame and builds anxiety. Stigma prevents teens from reaching out and creates reluctance to seek help. Know the facts about mental health disorders and recognize the biological basis as opposed to behavioral choices. Choose your words carefully. Avoid labeling people or using mental health terms casually. People often say things without thinking: "What are you, crazy?" "You're psychotic." "Schizo!" (People are not schizophrenic but rather people living with schizophrenia.) The way we lead in our speech influences the attitudes of others. Challenge stereotypes when you hear them. Treat others with dignity and respect.

Choose to empower your teen to be confident
about any diagnosis they may have, knowing they're
equipped to learn more about their condition and
access resources without harboring self-stigma.

Seek counseling or care for yourself if you're struggling personally or struggling to accept your teen's mental health condition. Lastly, never see your child's mental health through the lens of your parenting success or failure. That's a dangerous trap.

BEHIND THE HOME DOOR

My kids often start a conversation with, "Mom, I have an awkward question for you." (And, wow, do they!) My kids have asked me about *junior high* lunchroom talk including emojis for sex organs, "fingering," and "breaking a girl's virginity" (insert wide-eyed emoji here). I always start these conversations with "What do you think?" to tell me where to start. I've seen a teen who searched "rape" on the internet because they didn't know what it was and felt no open invitation to ask their parents. Are you feeling awkward yet? Don't worry, there is plenty of sex talk ahead to equip and prepare you for these conversations.

Parents, teens desperately need you to
initiate these conversations with confidence
and grace while sparing their dignity.

Conversation Doors
- If you feel a tug and know you need to initiate steps to make an appointment, put this book down *right now* and go do it.
- If face-to-face conversation feels awkward, try texting. Find a story about mental health that might interest your teen. Intentionally transition the conversation to in person.

- If you know someone with a mental health condition who is open to sharing their experience, plan a conversation in a private, comfortable setting.
- Research celebrities who are outspoken about their own mental health struggles. (Chris Evans, Lil Wayne's conversation with Emmanuel Acho, Kevin Love, Brooke Shields, J. K. Rowling, Simone Biles, Dansby Swanson, Demi Lovato, Lady Gaga, Olivia Munn, and Sophie Turner—for starters.) Every family is different and has different views on these individuals. Some of you may have an intense aversion to celebrity culture. That's okay! Skip this option. Many will be well known to your teen, and exploring this together can give you opportunities to influence your teen's views.
- Choose a film about mental health (I recommend parental previewing first) such as *A Beautiful Mind*, *Inside Out*, *Matchstick Men*, *It's Kind of a Funny Story*, or *Perks of Being a Wallflower*. Have a movie night with discussion to follow.
- Host a teen night at your home, school, church, or community group to raise mental health awareness using the Say It Out Loud tool kit from the National Alliance on Mental Illness.

Conversation Keys

After you complete your activity, schedule time to go for a drive or a walk together for a follow-up chat. Sometimes it's easier to talk about hard things side by side instead of face-to-face. Get a snack or a drink. Fish off the dock. Ride your bikes. Take a scenic route. Remember to LOVE your teen:

Listen with your face:
- Tell your teen you set aside time together for talking with no distractions.

- Listen carefully as they talk. When they finish say, "What I hear you saying is . . ." and repeat back to them what they said in your own words.
- Resist the urge to explain, fix, or argue. Just listen without judgment.
- Thank your teen for being willing to explore a difficult topic with you.

Offer open-ended questions:
- "What did you think about (your experience together)?"
- "On a scale of one to ten, with one being terrible and ten being terrific, how would you rate your mental health? What made you choose that number?"
- "How have you seen others struggle with mental health issues? How did that make you feel?"
- "Can you describe a time you've been concerned about your mental health or the mental health of a friend or family member?"
- "What can I do to support your mental health?"

Validate feelings:
- "That must make you feel (fill in the blank: sad, frustrated, lonely, angry)."
- "I can see how you feel that way."
- "I admire the way you handled yourself (or the way you're thinking) in this situation."
- "Thank you for being brave enough to trust me with your feelings."
- "I understand this has been a hard week/month/year/time/ challenge."

Explore some next steps together:
> If your teen discloses feelings of concern about mental

health or if you uncover concern after reading this chapter, gently but firmly tell your teen you're committed to seeking counsel on the next steps. Follow through using the guidance outlined above. If your teen discloses concern about a friend's mental health, follow up with that teen's parent, school, or other authoritative figure. Discuss ways you can be more open to conversations surrounding mental health, making your family and home a safe, accepting place.

BEHIND THE HEART DOOR

You might have a short conversation with your teen or it might open a floodgate you didn't know existed. Rest assured even if the conversation was ho-hum, your teen is now better prepared to act in the future. Maybe this was a difficult subject to discuss because you or a family member has a diagnosis previously undisclosed to your teen and it brought up difficult emotions. If you've never sought help for yourself but are wondering if maybe you should, the answer is unequivocally *yes*. Reach out to someone who loves you and take steps to seek professional resources.

Devotional

We often oversimplify mental health as an easily controlled spiritual choice, especially when we lack personal experience. People ask in a puzzled way, "Why are you anxious/depressed?" or say "Be anxious for nothing!" with a casual, confident shrug while leaving people suffering in what they now perceive to be a personal crisis of faith. Scripture does tell us not to be anxious. However, there are two very important words there: "*but in* every situation, by prayer and petition . . . present your requests to God. And the peace of God, which transcends all understanding, will guard your hearts and your minds in Christ Jesus" (Phil. 4:6–7, emphasis added). Did you get that? We don't have to be thankful *for* every situation, but we can be thankful *in* every situation. We don't have to be thankful *for* mental health conditions, but we can be thankful *in* the midst of them. Spiritual health is an important part of wellness. Science supports Scripture. Grateful people experience less pain, lower levels of anxiety and depression, cope more effectively with challenges, and sleep better. Grateful people are more satisfied with life. Their families are more satisfied with the quality of their relationships. Gratitude enhances empathy while reducing retaliation, aggression, and envy.

Being grateful leads to the *peace* of God that transcends understanding, literally guarding our hearts and minds. The word *peace* is difficult to define. We mostly think of it as a passive absence of conflict. The Hebrew word for peace (*shalom*) is much more beautifully complex. It's the last word used in the oldest known fragment of biblical text, also known as the Blessing. Shalom is used in Scripture more than two hundred times to convey a sense of completeness, safety, deep well-being, and reconciliation. Shalom conveys expectation and the hope for wholeness and the fullness of restoration in Christ. Mental health issues rob us of our sense of shalom. We feel unsafe, unwell, and unsettled. In this world we will have trouble, but we have shalom in Christ, who has overcome the world. Jesus is a Wonderful Counselor and Prince of Peace. He can give you peace at all times in every way, even when you're struggling with mental health.

Reflect

In the secret spaces of your heart, what are your true feelings about people with mental health conditions?

What language, words, phrases, or attitudes do you use that may be harmful to people with mental health struggles?

How can you make your home a safe space for respectfully discussing issues related to mental health?

Pray

(From Psalm 23) God, thank You for being my Shepherd in this parenting journey. Remind me when I'm following You, I want for nothing. Help me lie down in green pastures, seeing growth in my teen. Lead me beside still waters during times of conflict. Restore my soul when I feel broken and hopeless. Guide me in the right paths to lead my teen faithfully with sure steps for Your name's sake. When I walk through valleys shadowed by darkness and sadness, help me not to be afraid of evil. Remind me daily of Your presence with me, that I am not alone. Your rod and Your staff will comfort and guide me. Prepare a table before us in the presence of enemies who wish to tear us down and harm us. Anoint our heads with oil until our cup overflows with abundance. Let goodness and mercy follow us all the days of our lives as we dwell in the house of the Lord forever, amen.

Act

(Legacy Letter) Choose seven, fourteen, twenty-one, or thirty days (whatever time frame feels right) to keep a gratitude journal. It can be simple or elaborate. Print a blank calendar page, simply use notebook paper, or design something custom on a website or computer application. Each day thank your teen for something specific. It doesn't have to be poetry in motion, although feel free if you're artistically inclined. Leave it for your teen to find *privately*. I'm amazed when simple notes I leave on my teens' beds end up pinned to their bulletin boards. However, give it as a free gift, with no strings attached or response expected, trusting God with the outcome while following Him in the journey.

SOCIAL MEDIA

How to Be a Tech-Savvy Parent in an i-Gen World

She was eleven years old, a splash of freckles dancing across her smiling face. Her cheerful ponytail gave a friendly, carefree greeting as I entered the exam room. Her legs swung playfully in distressed jeans as she bounced along to a song, earbuds blasting music only she heard. Her mother sat in the corner, purse on her lap with contents spilling out, grocery list half-written. She was uniformed in official mom attire: yoga pants, school spirit T-shirt, messy bun pulled through a ball cap, and a dash of mascara and lipstick. She greeted me with a half smile, affectionate eye roll, and head nod toward her bubbly daughter, still dancing to music we couldn't hear. Leaning against the exam table, I saw social media open with filtered bunny faces being exchanged in rapid fire for flower-crowned heads. They were harmless pictures, adorable in fact. She excitedly shared with me her new social media platforms and how many followers she had (1,132 to be exact). I asked

Mom, "What privacy settings do you use to help keep your daughter safe online?" Ah, there it was. A common reaction to this sort of pop quiz. A blank stare with mild confusion starting to wander into mild alarm. Her concern was justified, although she didn't know that yet. With a reassuring smile, I pulled up a stool and invited Mom into our circle as I mentally pushed Play on the talk from my pediatric nurse practitioner toolbox.

BEHIND THE CLINIC DOOR

Hear me up front. Smartphones and social media are not *evil*, just as a car is not inherently bad. A car can be immensely helpful, essential even. But would you toss your car keys to your eleven-year-old and say nonchalantly, "Be careful. I'm trusting you"? I don't think you would, yet this is exactly what we do when we give smartphones and social media to teens without proper preparation. Then, when they get in an accident, we stand there with an exasperated look and say, "I can't believe you did that! I told you to be careful!" They feel shame but don't quite understand why.

Maybe you're thinking, *This doesn't apply to me. My tween/teen doesn't have a phone yet.* In reality, maybe they do. An estimated 95 percent of teens have *access* to a smartphone, and 45 percent say they are on them "constantly."[1] Maybe they use a friend's phone. Your teen's friends think not having a smartphone or social media is the cruelest punishment on earth, so they may offer your teen one of their old phones or the luxury of sharing a phone to communicate through social media. Just because your teen doesn't have their own phone doesn't mean you don't need conversations about boundaries and risks.

Seventy percent of teens report hiding online activities from their parents.[2] This shouldn't surprise us. We *all* did foolish things growing up, but we don't have to see those moments living on in perpetual digital infamy. When I was in ninth grade, I sneaked out with my friends to wrap a house. (Never mind I was so guilt-stricken I immediately unwrapped it and prayed in the yard for forgiveness before coming back with brownies for my classmate's mother to assuage my conscience.) My mom was not tracking my iPhone to see where I'd gone. She just drove down the street and yelled out the car window until she found us. Before caller ID, you'd call home and tell your parents where you "were." Need I say more?

Ways to hide simply evolve. Just ask your teen about their Finsta (Translate: "fake Instagram") account. To make this more confusing, real Instagram is actually fake, showing a perfect life with carefully curated vacation shots and filtered photos. Fake Insta is "real" and used as a forum with closer, trusted friends to share more candid posts. Some teens call this a spam or a ghost account where they post trash or unflattering photos, feeling free from pressure to be insta-ready. A mom once asked me how her teen had more than seven thousand followers but never posted anything. I gently broke it to her that she was blocked! Throw in secret photo-sharing decoy apps that look like calculators, ghost browsers, finna, flex, glow up, yeet, self-destructing message apps, and Snapstreaks. Confused yet? Hang in there. Help is on the way! You can be a tech-savvy parent in a digital-native world.

How Did We Get Here as Parents?

Our world has drastically changed since we were teens. You probably grew up with no call waiting or caller ID. Long, curly cords made their way from our kitchen into whatever door down the hall would close for the slightest bit of privacy. I wrote my nursing school papers on a typewriter (gasp!). I didn't have email until I was married. Even then, it was via an unreliable dial-up modem, and you couldn't use the phone and internet at the same time. I stood in line to register for college classes, moving from table to table in large hallways clutching the ever-important paper catalog I had carefully highlighted. My children now refer to this specific era in time as "back then" or "the era before the internet." My first cell phone was like a brick in my purse. My in-laws waited three days to see a photo of their first grandchild because we used a 35mm camera and sent snail mail from Texas to New Jersey. How did we survive as a civilization in such primitive conditions? my children wonder.

When the worldwide web first emerged in 1989, it was intended for consumption. MapQuest replaced Rand McNally. Websites replaced Moviefone. DoorDash replaced worn, stained menus in the junk drawer by the phone. Google was created in 1998! Around 2004, Web 2.0 was introduced, changing static web pages to dynamic user-generated content. The world has never been the same, taking off at lightning speed down the information superhighway. The iPhone debuted in 2007, followed by the iPad in 2010. How did we parent before iPhones? Is it even possible to take a toddler to the grocery store without electronic accompaniment now? Social media sites loudly advertise their reach. Facebook, created in 2007, boasts more than 2.45 *billion* daily active users. YouTube sees 5 billion videos watched *every day* with 300 hours of material uploaded *every minute*. Twitter has 330 million monthly active users sending 500 million tweets *per day*. Snapchat was once the up-and-comer in social media with 319 million daily active users. It's now surpassed by TikTok, a global sensation attracting more than *one billion* daily active users! There will be new fads to follow this writing.

Consider the cultural context of this new world our teens are navigating. The word of the year in 2009 was "unfriend," followed by "app" (2011), "GIF" (2012), "selfie" (2013), and "vape" (2014).[3] These words seem like they've always existed in our vocabulary, but they emerged in less than a decade. Frankly, I have T-shirts older than that. In 2015, the word of the year went to a new level as "face with tears of joy" emoji—a new word in and of itself. Did you catch that? The word of the year was, in fact, not even a word but a little yellow circle with use now relegated by Gen Z as a mark of being old, along with side-parts and skinny jeans.

In the world where digital-native teens are growing up, technology is not novel. Having a smartphone is not only normal, it's expected. Just ask my teens about their required entry into building responsibility with a flip phone. They'll gladly tell you of the humiliation of texting (44–444-6-666–60), translated as "Hi Mom." Parents worry about communicating in an emergency, pickup from school, and a million other reasons, while forgetting we survived our teen years without phones.

When my oldest daughter was in fifth grade, social media was emerging. She asked me if she could have an account because *everyone* in her class had one. I told her what every parent knows to say, "Not *everyone* in your class has social media." I said this with prerequisite parental eye roll, clucking tongue, and shaking head. She challenged me with her class roster, and sure enough, *every* kid had an account. I reverted to standard line number two in the parenting handbook: "Well, if everyone jumped off a bridge, would *you* do it?" Answer? No social media. Fast-forward to her freshman year, and we circled back to this request. I had learned quite a bit because wisdom accumulates in dog-year scales while parenting teens. This time I asked her to write a three-page report with references, assigned objectives, and evaluation rubric (poor kid with a professor mom). After a week, she returned with a much longer paper. I evaluated the criteria on safety issues. Check. Rules on posting? Check. Who to friend or not? Check. What to do if she witnesses bullying or threats of self-harm? Check. I began to feel a little smug, always the first sign of pride going before a fall. On the last page, I began to read the conclusion, expecting a terrific sales pitch. Instead, I saw, "After doing this research, I realize I am not ready to accept these responsibilities and decline social media at this time." This was one of my most humbling but satisfying parenting moments. A year later she brought it up again, feeling ready. She is now in a healthy relationship with social media, using it responsibly but struggling with screen time, as we all do. Those crafting, recipe, and sports blooper videos are so satisfying, right?

Once when my teens had friends over, they sat on the couch side by side, completely nonverbal, glued to their phones, thumbs flying. Exasperated, I said, "Why don't you just talk to each other!" Without looking up, in unison, they eerily said, "You can't speak emoji, Mom." That day in my house, with young teens at the beginning of smartphone days, I knew the phone thing had to change. Immediately.

Health Impacts

Social media has great potential benefits. Online connections foster healthy social interactions, build and maintain long-distance friendships, provide access to education, facilitate contributions to online community, teach principles of global digital citizenship, encourage budding entrepreneurs, and foster healthy image crafting. However, excessive use creates health risks. Teens can be groomed, recruited, or exploited in abusive situations, creating complex emotional trauma, including cyberbullying, human trafficking, and sexting (more on those later).

Physical health risks arise when using a phone while driving or walking. Who remembers the onset of Pokémon Go? The first time I saw it in a park I thought it was a zombie apocalypse. A teen in my community was almost shot as an intruder in a neighbor's backyard at 2:00 a.m. while trying to catch a Pokémon! Look no further than nightly news to see tragic stories of death by selfie, in which people die trying to get the perfect social media shot. This happened while my family was in Vancouver, where a popular YouTuber tragically fell to her death. I see teens in the clinic with "texting neck," sleep deprivation (checking social media constantly in the night for FOMO [fear of missing out]), poor school performance, and impulsive binge-watching of pornography. These are all documented health risks associated with excessive social media or online activities.

The American Academy of Pediatrics uses the term "Facebook Depression" to describe risks for teens who spend excessive time on social media sites.[4] There are also higher risks of anxiety and self-harm. Today's teens spend approximately nine hours a day consuming some form of digital media.[5] There are 93 million selfies taken per day[6] and apps are dedicated to editing your body to be more desirable. Consider social media messages. Facebook: "Like me!" TikTok: "Discover Me!" YouTube: "Watch me!" Instagram: "Follow Me!" Social *me*dia is all about *me*!

Now you're thinking about how to live off the grid, cut the cord on technology, or at the minimum, restrict phone use for your teens until age forty. Hang on! There are some remarkably simple actions to help protect your child and promote a healthy and safe online experience.

When Should I Allow My Child to Have Social Media?

This is one of the most common questions I get in clinical practice. Truthfully, I often need to talk to parents more than teens. Your teen already knows what I've shared with you: we are painfully behind. So let's start with the basics. There is currently no approved social media platform for children under thirteen years of age. Period. (Okay, technically there is a Facebook Messenger app for kids, but I've never met a kid who uses it.) Thirteen years is the age set by the US Congress in the Children's Online Privacy Protection Act (1998).[7] So thirteen is the minimum age for a *conversation*. And listen, while we're here, each teen is different. Don't make a practice of setting a standard age for each milestone (like dating at sixteen). One of my kids likely could have handled a phone at age seven while another might be forty-seven before they're ready! Make a habit of saying, without promises, "We can have a conversation about it when you're (insert age here)."

Let's revisit our cheerful eleven-year-old at the beginning of this chapter. She was on Snapchat, concerned about keeping her Snapstreak ("snap" your "contact" at least once every twenty-four hours for three days, and a fire emoji appears along with the number of days of your streak). I asked her when she created the account if she saw a prompt to verify she was thirteen years old. She affirmed and her mother quickly added her daughter was trustworthy and the account was monitored closely. I didn't doubt either of those things, but *the law doesn't make exceptions for trustworthy kids or vigilant parents.* By violating the terms of use, you potentially void legal protections should your child experience exploitation, abuse, cyberbullying, or other harm. I see this happen, always with painful regrets. Risk of sexual exploitation is very real and something we will explore later.

Now, before we get into guiding your teen through social media use, it's time for a little honest self-examination. I'll go first. Once, I was talking (sanctimoniously) to my son about the potential for a popular video game to become all-consuming and the importance of setting healthy boundaries. He listened carefully and then said,

"Mom, social media is just gaming for adults." Arrow pierce heart. How many times am I at a baseball game only to see the tops of parents' heads? They are more engaged in their online life than the real life occurring right before their eyes. How many times have you yelled at your kids in frustration during an outing where everyone is miserable and fighting, but you're trying to get that perfect social media picture? "Stop touching your sister!" "Put your arm around him!" "Smile!" "Come on, cut it out!" Then immediately goes the post on your social: "Having a wonderful day together at the Christmas Tree Farm! #familytime #makingmemories #traditions." Meanwhile, the parent you carpool with is at home, looking longingly at your photo and wishing their family was as close as yours. Parents, we need to own our culpability here and approach our teens with empathy as they navigate this social mirage.

Social media is a reality of twenty-first-century parents. It's a great way to connect and seek support. But as parents, we often don't give posting much thought. It's called "sharenting": venting frustrations about teen drama, funny bath photos, relief over being "kid free" for the moment, asking advice on personal struggles, angst about teen dating or driving, posting awkward photos making gentle fun of your teen. Here's the thing. You are the literal caretaker of your child's digital footprint. One day they will look at everything you posted and see themselves through your eyes. What will they see? A narrative that conveys approval only through accomplishments? Dirty laundry aired about conflicted relationships? A parade of embarrassing moments? That's a big responsibility. So think *before* you post. It's okay to be authentic and vulnerable. But ask yourself, is this a moment I want to preserve forever? Think of *Hamilton*. Who tells your story? Steward the extraordinary privilege of telling your teen's story well.

Parenting Pro Tips

How do you safely navigate this swiftly moving current? In the early teen years, brain development starts a process of abstract thinking called *formal operations*. Before this happens, children are literal thinkers (*concrete operations*) and take things at face value. Translating to social media, if teens meet someone online who says they're a fifteen-year-old friend of a friend at a neighboring school, they believe it. Just look at YouTuber Coby Persin's Social Media Child Predator experiments[8] (not before bedtime or while your teen is out—it will scare you). I assure you I see scenarios like this in real life. As formal operations develop, older teens learn not to take everything at face value and to appraise each situation critically, meaning improved self-safety. Developing abstract thinking doesn't happen at the same time for everyone but will generally begin around age ten to twelve and progress into the early twenties. Abstract thinking is an important online safety skill and could make the difference in protecting your teen from being susceptible to harm.

How do you know your teen is reaching formal operations stage, increasing their confidence to function more independently? Ask yourself: Does my teen do any of the following:

1. Actively consider new possibilities or explore new ways of doing things?
2. Independently form new ideas or ask questions about family beliefs or rules?
3. Consider many viewpoints and the feelings of others when thinking about a situation?
4. Share this thought process aloud when making decisions?
5. Ask questions about global concepts such as justice, history, and politics?
6. Talk about long-term plans and goals?

If your answers are mostly yes, your teen is better equipped to handle an online presence. Other considerations include your teen's sense of self. If they struggle with insecurity, low self-esteem, and lack of confidence, social media is *not* going to help. If they're generally confident and responsible, it *might* be appropriate.

If your teen is ready for social media, adhere to platform age requirements, demonstrating honesty and integrity. If your teen uses a platform, you should use it too. Teens often hide things because they fear you'll see risk and remove access. If you create open channels of communication and ground rules for disclosure, they will share more. Explore creating a written contract to clearly outline your expectations and the consequences for infractions.

Ten Tips for Safe and Healthy Social Media Use

1. Set accounts to "private." Don't allow teens under eighteen to have a public account without serious consideration and professional legal consultation.
2. Use stock photos for profile pics. This is something generic: a tree, beach, puppy, geometric pattern. Something that doesn't say "I'm a twelve-year-old naive kid looking for followers!" Seeing a minor, especially with a public account, is a gift for online predators who spend their day surfing social media for vulnerability and easy access.
3. Never "friend" anyone who isn't your friend in real life. It doesn't matter if they're Johnny's uncle's friend's cousin's brother's girl-friend or if the most popular kid in school "vetted" them. *Only* friend your *real-life* friends. *Never* agree to meet a stranger. Ever.
4. Don't post personal information such as a birth date, school name, or home address that could encourage exploitation or identity theft. Don't publicly post school sports team uniforms.

It's easy for a predator to look up a schedule on a website and show up. Sadly, I've seen this happen too.

5. Avoid apps allowing anonymous users. These are notorious for predators. Also be aware of chat functions in online gaming systems or anonymous messaging apps, which are easy to use to exploit or extort teens.

6. Create a family media plan, and *everyone* should stick to it. (Yes, you too.) Designate tech-free zones and tech-free times. In my house, tech-free zones are the dinner table, the car (hello, captive audience), and bedrooms, which should be for sleep and rest. I get it, people use their phones as alarms. But there are amazing little things sold in stores called alarm clocks that wake you up in the morning. I have a tray on my kitchen counter where teen friends check in their phones. I have plenty of chargers and they have access, but not in my kids' bedrooms. (Would you allow your teen to have a party at night with two thousand people—including strangers—in their room, plus ten thousand of their closest friends' followers? Of course not, but this is what we do with social media.) I see teens inadvertently exploited with pictures of their most sacred spaces and in various stages of undress because friends take selfies without noticing who is in the background.

7. Model being a good digital citizen. Put your phone down and listen with your face during conversations. Adopt healthy boundaries. Ask permission before posting a photo of your teen on social media. Teach your teens to give the same respect to others. Ask before posting. Make sure they feel good about what you post and that your narrative is in sync with their self-image. Sometimes our posts create pressure to live up to a narrative or image we are creating for them or generalize a struggle in character traits.

8. Set firm boundaries. Advise of dangers engaging online while distracted and walking, biking, or driving. Enable software to protect teens from receiving texts while driving. Ask friends and siblings to hold them accountable and ask them to hold you accountable too. Don't let devices distract from good sleep. Disengage at least an hour prior to bedtime. I see teens with sleep deprivation because they get up in the night to keep a streak or check notifications. Did you know sleep deprivation has similarities with the effects of being drunk?[9] Both slow reaction time, cause difficulty focusing, and create feelings of restlessness and irritability. It's not acceptable to send intoxicated teens to school, but most teens go to school sleep-deprived every day. Students with less sleep are at higher risk for academic difficulties,[10] physical injury, car accidents, mental health problems, immune dysfunction, and heart disease.

9. Talk about the quality of information on social media. I often see teens with questions about sensitive subjects they may not want to ask their parents, so they use online or social media sources. Talk to them about clickbait, phishing, and online scams. I've fielded Google search advice gems from teens like "you can't get pregnant if you have sex in a swimsuit," "using nail polish as effective birth control" (yes, really, and we all have questions), and "drinking black coffee helps grow chest hair." Teens have a hard time telling real news from fake. Help them acquire this skill.

10. Recognize and discuss the implications of a permanent digital footprint impacting college admissions, military applications, scholarships, coaches/recruiters, employers, and identity theft. A momentary indiscretion creates permanent impact. I assure you, as a university admissions committee member, I absolutely

looked at the social media profiles of applicants. I also called roll in my class one day using social media profile pictures. It was very effective, as drunken photos and obscene gestures paraded across the screen.

Maybe you're sitting here thinking, "Wow, I haven't done any of this." "I've blown it." "We've done everything wrong." "I've ruined my kid!" "What do I do now?" First, give yourself grace. These are new things that are changing constantly. We don't know what we don't know. It's hard to know what we need to know. A mom once asked me to recommend smartphone monitoring software because her teen successfully removed seven previous programs. I gently suggested maybe the answer wasn't software but to take away the phone. When I die, my kids will commiserate over my mantra, "iPay, iSay."

It's perfectly okay to reset boundaries.

You can say, "I learned some new information to help better guide our decision-making and we're going to reset some boundaries for your health and safety." Then reset them. They may complain in dramatic fashion. But that's okay. This isn't about being the phone or social media police. No matter what happens, it's *never* too late for a fresh start.

This journey is about building relationships in which your teen is comfortable asking you uncomfortable questions.

BEHIND THE HOME DOOR

Asking your teen to teach you something creates a dynamic power shift. It's empowering to be in charge and feel valued for one's personal expertise. Most teens know more about social media than you do, so leverage that knowledge to create a bonding moment. Resist the urge to address anything negative you see in the moment. If you don't like the pose they chose or words they used, tuck it away for a later conversation—unless something is truly alarming.

Conversation Doors

- Try a new social media platform, ideally one your teen is already on. Ask your teen to help you create a profile.
- Create crazy trick-shot videos together or maybe science experiments, karaoke, cooking, or a time-lapse project. Create a sports highlight reel if you have an athlete.
- Ask your teen to teach you how to take photos with selfie filters. Print a photo and put it in their room with a thank-you note.
- Ask your teen to make a TikTok or dance video with you. Rely on their expertise and creative direction to make it happen. Step out of your comfort zone and be vulnerable.
- Start a Pinterest board together. Choose a topic such as planning a family vacation, room redecoration, or Christmas wish lists. It's a great way to see what captivates your teen's interest.
- Find your old notes from high school, the kind so carefully and intricately folded. Think MASH. You know the type. Share these with your teen as your version of social media.
- Host a group social media photo shoot in a fun location. Teens know what to do!

Conversation Keys

After you complete your activity and hopefully laugh until your bellies hurt, initiate a conversation. Remember to LOVE your teen.

Listen with your face:
- Thank them for teaching you something new.
- Say specifically what you enjoyed about the experience.
- Share one new thing you learned or observed about their personality and compliment it.
- Tell them something you learned that surprised you.

Offer open-ended questions:
- "What do you like best about using social media?"
- "What is your favorite selfie and why?"
- "How do your friends encourage you or make you laugh on social media?"
- "What makes you anxious, depressed, or discouraged about what you see posted?"
- "How do you feel about what you post?"
- "What else would you like to share?"

Validate feelings:
- "I'm sorry you experienced this."
- "That must have been hurtful."
- "I can understand your frustration."
- "I'm so glad to see you enjoying this experience!"
- "The way you responded showed courage."

Explore next steps together:

Encourage your teen to come to you with any questions or concerns. Acknowledge they'll make mistakes but emphasize you're a safe place to share. While mistakes may have consequences, your love is unconditional. Work together to create a plan for safe, healthy social media use.

BEHIND THE HEART DOOR

You might have a great experience or you might learn things that will break your heart as a parent. If there are concerning issues, seek counsel from your health-care provider, school counselor, psychologist, spiritual leader, or other trusted source. Teens today struggle mightily with the pull of social media. It's important to help them develop a healthy and realistic self-image, rooted and grounded by faith in Christ. We are His image bearers, and each of us is fearfully and wonderfully made.

Devotional

Imago Dei is a theological term used to convey the incredible truth that we are created in the image and likeness of God. The word *image* means mirror or reflection. Many times, though, when we look in the mirror, we don't see imago Dei. Instead of seeing the fingerprints of God through His unique creation, we see only imperfections. Our mirror self-talk is crueler than anything we would say to anyone else's face.

"How could you be so stupid?"

"You're ugly and fat and no one likes you."

"Your hair is hideous."

"You're so old."

"You're out of shape and slow."

"No one wants you."

But God says, "You are *called*." "You are *chosen*." "You're a *new creation*." "You are *forgiven*." "You are *blessed*." "You are *set free*." "You are *redeemed*." "You are *beloved*." "You're being *transformed*." "You are the *apple of My eye*." "You are *pursued*." "You're a *child of God*." "You are *adopted, no longer an orphan*." "You are *pleasing*." "You are *never alone*." "You are a *masterpiece*."

Our identity in Christ is much more powerful than our own image crafting. Put these on sticky notes on your teen's mirror (and yours too!) as a powerful reminder.

Reflect

What image are you crafting for your teen through your social media use?

What media habits in your family need to change to promote healthy use and boundaries?

How can you intentionally help your teen to see their self-image through the eyes of Christ?

Pray

(From Psalm 139) God, I thank You for this fearfully and wonderfully made teen who bears Your image. Your eyes saw and knew _____ in the womb, intricately woven. You have every day of their life in Your hand. You know when _____ sits down and when they rise. You know their thoughts from afar, even when I don't. You search their path and are familiar with all their ways.

Even before a word is on my tongue, You know what it will be. You hem me in as a parent, going behind and before me, leading me, Your hand holding mine. How precious are Your thoughts, O God! Search my heart. If my words or actions grieve _____, lead me on the wings of the morning. Help me reflect in _____'s eyes the image You created them to be. Amen.

Act

(Legacy Letter) Write an I Am poem for your teen.

> I am your (mom, mama, godmother, pops, bonus
>   dad . . . what does your teen call you?).
> I wonder (something you're curious about
>   your teen).
> I hear (sounds that remind you of your teen).
> I see (good things you see your teen doing).
> I want (a desire for your teen).
> I am your (repeat the name from earlier).
> I pretend (something you pretend to be or do that
>   they may not know).
> I touch (something special belonging to your teen).
> I worry (something that worries you about
>   your teen).
> I cry (something that makes you cry for your teen,
>   whether tears of joy or sadness).
> I am your (repeat your name).
> I understand (something you know to be true
>   about how your teen feels).
> I say (something you believe in strongly).
> I dream (something you dream for your teen's
>   future).
> I try (something you make an effort toward with
>   your teen).

I hope (something you hope for your relationship
    with your teen).
I am your (repeat your name).
You are (your child's name).

Put this poem somewhere your teen will find it privately. If you're artistic, feel free to be creative in the design. You can personalize it or print it with graphics. You can write it on a napkin if you're not the sentimental type. Commit to not expecting a response. Give it as a free gift, trusting God with the outcome while following Him in the journey. This is another seed you've planted for a later harvest.

three

CYBERBULLYING

How to Create a Safe Space in an Unsafe World

The larger-than-life smiling face of a beautiful twelve-year-old girl shined down at me from the oversized screen on the conference stage. This was the first time I saw Megan. Her mother took the podium and shared Megan's story of being severely bullied at school—to the point her parents changed schools. As is the case with most bullying, it exposed and exploited deepest insecurities. After experiencing social rejection, Megan was befriended online by a boy in their community who was homeschooled. Her parents monitored this budding relationship closely on social media. After a time, the friendship soured without explanation. The boy began to send negative messages, eventually telling Megan everyone hated her and even more cruel things. After telling Megan the world would be better off without her, she died by suicide in her bedroom while her parents were downstairs making dinner and discussing ways to support her.

This is beyond tragic, but, unbelievably, the worst part of the story is still to come. It turns out this boy who befriended Megan

41

wasn't a real person but a digital creation dreamed up by a mother and daughter living four doors down. They created a plan with friends to form this friendship as a "joke," using information gained to manipulate social circumstances.

So here I was, face-to-face with Megan's mother, side by side with her health-care provider, listening to them courageously share their story to prevent other parents from experiencing the same kind of devastating pain.

BEHIND THE CLINIC DOOR

Electronic (or digital) aggression is a new term that broadly describes modern phenomena occurring in online experiences. Teens who experience this are at greater risk for depression, substance abuse, aggressive behaviors, and suicide. On the flip side, teens who act as online aggressors have relationship problems, including damaged emotional bonds with parents and lower self-esteem. They engage in risk-taking behaviors such as property damage and substance misuse or abuse while experiencing higher rates of depression and suicide. Even more complicated, some teens are both victims and perpetrators, creating a complex web of consequences not easy to address. Teens need effective response strategies and protective factors to develop resilience and avoid the negative outcomes of toxic stress arising from digital aggression.

At some point when you were growing up, you probably experienced some sort of bullying. As embarrassing as this is to share, I remember being in eighth grade and being called RBB for the entire year. I had *no* idea what that meant, but I knew everyone was laughing except me. I finally overheard a conversation revealing their secret joke.

Road Block Butt. I was mortified. Truthfully, I wanted to die. Looking back now, with adult perspective, I can see this seems mild, but it was nonetheless traumatic to me at the time. I can also see how this moniker was started by a classmate who responded in an unhealthy way to her own insecurity over her lack of pubertal development and jealousy over my early arrival in that space. But I didn't know that then and, frankly, it wouldn't have mattered anyway.

Here's the thing though, my boomer, Gen X, and millennial friends, at least we had some sort of safe space where we could lock ourselves away from this kind of exposure and treatment. Maybe that was home, summer camp, or even grandma's house—somewhere you didn't have to worry about Big Mike beating you up behind the school or Mean Jean eviscerating your outfit. Out of sight, out of mind. Today, things are different. Your teen may not even know their bully because they hide in online profiles. The largest audience for bullying used to be the school cafeteria, but now humiliation easily goes viral for audiences of *millions*. As parents, our hearts are sick with dread thinking about the ways school has changed since we were there. We experience anxiety over lockdown drills and school shootings, but there is a weapon in the school environment daily carried in the pocket or backpack of nearly every student that is far more dangerous and deadly: the smartphone.

Today's teens face bullying 24/7 in online forums. You might be thinking, *But my teen doesn't have a smartphone or social media.* Parents, it doesn't matter. Teens shoulder surf constantly, looking at screens of friends. They can still be bullied online, and those pictures or comments can pop up at any time in any place in their social circles. *There is no escape.* The slam books of yesteryear are now online anonymous forums. There are social media sites dedicated to albums of unflattering photos. Your teen has absolutely no control over other people taking photos and is constantly at the mercy of a renegade paparazzi ready to post with enthusiastic onlookers, influencers, keyboard warriors, and trolls. That's a lot of pressure.

My daughter hosted a slumber party for her birthday in fifth grade. One of the girls decided to draw a mustache on my daughter with a Sharpie à la Ross and Rachel of *Friends*. This was not done out of cruelty but simply immaturity. She's a sweet and precious girl who made a snap decision. It was before the social media craze, and I shudder to think of the viral potential in their social circle that would have made this unnecessarily live in infamy. As it was, the girls reconciled and moved on with no threat of lingering photographic evidence.

Health Impacts

Online forms of digital aggression include catfishing, trolling, flaming, outing, trickery, and cyberstalking. Are you feeling lost and maybe distressed? Hang in there, my digital immigrant friend. Help and hope are on the way!

A colleague, Melvina Brandau, is a pediatric emergency room nurse and researcher who studies electronic aggression. Some of this information is shared from her publication for nurses,[1] translated here for you as parents using real cases from my clinical practice. I am also sharing information by Drs. Justin W. Patchin and Sameer Hinduja, criminal justice professors and cofounders of the Cyberbullying Research Center.[2]

Cyberbullying

Cyberbullying occurs online through computers, cell phones, and other electronic devices. It's a critical health concern among teens with significant connection to physical, emotional, social, and psychological health concerns. The best definition includes the following elements: willful (deliberate, not accidental), repeated (a pattern of behavior, not an isolated incident), and harmful (as perceived by the victim). Basically, it's using electronic means and forums to harass peers.

Cyberbullying is common and makes it difficult to learn or feel safe at school. It overwhelmingly impacts self-esteem and friendships. When you think about in-person bullying, you can usually imagine a physical power differential such as size or stature. This is where bullying has changed, and we need a new mind-set.

In online bullying, the aggressor usually has a power differential. They are more tech savvy or an influencer who has followers with which to inflict social or emotional harm.

Teens can easily use an anonymizer, an intermediary website disguising the IP address of the poster, which leaves no easily traceable digital footprint.

In my practice, I've seen countless instances of cyberbullying:

- Slam book (anonymous bash boards)
- Blogobullying (creating a blog to demean and embarrass)
- eIntimidation (posting and sharing threats)
- Griefing (cyberbullying during video games)
- Password theft (posing as someone else and posting content to harm others or get someone else in trouble)
- Slut shaming (taking pictures without consent to portray someone as provocative)

I encountered password theft as a nursing instructor when a nurse reported he believed a student had stolen his password to watch pornography on a hospital computer. He was in deep trouble and irate. I was skeptical. I called in the student and laid out the charges, and to my shock, he nonchalantly said, "Yeah, I did. Was that not okay?" Young adults have trouble seeing the long-term impacts of impulsive decisions, especially growing up in a world where online chatting is unfiltered and has no expectations for privacy. I've seen many teens traumatized by the unanticipated impact of their decisions, saying it was only a joke. These encounters lead to psychological distress, self-harming behaviors, and school expulsion, and some degree of compassion is warranted.

Catfishing

Catfishing is probably not what you're thinking right now. It's not what you did with your grandpa. Hear your teens saying, "Okay, boomer," right now. IYKYK. If you don't get that, ask your teen. They'll get a kick out of your request but will think it's sus and wonder why you're asking. (Now you probably have to ask them about sus—insert laughing face with tears emoji.) Lest you think I'm too savvy, I once bought my brother a shirt when he was in high school, and when I asked him if he liked it, he replied, "It's tight," to which I replied, "We can get a bigger size!" Insert hysterical laughing from my younger siblings telling me "tight" had replaced "cool." (#Old. By the way, my hubby still calls that a pound sign.) Catfishing is a fake online persona to lure someone into a false romantic relationship or friendship with a goal of blackmail or theft. MTV even has a show exploring these stories. Other high-profile cases include Manti Te'o (a 2009–2012 Notre Dame football player and Heisman candidate), Meri Brown from *Sister Wives*, Thomas Gibson, and R. Prophet. Kimberly Williams-Paisley, actress and wife of country music star Brad Paisley, was painfully catfished by a woman who convinced them her daughter was dying of cancer. Because of the novelty of this exploitation, there are often limited legal pathways with which to respond. This is why it's so important for teens to never friend anyone online they don't know in real life.

Flaming

Flaming is a direct and personal online interaction that violates social norms and hurts the recipient. In other words, it's a nastygram. It's a lot easier to say things to someone online that you would never ever say in person! Flaming elevates into flame wars where teens roast each other. There are social media galleries dedicated to acclaiming the best roasts (or sick burns). One of my teen patients told me her peers perpetually flamed her, always adding #Loser. She actually carved that hashtag into her arm with a pen knife as she wrestled with the pain of that label.

Cyberstalking

Cyberstalking is using online devices for repeated, unwanted pursuit or tracking of someone. Three defining elements include (1) *repeated* threats or harassment, (2) online access to that person in digital forums, and (3) fear for safety. This happens by using geotracking, including geolocating (identifying geographic location), geopositioning (tracking by GPS location), geofencing (setting boundaries to alert when someone is entering or leaving a physical area), or geotagging (latitude, longitude, bearing, altitude, and distance—basically exact location when making a social media post). This is very scary stuff that needs law enforcement involvement promptly.

Trolling

Trolling is hanging out in online forums and leaving comments intended to provoke a negative emotional response in another user. Often this is for no other reason than narcissistic amusement as trolling is usually done in the absence of any relationship. In other words, trolls look for people they don't know and intentionally provoke the conversation (aka keyboard warriors). Enter the celebrated art of the clapback. Even companies have gotten into this on Twitter. Consider these trolling examples (if you're honest, some will make you laugh).

> **Old Spice:** @tacobell Why is it that "fire sauce" isn't made with any real fire? Seems like false advertising.
>
> **Taco Bell:** @oldspice Is your deodorant really made with "old spices"?
>
> **Twitter User:** @mcdonalds How much does a Big Mac cost?
>
> **Wendy's:** Your dignity
>
> **Anonymous User:** @jk_rowling Caught this article on yahoo. I will now burn your books and movies too.
>
> **@jk_rowling:** Well, the fumes from the DVDs might be toxic and I've still got your money, so by all means borrow my lighter.
>
> **Twitter User:** @tesco Who the *&$% uses Tesco mobile
>
> **Tesco:** Only about 4.7 million users, about the same odds as you getting a date this weekend
>
> **Twitter User:** @moonpie Your time is wasted on social media accounts
>
> **MoonPie:** Buddy, it's Saturday night and you're talking to a marshmallow sandwich on the internet

While some of these zingers elicit a chuckle, the narrative inevitably turns to debating when someone has crossed the line. These are highly resourced corporations. How are teens supposed to navigate the nuance of differentiating between a clever comeback and unkindness or cruelty?

Outing

Outing is sharing someone's sexual identity without their knowledge or consent. The most well-known case of this is Tyler Clementi, a freshman at Rutgers University whose roommate filmed and shared a video of a sexual encounter with another male student without Tyler's knowledge or consent. Within seventy-two hours, Tyler died after jumping off the George Washington Bridge.[3]

Trickery

Trickery happens when someone gains the trust of a teen and gets them to share secret, deeply personal, or intimate content, which that person then shares publicly, without their knowledge or consent. This can include sexting or image-based abuse.

Fraping

Fraping is commandeering someone else's social media profile or posting and appearing to be someone else. For example, someone might create a profile that looks like a peer's and begin posting racist content to damage their reputation.

Human Trafficking

Currently, the majority of my professional nursing work is focused on human trafficking and preventive factors. I've published extensively about it,[4] helped write and pass laws about it, and speak about it literally all over the world. An anti-trafficking advocacy organization in Houston literally changed my life through their director, who asked me to write a continuing education program about human trafficking. I knew absolutely nothing at the time. Okay, less than nothing, because I actually believed all the wrong things! Now I'm an international trafficking advocate working with the US Department of Health and Human Services to establish national trafficking response standards for health systems.[5]

The risk for human trafficking is real, but parents are usually most afraid of the scary guy with the white van at the grocery store. Let me assure you kidnapping is not even close to the most common way teens are trafficked. While that scenario may depict nefarious behavior, you should be far more terrified of the thousands of followers you don't know who enter your child's bedroom every night through their social media. This is a trafficker's paradise—millions of accessible, easily influenced teens sharing their vulnerability openly and publicly and allowing a trafficker to easily gain entrance and trust while building a relationship. Almost three-fourths of several hundred thousand reports of online child sexual exploitation to the National Center for Missing and Exploited Children at the beginning of the pandemic came from social media messaging.[6] Most teens are groomed into trafficking by someone they know, either in person or online. Traffickers are highly motivated to invest months or years in these relationships because they are so financially lucrative. When you see headlines about teens being "rescued" from trafficking, read the fine print. Most have run away from foster care or juvenile justice. My husband can't bear to hear the unspeakable things I experience, but he prays constantly for me, every child I encounter, and those I don't encounter but who need help. I could write a book for parents just about human trafficking, and I just might, so stay tuned! In the meantime, there are easily adopted practices that go miles and miles in helping to prevent your teen from being groomed or recruited by a trafficker. We reviewed many of these in the social media chapter and will continue our exploration below, but you can find more resources on trafficking in the appendix.

Parenting Pro Tips

Prevention:

Monitor online activity closely during the early stages of social media use (think training wheels). Don't focus on being a social media warden with secret spying and unnecessary invasions of privacy while you hover over every text. Concentrate on building trust. As responsibility increases, keep the lines of communication open. Teach practical online tech tools such as privacy settings, password safety, and reporting bullying to online platforms (see cyberbullying.org for a directory of online platform reporting instructions). Frame this as a co-learning journey, leveraging their tech-savvy skills with your wisdom and experience. Adopt this mind-set with all posts, yours included:

T: Is it true?
H: Is it helpful?
I: Is it inspiring?
N: Is it necessary?
K: Is it kind?

Early Intervention:

Although it's wise to advise ignoring minor teasing, insults, and name-calling, repeated digital aggression won't go away. Parents struggle with how to enter this space, and police are hesitant to criminalize teen behavior. Teen social problems usually need social solutions. If the offense is serious or repeated, escalate to law enforcement. The bottom line is that teens need to feel comfortable talking to adults while feeling confident that meaningful steps will be taken to keep them safe. The best possible thing you can do is to promote safety and give emotional support.

Signs your teen may be experiencing cyberbullying include school avoidance or anxiety, mood changes after online activity, being unusually secretive, sleep disturbances, disordered eating (more to come on that), avoiding conversation, refusing to answer questions, anxiety or depression, and suddenly avoiding peer outings.

Getting Help

If there is potential criminality (sextortion, blackmailing, stalking, sexual exploitation), call law enforcement immediately. Internet service providers or social media platforms can offer assistance, provided your teen has not violated the terms of use (including being underage or violating posted community standards). Report any abuse on the platform. If another teen is involved, contact the parents if possible. The school is a critical resource in reporting and deterrence and is obligated to uphold state laws governing bullying. Consider school policy and engage them as a partner.

When responding individually to your teen, emphasize their strengths and abilities. Avoid solely focusing on the negatives. Teach them to delete, block, and report cyberbullies. Screen shot evidence on phones, computers, games, smartwatches, and any other electronic device (see cyberbullying.org for tutorials). Don't be afraid to report the matter to the appropriate authorities.

What If My Teen Is the Aggressor?

Teens engage in cyberbullying for many reasons: retaliation, power, vengeful angel mind-set to protect their friends, and mean girl culture (which all genders can adopt). Sometimes teens are impulsive and thoughtless and don't think through the consequences of their decisions. They may genuinely not see the harm in their behavior, or they may be swayed by cheers from peers. Don't jump to generalize behavior to their character.

Warning signs your teen may be an online aggressor include quickly hiding devices, using devices late at night, getting overly upset when access to devices is denied, being overly concerned with cultivating social status, and overtly bragging about their online tech skills. Progressing concerns include behavioral issues at school, with disciplinary action and threats or acts of violence toward others. You will likely be very angry if you discover this activity by your teen, but work to cultivate empathy. Enact boundaries with love. Help them to see their digital reputation as others do. Enact consequences with dignity. Cancel culture can harm teens as they feel one significant mistake can irreparably ruin their lives. Point the way back to restoration with grace.

BEHIND THE HOME DOOR

Taylor Swift's lyrics sagely note that sometimes "haters gonna hate" and you just gotta "shake it off." That being said, these experiences are traumatizing and online culture is here to stay. Even if your teen has zero social media presence, they can still be bullied online or see their friends harmed. Having a supportive adult present is the most significant predictor of resilience and healthy coping. Use every opportunity to speak words of life that will serve as a barrier against unkind words thrown at the heart of your teen.

Conversation Doors
- Create your own kindness campaign. Flood social media with positive comments. Mail encouraging cards. Leave sticky notes with encouraging messages in restrooms, on lockers, or other places they'll be found.

- Visit cyberbullying.org or stopbullying.gov and review the resources they provide as well as your state's laws.
- Start a secret kindness campaign for a teen you know has experienced bullying.
- Explore Megan Meier's story together and talk about your feelings.
- Print out Toby Mac's #SpeakLife posters and put them up somewhere where they will encourage others.

Conversation Keys

After you complete your activity together, initiate a conversation. Remember to LOVE your teen.

Listen with your face:
- Say, "I imagine this might make you feel scared or confused."
- Thank them for being willing to share their thoughts and feelings.
- Share with them one new thing you learned or observed about their fears.

Offer open-ended questions:
- "How have you experienced or witnessed any of these things?"
- "How have you responded before when you've seen bullying?"
- "How did those experiences make you feel?"
- "What do you think is the best response in these situations?"
- "What would make you feel more empowered to respond?"
- "What else would you like to share?"

Validate feelings:
- "This seems scary and overwhelming."
- "There are fun things about online engagement, but there are hard things too."
- "It's okay to be _____(confused, hurt, angry) about this."
- "You can always come to me if something is bothering you, even if it seems small or silly."

Explore next steps together:

Answer the following question together:

What is your teen's action plan if they experience or witness any of the scenarios above?

BEHIND THE HEART DOOR

Our human wisdom says, "Sticks and stones may break my bones, but words can never harm me." This is so very wrong. The truth really goes like this . . .

_____

Sticks and stones may break my bones, but words will wound my heart and soul forever.

_____

Words hurt deeply. Think for a moment about the meanest thing someone ever said to you. It might be your parent, someone in school, your spouse, or maybe even your teen. It doesn't matter how many years have passed. You can go back easily and play those words on the movie in your mind with immediate emotion. When you recognize that emotion, hear your body's cue telling you to recircuit your response. How do you do that to be a healthy model for your teen? Read on!

Devotional

God's Word is living and *powerful*, sharper than any two-edged sword, piercing to the division of soul and spirit, joints and marrow, discerning thoughts and intents of the heart. Think about this. God *spoke* the world into existence. He did not use a potion, a magic wand, or a cauldron. He simply said, "Let there be light." And there was. In just the third verse of the Bible, we're introduced to the power of words. In Genesis 37 we read the story of Joseph and how words changed the course of history. Listen to the words Joseph's brothers used as he approached.

> Here comes that dreamer! . . . Come now, let's kill him and throw him into one of these cisterns and say that a ferocious animal devoured him. Then we'll see what comes of his dreams. (vv. 19–20)

The Bible gives four chilling words: "and they hated him" (v. 8). They sold him into slavery. Many years later, the brothers came to Egypt, desperate for food, and Joseph forgave them. It wasn't easy and he was emotional.

> [He] looked for a place to weep. He went into his private room and wept there. (Gen. 43:30)

Despite Joseph's provision and grace, this still wasn't a happy ending. When Joseph's father died twenty years later, were his brothers happy to see him back for the funeral? Not a chance. They had more choice words: "What if Joseph holds a grudge against us and pays us back for all the wrongs we did to him?" (Gen. 50:15).

Joseph had every right to do so, but he relied on a power greater than himself, saying:

You intended to harm me, but God intended it for good to accomplish what is now being done, the saving of many lives. (v. 20)

The tormenters were still tormented while Joseph found peace and success. I want you to go back and think about your earlier memory. When that person spoke those words, they planted a seed in your life. Take a moment and consider a paradigm change. When you feel the emotional pull that wants to trample you and re-wound you with those evil words, say to yourself

---

But God meant it for good.

Reflect

Can you find something positive about your negative or traumatic experience?

What did it teach you? What fruit has that experience produced? What are reasons for which you can be thankful?

Pray

(From James 3): God, our words are a match that can set fire to an entire forest. Our speech is a gift from You to be stewarded well. Forgive us when we use our words to stain, burn, and harm others.

Forgive me for the times I've used my words as a parent to condemn and shame instead of blessing when _____is in need. Search my heart and give me wisdom and humility in my responses to my teen. Protect _____ from jealousy and selfish ambition. Bless our family conversation with peace, gentleness, reasonableness, and mercy. Help me to guide _____impartially and fairly as I help them navigate their words. Help us to harvest righteousness as we sow seeds with our words. Amen.

Act

(Legacy Letter) Create a social media feed for your teen (on paper or online) and ask people who love them to write messages of affirmation and share their favorite photos. Style it after your teen's favorite social media platform. Be creative!

SUICIDE

How to Find Hope and Peace in a Broken World

The silence was palpable as I walked into the exam room. He was slouched in a corner chair. Long, unwashed hair strands fell over a clean, scrubbed face, creating a screen shielding him from eye contact. His sweatshirt was rumpled but not dirty. His cowboy boots seemed to pull him down toward the floor. He didn't smile or say hello, just stared blankly. His parents sat in chairs across the room. His mother tapped her purse nervously as his father answered a work call. They just needed a form signed (a formality they said) to return to school. "Could you do this quickly," they asked. As I moved to the exam table, I saw documents from the local hospital.

Diagnosis: Suicide attempt.

Discharge Summary: Fifteen-year-old male with history of depression stole a bottle of diphenhydramine (Benadryl) while grocery shopping with his mother and ingested entire bottle in store restroom. Transported to the emergency department via ambulance in cardiac arrest. Status post successful resuscitation; discharged from intensive care.

I looked up at the parents and said, "I think we should talk about this a little more," to which they responded, "We're so lucky another boy with the same name at school committed suicide this week. If anyone asks, we can easily say they're confused. No one ever has to know." My eyes glanced at the young man in front of me, carefully watching his blank expression as he sank deeper into the chair. There was a massive void in his eyes as I doubted he'd ever felt really seen.

BEHIND THE CLINIC DOOR

The story above is heavy, isn't it?

This is reality in pediatric practice today. Tragically, this case is by no means unique.

The topics we're covering are difficult to discuss, and this is one of the hardest. For some of you there are simply no words to describe your grief. Take a breath here. Get in a comfy chair, someplace you feel safe. Let's walk through this together to look for hope in something that seems so hopeless.

Of all the topics I'm writing about in this book, this one hits me hardest emotionally. My first very personal experience with suicide came crashing into my life when I was nineteen and one of my best friends died by suicide. I never saw it coming. I had *no idea* she was struggling. None. I went to her funeral alone and cried so hard I lost my contacts and asked a stranger to drive me home. I was wracked with guilt, wondering what I could have done differently. This was seared into my conscience for years to come by someone who said to me at the funeral in my crisis of doubt, "I guess you weren't really her friend, were you?"

My daughter's experiences with suicide during her teen years are too traumatic and tender to share even still. The physical human brutality of death and gut-wrenching raw expressions of excruciating grief she witnessed are just too sacred a moment to spill carelessly across a page. These multiple tragedies shaped her worldview so significantly she wrote her college application essay about the impact of the losses she experienced. When she was a sophomore in high school, she received first place for her science fair project correlating screen time to depression and anxiety scores. She was brokenhearted at the results and discontent at the notion of winning. More than 10 percent of her peers reported suicidal thoughts *every day*.

In professional nursing practice, suicide was something I saw early in my career as an every-once-in-a-while sort of thing. In my recent practice, it is an *everyday* occurrence. A teen who survived an attempt to take his life tried to jump off the hospital roof. Another assaulted me with a telephone when I intervened for her safety. Another was eleven years old and tried to strangle herself with a sock. I could fill a book with stories of my experiences of caring for these children from all walks of life. There's no doubt suicide is a public health crisis.

Health Impacts

Shockingly, suicide is the second leading cause of death between the ages of ten and twenty-four, superseded only by accidents.[1] Since 2007, suicides in this group have increased by up to 60 percent.[2] Approximately one in five teens report suicidal thoughts or behaviors, while one in forty are serious enough to need medical treatment.[3] For every suicide death, there are an estimated one hundred to two hundred survived experiences.[4] Researchers cannot agree on a single cause, although ongoing investigations include social media, economic stress, and mental health conditions. The leading methods of suicide include firearms, suffocation, and poisoning. Although females attempt suicide more often, males often use more lethal methods.

What Are Signs of Suicide Risk?

It's absolutely okay to talk about suicide risk. We can't assume a false sense of security and adopt the "not my kid" mind-set. Keeping an open mind that's receptive to feelings or experiences your teen might have is always a wise course of action. Although any teen is vulnerable, certain characteristics and experiences increase the risk. If your teen experiences a significant loss, including the death of a loved one, divorce, romantic betrayal, significant illness, or life-altering injury, a conversation to signal it's okay to talk about suicide thoughts is warranted. A case that stays with me is a high school senior basketball star who was signed for a college scholarship and presumably on his way to the NBA when he hurt his leg in the last game of the season. The surgeon gave the family a detailed operation report. "Any questions?" he asked. "When can I start playing?" the boy replied. The surgeon looked genuinely confused. "Never. You're lucky to have your leg, son." After he left, the family stood in shock, sharing they sold their house to move with their son to college to watch him play. Sadly, this teen died by suicide shortly thereafter. This was a long time ago, when we didn't talk about things like we're trying to do now. My heart still aches over this boy.

A family history of mental illness, substance abuse, or suicide can negatively impact your teen. Talk to your health-care provider about genetic and family risks. Teens with prior traumatic experiences such as abuse and neglect and teens in foster care or juvenile justice are vulnerable. Lesbian, gay, bisexual, transgender, queer, intersex, and other gender nonconforming (LGBTQIA+) teens face a greater risk than their peers.[5] Teens engaging in alcohol or substance misuse or abuse are at risk for impaired decision-making and impulsive choices leading to suicide. Having access to guns at home is a significant risk factor, as an average of 60 percent of all suicides in the United States occur by firearm.[6] Recently, concerns are emerging indicating a correlation between girls under thirteen years of age who use social media three hours or more per day and an increased risk for suicide as an adult.[7]

During a new onset of depression, the risk for suicide is greatest in the first four weeks. Most medications that treat depression improve energy before they improve mood. This can create a short period of time called emergence, when people with suicidal thoughts have the energy to act on them. Medication increases feelings of energy, but feelings of despair and hopelessness are still very real. Medication is an important therapy option for depression, anxiety, and other mental health disorders, including suicide behaviors, but you should have an honest conversation with your health-care provider about the potential risks. The general rule of thumb with medication is to start low and go slow. In other words, a prescription is not a quick fix. It usually takes four to six weeks to know if medications are working, and each adjustment takes two to four weeks to evaluate for effectiveness. Medication requires patience for the long game and can't be a singular strategy. During this time, extra care and attention should be given to watching for suicide thoughts and behaviors. Cognitive behavioral therapy, dialectical behavior therapy (recognizing when feelings or actions are unhealthy and learning how to confidently cope with distress), and brief intervention strategies (safety and crisis response planning) directed by your health-care provider are effective options to consider alongside medication therapy.

You might be feeling very concerned now, wondering if medication really is okay to take. You might be worried about someone you know and love who is struggling with mental health, and you are trying to quiet any secret deep fears about suicide. First, rest assured, many medications have strong safety profiles and widely accepted recommendations for effective therapy. Second, it's important to remember, although mental health conditions increase suicide risk, the vast majority of people living with mental health disorders will *not* attempt suicide. Third, it's okay to ask about suicide. I'll tell you how to do that shortly.

If you're worried about your teen, look for these warning signs: talking about dying, giving away special belongings, personality changes, exaggerated mood swings, sleeping all the time or not at all, not caring about personal appearance, academic struggles, isolation from peer groups, new risk-taking behaviors, using drugs or alcohol, a preoccupation with guns and weapons or violence toward themselves or others or animals, or writing, drawing, or viewing media depicting suicide. Seeing these warning signs in your teen is terrifying, but what we fear even more is saying it out loud. We think our silence somehow mystically keeps danger at a distance.

When my kids' youth pastor was in seminary, he discussed suicide after several tragic deaths in our community. His professor asked him a life-changing question: "What are *you* going to do about it?" Our youth pastor gathered the community leaders and planned a Sunday night event called Find the Hope, where we spoke openly about suicide. It featured the school superintendent expressing support, me as a pediatric nurse practitioner talking about risk and prevention and early intervention, a psychologist demystifying mental health, and a pastor offering spiritual counsel. It's a heavy topic for a Sunday night. We had no idea what response we would get when the event was announced, so we were absolutely shocked when we saw the school auditorium was packed with hundreds of people, all hungry for information and desperate for hope. Having an open conversation about this was powerful. After I spoke, a line of parents waited to share their teens' stories of struggle. They all had one thing in common: "I've never shared this with anyone before."

Parenting Pro Tips

It's hard to understand suicide thoughts when you haven't been there. We judge and assume and placate, mainly because we want to help, but we don't know what to do exactly. Our first response is usually dismissive because we subconsciously don't want it to be true.

You have to realize someone you love may be more scared of life than they are of death.

Living with this pain for their whole future is unimaginable. They see their struggles as an incredible burden to you. Ending their life would ease your pain, too, they think. Fear of stigma keeps teens from making an outcry for help. Among the people who die by suicide, 38 percent had a health-care visit the week prior to their suicide and 64 percent the month prior.[8] Stigma prompts silence.

What Is Stigma?

Let's have a heart-to-heart about that. The dictionary defines stigma as "a mark of disgrace associated with a particular circumstance, quality, or person."[9] That's still a little cerebral. I think about it this way:

Stigma is an unhealthy coping mechanism used to deal with our fear that something bad will happen to us or someone we love. Stigma, at its core, is simply social rejection.

When we hear the unthinkable happened to someone we know, if we're honest, our minds immediately start an internal ticker tape. Alcoholic? Mental illness? Abuse? Debt? Your brain clicks to a stop when you find the thing you see as completely different from you. You get relief with self-adopted comfort from the thought that it would never happen to you. You usually proceed to share that observation with your teen. Subconsciously, you're trying to reassure them (and yourself) that this couldn't happen to your family. This psychological shift is critical.

This moment of social rejection births stigma, placing someone in a different imaginary category based on a characteristic you see as undesirable and threatening to your construct of security.

These are ways I've heard stigma expressed when teens share news of suicide with their parents:

"How did they do it?" (**Never** ever ask this question! It helps absolutely no one.)

"I'm not surprised. I saw that coming a mile away."

"What a shame, but you know her father is crazy."

"How did you not know? Are you sure you didn't see any warning signs?"

"Why in the world would _____ commit suicide? They had so much to live for!"

"How could he do something so selfish? His poor mother!"

Contrast that with:

"I'm so sorry. That must be unimaginably hard."

"I'm sorry to hear this. How are you feeling?"

"This news is so shocking and sad. I'm here for you whenever you need me."

"I don't know what to say, but I want you to know I'm sorry and I care."

Parents, we have to be so intentional and thoughtful in the way we present our judgments of others to our children. One day they might walk in those very shoes, and their core memories of your response will influence what they tell you. The Pixar movie *Inside Out* is an adorable tearjerker story that explores the complex emotions of eleven-year-old Riley after a family move. Joy, Sadness, Fear, Anger, and Disgust become touchingly personified as they explore Riley's core memory orbs. They represent significant moments that permanently shape her personality and coping skills. If you haven't seen it, it's worth watching after reading this chapter, no matter your age. Now is a prime opportunity to create core memories of grace, compassion, and kindness in response to hard moments. This was on my mind as I picked up my daughter early from school one fateful day when suicide crashed into her world, saying, "What I'm about to tell you will change your life forever. I want you to know I'm here for you and we will get through this together." That's what she remembers most about that day. I'm not always that eloquent or self-controlled. Our first emotional responses as parents tend to be unhealthy human coping mechanisms searching for a way to separate us from the unthinkable.

Significant fear and misunderstanding engulf suicide. An estimated 30 to 40 percent of adults label suicide with words such as *selfish* and *cowardly*.[10] The words we use matter. Can you imagine, as a parent, thinking of your child in the most desperate imaginable emotional state and someone uses those words? No! Saying "committed suicide" is like saying "committed a crime." Labeling suicide as "failed" or "successful" is harmful. People with suicide behaviors already feel hopeless, and now we say they *failed* even to kill themselves. Shudder. It's no wonder it's difficult to speak up.

You can start casting stigma aside with something as simple as the language you choose. Instead of "committed suicide" say "died by/of suicide" just as you would say "died of a heart attack." You can also say "suicide behaviors" or "suicide thoughts" when talking to your teen about concerns they have about their friends. Suicide contagion (exposure to suicide behaviors through family, school, peers, community, or media coverage followed by more teens expressing suicide thoughts and behaviors) is real, although it can be minimized by factual reporting, limiting discussion of suicide methods, and implementing evidence-based crisis intervention efforts in schools and communities after a death. Let me say again, *never* ask about method, much less make it your first question.

If the thought "Would they . . .?" crosses your mind about your teen, then you *absolutely* need to find some way that's comfortable to ask, whether it's you, a trusted friend, counselor, minister, or health-care provider. It feels *terrifying* to ask about suicidal thoughts. It seems so awkward, intrusive, and somehow accusatory. You might be afraid to ask because you think you'll give someone ideas. Hear me say this loud and clear:

Asking plainly about suicide does *not* increase the risk of suicide or generate new thoughts of suicide that weren't there before. *Asking saves lives!*

Asking gives an important opportunity for connection and intervention. Here's the catch. If you ask, you need to know what to do should the answer be yes.

Suicide thoughts and behaviors occur on a continuum. Threat levels are assessed by considering several elements, such as intensity and frequency of suicide thoughts, perception of hope for the future, and detail in planning a suicide act, including access to lethal means and the ability to resist suicide thoughts. Intervention ranges over expressing empathy and messages of hope, connecting with mental health and social support services, safety planning, means restriction, and hospitalization. Always err on the side of caution and consult a health-care professional for any suicide concern.

Emergent:

If anyone mentions suicide, even if they appear to be joking, your teen should *always* take them seriously and feel comfortable asking about it *and* telling an adult. Simply say, "Are you thinking about killing yourself?" If the answer is yes, the follow-up question should be, "Do you have a plan?" If that answer is also yes, this is an emergent, life-threatening situation. If you don't have access to immediate mental health resources, call 911 or go to the hospital right away. You can also call the National Suicide Prevention Lifeline (800-273-8255), a 24/7 free hotline. Put this number in your phone *now*. If there is a plan, intent, and access to lethal means, hospitalization is usually warranted for safety.

Urgent:

If your teen is struggling with depression or demonstrates suicide language or behaviors, urgently connect to mental health services. Research suggests a decision to act out suicide behaviors happens less than an hour prior to an attempt 74 percent of the time, and 24 percent decide less than five minutes prior.[11] Create a safe environment to the best of your ability. Remove all firearms, knives, and dangerous chemicals from your home. Lock up all medications, including vitamins and over-the-counter pain medications. This is called *means restriction*. It doesn't eliminate all suicide risks, but think about when your teen was very young and perhaps you had a fence around the pool or a special door lock. Means restriction increases the amount of time and effort required to act out suicide, giving someone extra time to intervene.

Important:

If your teen experiences the death of someone close to them, seek professional counseling. Some may just need a few sessions to work through their grief while others need longer therapy. Early intervention promotes resilience and recovery. Your teen may resist counseling. It's your job to get them to the appointment; it's the therapist's job to get them to engage. If they won't go to therapy, go in their place to acquire the skills and support to meet them where they are.

If any teen expresses suicidal thoughts, stop the conversation immediately and ASK, an acronym used to label the three steps described in detail above:

1. Ask about suicide.
2. Seek more information and keep safe.
3. Know where and how to refer for help.

If your teen is exhibiting any risk factors, open a conversation with your health-care provider. They are equipped with helpful screening tools to determine the appropriate level of concern and intervention.

BEHIND THE HOME DOOR

Talking openly about suicide means reduction (preventing access to lethal methods), connecting to support services, and checking in frequently on friends and loved ones are effective ways to prevent suicide. Be kind and compassionate as you help your teen navigate these turbulent emotional waters. Express concern, listen authentically, maintain relationship connections, trust your gut, and prioritize safety.

Conversation Doors
- Plan a hike. It can be a mountain or a neighborhood trail. Plan milestones in advance where you leave something (a small gift or signs) for your teen to find. Correlate these to important life milestones to celebrate together.
- Throw a random Life Celebration party. Make your teen's favorite food, just because. Highlight photos from different years

and celebrate big milestones. Alternatively, buy a card or a gift just to celebrate life.

- Watch *Dear Evan Hansen* together and use the published study guide to explore questions and themes.
- If you were impacted by suicide but haven't shared this with your teen, consider taking them somewhere meaningful in the context of that relationship and thoughtfully share your story in an age-appropriate way. Your health-care provider or pastor may advise you.

Conversation Keys

After you complete your activity together, initiate a conversation. Remember to LOVE your teen.

Listen with your face:
- Tell your teen you know this is a hard topic.
- Thank them for being willing to share their thoughts and feelings.
- Share one new thing you learned or observed about their personal strength of character.
- Offer a hug or gesture of physical affection.

Offer open-ended questions:
- "How has suicide impacted you?"
- "What is your greatest fear about suicide?"
- "What would you do if a friend told you about thoughts of self-harm?"
- "When, if ever, have you experienced thoughts of harming yourself?"
- "What else would you like to share?"

Validate feelings:

- "I'm sorry you experienced this."
- "I don't know what to say, but I want you to know I care."
- "I know I can't make this situation any easier, but I want you to know I love you."
- "You're right. It's not fair."

Explore next steps together:

Make sure your teen has a clear plan of what to say if someone expresses suicide thoughts. Agree on which adult to share these concerns. Make sure they have the teen suicide hotline number in their phone for personal use or to share with friends. If your teen expresses suicide behaviors or thoughts during this conversation, it's critical you seek mental health services immediately.

BEHIND THE HEART DOOR

Right here, right now, before we go any further, if you've lost a loved one to suicide, there simply are no words to describe your pain, but this message is for you.

WHAT HAPPENED IS NOT YOUR FAULT.

Second, grieving is a process. It comes in stages we all know: denial, anger, bargaining, depression, and acceptance. That process is not like moving through one door and closing another behind you. It's messy. It's unpredictable. Triggers will come unwarned. Give yourself grace and space to grieve. It doesn't matter if it's been three months or thirty years. Everyone grieves differently. It's hard.

Third, if you're struggling but haven't sought counseling or mental health support, I encourage you to take that step. Talk to someone. Find support, whether a minister, friend, counselor, or support group.

Devotional

Suicide is not a new phenomenon. Did you know seven instances are recorded in the Bible? As God's image bearers, we must be aware that Satan seeks to steal, kill, and destroy. He is called the father of lies and a murderer, whose native language is lies. He whispers convincing deceptions to destroy God's image in you—they're better off without you . . . no one cares . . . you're all alone . . . there's no hope. All of these are lies.

But God's love surpasses our ability to even comprehend it. Jesus gave His own life so we could have life more abundantly and experience the love of Christ and fullness of God. *Nothing* separates us from the love of God through Christ, *even death*. We can call this to mind and have hope. Because of the Lord's great love we are not consumed, but His mercies are new every morning, not every week or every year, but *every single morning*.

Reflect

What secret fears or unresolved pains do you have about suicide?

Have you seen or heard suicide behaviors or thoughts in someone else that need to be addressed?

How can your speech and actions convey empathy and decrease stigma and shame?

Pray

(From Romans 8) God, we know there is no condemnation for those who are in Christ Jesus. With Christ in us, even though our bodies may die, Your Spirit gives life and adoption into Your kingdom as children, heirs of God, and co-heirs with Christ. In all things, You work for the good of those who love You and are called according to Your purpose. Neither death nor life, angels nor demons, neither present nor future, nor any powers, neither height nor depth, nor anything else in all creation, can separate us from the love of God that is in Christ Jesus our Lord. Help us not to lose heart but to take refuge in You, a very present help in time of trouble. Be near to the brokenhearted and those who are crushed in spirit. Amen.

Act

(Legacy Letter) Create a life time line for your teen, noting significant milestones. This can be as simple as writing on a piece of paper, crafting with photos/stickers, or artistically using hand drawings or graphic designs. Instead of traditional accomplishments such as sports accolades or academic awards, focus on character milestones to frame your teen's life journey. Use these prompts to get started: moments of extraordinary courage, resilience, forgiveness, humility, integrity, honesty, loyalty, responsibility, compassion, selflessness, generosity, perseverance, kindness, creativity, and self-control.

five

VAPING

How to Recognize the Health Threat You Never Saw Coming

He was one of the best nursing students I ever taught in pediatrics. He was always on time and prepared, friendly yet respectful, eager to learn. He even ironed his scrubs, creating a crisp crease down the front of his pant legs. His badge was perfectly placed on his scrub top pocket with a smiling picture reflecting the smiling face above it. His last question each day was, "What can I do tonight to better prepare for tomorrow?" Children loved him, parents welcomed him, and staff appreciated him. On the last day, as other students said their goodbyes at an informal party in our conference room, he lingered. A shadow crept across his demeanor, and for the first time in six weeks, hesitancy slumped across his shoulders. His hands fidgeted nervously as he took too long to collect his things. I pretended not to notice and said goodbyes as I walked the others out. I turned back, instinctively knowing he'd be waiting. He couldn't look me in the eye. I sat across the table and waited patiently. He hesitantly asked for a letter of reference, which was common when students near graduation, and this student had well earned one. Tears welled as he shared with a broken spirit that he needed it for the Board of Nursing to appeal for his nursing license. He disclosed an underage criminal conviction for possession of vaping paraphernalia with marijuana. Even though it was a misdemeanor, if it was not expunged or sealed, this could impede or even prohibit his obtaining a nursing license, depending on the circumstances. While there are ways to successfully navigate appeals, and many do, it's stressful and humiliating, with no guarantees. In that moment, he could not escape the sea of regret threatening to drown his career aspirations.

BEHIND THE CLINIC DOOR

Vaping is a major concern I see in practice. We will talk about alcohol and drugs in chapter 6, but vaping deserves its own exploration as a significant health threat facing today's teens.

Everyone today knows the dangers of smoking, but it hasn't always been that way. It wasn't until 1964 the US surgeon general issued the first official report linking cigarette use with lung cancer.[1] Even so, smoking continued to be accepted for decades. My daughters were recently watching first-season (2003) reruns of *America's Next Top Model* and were incredulous to see incessant smoking indoors, asking if it was staged for television. It wasn't until 2009 the Food and Drug Administration began regulating tobacco products and restricting the marketing and advertising of cigarettes.[2] It wasn't until 2012 (after the iPad was invented) that the Centers for Disease Control and Prevention (CDC) launched its first-ever paid national tobacco education campaign,[3] around the same time individual states started banning smoking in public buildings. Cigarettes are still the leading cause of preventable death, killing nearly eight million people each year.[4] My great-grandmother heartbreakingly succumbed in her early seventies to emphysema from smoking.

Teens today know *smoking* is bad for your health, and, in fact, young adult smoking rates are at a historic low with less than 5 percent of high school students smoking cigarettes[5]; however, they do not, I repeat, *do not* consider vaping or using the many other forms of tobacco and nicotine products on the market to be a form of smoking. Most teens don't know vaping liquids deliver nicotine. Twenty percent of young adults think vaping is harmless—it's just water—and nearly half believe it's a healthy alternative to smoking.[6] This means you don't need to talk to your kids about smoking. You need to talk about e-cigs, disposables, bidis, vape juice, Juul, Pod refills, hookah, and puff bars. Did I lose you? Hang in there, here we go!

Health Impacts

Vaping is using an electronic cigarette (e-cig). Although vaping was introduced in 2003, its popularity began to climb exponentially among American youth in 2014. By 2020, almost one-third of high school students reported trying a tobacco product, with e-cigs being the most popular method by far.[7]

My first awareness came as a nursing instructor in labor and delivery. A colleague rounded the corner to find a student at the nurses' station, e-cig in hand and a vape cloud billowing into the hallway as she casually read through a chart. The faculty said incredulously, "Smoking is not allowed in clinical!" The student replied equally as incredulously, "I'm not smoking!" Vaping was harmless and, in fact, healthy in her estimation. It wasn't even a violation of the student handbook, which only covered smoking.

What Are E-cigs?

An e-cig (aka vape device) is an electronic device with an atomizer, battery or other power source, and something to hold liquid—a cartridge or tank. Vapor is inhaled from the device. Other forms of smokeless tobacco include dip (snu, snuff, chaw), hookah (a water pipe with a smoke chamber), nicotine dissolvables (called lozenges, strips, or sticks), and Juul pods (a potent e-cig resembling a computer flash drive). From this point on, I'll address vaping generally, but ask your teens about the other forms mentioned. I was genuinely surprised to hear about the popularity of hookah. Apparently it makes for an exotic party game.

E-cigs, though advertised as safe alternatives for adult smokers, are obviously marketed to young people with vape juice flavors such as gummy bear, cotton candy, waffles, and unicorn milk. In February 2020 a nationwide ban went into effect on flavored vape juice, although some fruit, mint, and menthol flavorings are still legal. The ban covers only cartridges or pods, with flavors for all other devices remaining on the market.[8] This made disposable e-cigs wildly popular as teens prefer flavored and less expensive products. It's surprisingly easy for teens to purchase nicotine. More than three-quarters of underage Juul users report purchasing the device at a physical store, while half receive them from a friend and only 6 percent are acquired from the internet.[9]

It's important to say there is an ongoing debate about the benefits of vaping in helping adults to stop smoking by transitioning to e-cigs versus the dangers of teens starting nicotine use with e-cigs. However, tobacco-free and nicotine-free options are the only healthy choice for still-developing teen brains.

E-cigs contain harmful chemicals: formaldehyde, heavy metals, benzene, lead, nickel, paint thinner, or volatile organic compounds in addition to nicotine (not to mention the devices themselves can explode). Herein lies our problem: teens don't think of vaping as tobacco or nicotine or anything dangerous at all. When you say "vaping," teens hear "vapor," and that just means water, right? Throw in flavor and we're talking about flavored water, right? Think of it in these ways: Has your teen ever tried an energy drink? Has your teen seen you use flavoring powder or drops in your water? It's not a far stretch for a teen to see these as similar. However, e-cigs don't produce true vapor but an ultrafine aerosol that buries itself deep in the lungs.

Juuling (pronounced "jeweling") is a particularly potent form of vaping. One standard Juul pod (around two hundred puffs) or a disposable e-cig contains the same amount of nicotine as an entire pack of cigarettes. It delivers nicotine faster than other e-cigs. A challenge for parents is that e-cigs are easy to conceal, because they're discreet and mimic everyday household objects such as cell phones, car fobs, lipsticks, remote controls, and even asthma inhalers. Hoodies are specially made to deliver vapes through drawstrings (look online for photos). Many students don't realize these seemingly harmless-looking items are, in fact, illegal for minors. I encounter families whose students were in possession of vaping devices and criminally charged when they were holding what they thought was a harmless object for a friend. It's traumatizing.

Dripping is a new, dangerous trend. Instead of inhaling from the mouthpiece of a vaping device, vaping liquid is dripped directly onto the battery-powered coil. Imagine taking the plastic cover off your hair dryer and dripping essential oils directly onto the coils so you could inhale the vapor. Dripping heats a liquid to a higher temperature, gives a stronger "hit," and produces larger vape clouds. Believe it or not, there's a real event called the Vape Olympics. Internet search if you dare, and see worldwide cloud-chasing competitions with crazy vaping tricks that will shock most adults and impress teens.

What Are the Health Risks of Vaping?

Student e-cig use is linked to marijuana use, and alarmingly, e-cigs can deliver cannabidiol (CBD) or other marijuana forms. More than 20 percent of high schoolers report vaping marijuana. Vaping marijuana appears to increase the risk of using other drugs.[10]

In 2019, a new and potentially fatal disease called e-cigarette or vaping product use–associated lung injury (EVALI) was identified by health-care providers. All fifty states reported EVALI cases. Most weren't associated with nicotine vaping but with tetrahydrocannabinol (THC), a psychoactive component in marijuana. In addition, vitamin E oil additives seem to be the leading culprit of EVALI lung damage.[11]

Youth under twenty-five are more likely to struggle with addiction because adolescent brains respond to new experiences in more powerful ways than adults. Teens feel naturally invincible ("Bad things happen, but not to me"). The prefrontal cortex, the area of the brain responsible for emotional regulation and impulse control, doesn't fully develop until the midtwenties, challenging sound decision-making and peer pressure response. The prefrontal cortex is vulnerable to nicotine's effects. Nicotine changes the way connections are built in developing adolescent brains.

Hang in here with me for a minute. In a brief and simplistic explanation, nicotine literally changes your brain. Nicotine activates receptors that release dopamine, a chemical that makes you feel good and experience pleasure. It's an instant hit, about eight to twenty seconds from mouth to brain. As nicotine ingestion continues over time, the number of nicotine receptors in your brain increases by *billions*. The more receptors you develop, the harder it is to quit, because all those receptors crave a nicotine connection. Withdrawal causes anxiety, irritability, and problems sleeping and eating. The fastest way to feel better is to use nicotine for a quick dopamine release. Nicotine decreases attention, memory, and impulse control while increasing the risk of abusing other substances and experiencing depression and anxiety. If you quit, and especially the earlier you quit, the number of receptors eventually return to normal and the cravings fade.

Nicotine is extremely toxic when ingested orally or *through the skin*. A small amount can be fatal for a child (or a family pet). It's absorbed through the mouth without swallowing or simply by touch and is much more potent in liquid form than in cigarettes. I saw a toddler nearly die from nicotine ingestion after a teen spilled some vape juice while refilling a cartridge. This baby touched the pooled liquid and within an hour was critically ill. Reports of poisoning events related to accidental nicotine ingestion are increasing dramatically.[12] Early signs of toxicity include nausea, vomiting, rapid heartbeat, shortness of breath, wheezing, agitation, and seizures, and if untreated these symptoms are severe and can be fatal.

If you suspect your teen is vaping, look for such side effects as dry mouth, cough, sore throat, headache, weight fluctuations, lethargy, nausea, and vomiting. Vaping decreases learning memory, negatively impacting school performance. Signs of withdrawal include sweating, stomach cramping, constipation, difficulty concentrating, agitation, irritability, anxiety, and depression.

Parenting Pro Tips

According to federal law, you must be at least twenty-one to purchase e-cigs. But if teens don't think vaping is harmful, they'll do it even if it's illegal. Almost every week in my local school districts, the police report teens being charged for possession of vaping devices. In some cases, it's a misdemeanor, but in others it's a felony, especially when THC is involved. I've seen teens prohibited from participating in extracurricular activities and even expelled. The severity of police involvement and criminality is always shocking to both students and parents. It can further impact high school graduation, college applications, and, as you read earlier, harm professional paths.

How Do I Talk to My Teen About Vaping?

Even if you think your teen would never vape, it's important to inform and equip them to be aware of and responsive to situations where they could be unknowingly implicated. Many parents think talking about these things with teens may make it more alluring, but I *strongly* disagree. Knowledge is power. The more you empower your teen with advanced decision planning to act, the more confidently they can navigate that situation.

When e-cigs first emerged, I passed a mall kiosk selling vaping devices. I made the mistake of showing a tiny hint of curiosity, making eye contact for a millisecond. That was blood in the water, and the salesman came after me quickly. The first thing I noticed was his perfectly styled designer clothes and his Rolex watch, which was probably a *Rolox*. He had an air of confidence and charisma I found about as appealing as a thirteen-year-old drenched in Axe, but I could see how teens would want to emulate his self-assuredness. This was an attractive and charismatic guy. He touched my arm, encircled my wrist, brought my hand to his heart, looked me right in the eyes, and with all the Eugene from Disney's *Tangled* kind of smolder he could muster, he asked, "Do you vape?" I was horrified. I was a grown woman, a mother of four with a doctoral degree, and all I could do was sputter indignantly, "N-n-n-n-no!" He did not miss a beat but moved in closer, encircling my wrist tighter and said in a seductive "Most Interesting Man in the World–Dos Equis" way, "Do you want to start?" I still remember the cold chills running from the base of my neck to my feet. I jerked my wrist away with a self-defense move I had learned from a police officer at a mom's club and ran away. I realize this was not me at my best, but that moment stuck with me as I witnessed in a powerful way what our kids are up against. How can a teenager resist that?

What If I Find Out My Teen Is Vaping?

If you discover your teen is using e-cigs or other tobacco, stay calm. I know that's easier said than done, but our reaction as parents often goes from zero to sixty in nanoseconds. It comes from a place of protection. We aren't truly angry at our kids. We are angry that something threatens to derail their future. Let's direct that protective spirit, but not at the heart of our children. Don't lead with statements such as "How could you do this?" or "What were you thinking?" Don't lead with a litany of meaningless punishments: "You're grounded for life!" or "Your life as you know it is over!" Those are not helpful in this moment. I'm not saying there shouldn't be consequences, but discipline should *never* be delivered from a place of anger.

How you react in this moment shapes your teen's self-image, behavior, and future willingness to share openly with you.

Upon discovering your teen is vaping, immediately schedule an appointment with your health-care provider for evaluation and connection to resources or services. If your teen experiences legal consequences related to vaping, consult with your trusted health-care provider and seek legal advice. This is a traumatic experience and counseling is helpful. When teens have adverse childhood experiences, depression and anxiety are common. Reassure them this is a normal bodily response to stress. Remove any stigma from seeking help. Early intervention builds resilience, improving the outcome of long-term mental health.

BEHIND THE HOME DOOR

Prevention is best but requires proactive conversation. Instead of interrogation, ask genuinely, using curiosity as an initial approach. Don't come across as an expert with newly acquired knowledge. Invite them on a co-learning journey. Teens crave active listening and the chance to speak freely without the constraints of weighing words through the lens of their peers. They might be able to tell you how vaping works but might genuinely not know how dangerous it can be.

Planning a conversation in advance avoids feelings of urgency and anxiety when you discover a concern. Allow teens to use you as an out: "My parents would freak out if I got anywhere near that." Their planned response needs to be comfortable to their personality and appropriate for the situation. Don't tell your teen what to say. Help them craft their own response.

Conversation Doors
- Together, create a script for how your teen would refuse if asked to try e-cigs. Practice with lighthearted role play or invite friends

over to make a video. It's okay to be silly. They may roll their eyes and protest, but it gets the point across.

- Visit http://powertotheparent.org/be-aware/hidden-in-plain-sight with your teen. Identify clues for potential substance abuse in a teen's room.

- If you know someone who is struggling with nicotine addiction and is willing to share their experience, visit them together and listen to their story. Personal stories are powerful, and hearing from a trusted adult reinforces the messages coming from parents.

- Search news stories of teens who had EVALI. Explore their stories together and share your feelings. There are several children's hospitals that feature video stories.

Conversation Keys

After you complete your activity together, initiate a conversation. Remember to LOVE your teen.

Listen with your face:
- Thank your teen for being willing to engage in an awkward conversation.
- Tell them specifically what you enjoyed about the experience.
- Share one new thing you learned or observed about their thought process.
- Offer a compliment about that attribute.

Offer open-ended questions:
- "How do you and your friends feel about vaping?"
- "Why do you think so many teens find vaping appealing?"
- "In what kinds of situations have you seen people vaping?"

- "How would you respond if someone asked you to try a tobacco product?"
- "How do you feel about being in that kind of situation?"
- "What else would you like to share?"

Validate feelings:

- "I'm sorry you experienced this."
- "That must be hard. We'll get through this together."
- "I can understand your worry."
- "I'm proud of you for expressing your convictions."

Explore next steps together:

Encourage your teen to come to you with any questions. If your teen has used e-cig products and not disclosed that, create an environment where they can tell you without fear of anger. Predetermine fair, appropriate consequences. While mistakes have consequences, your love is unconditional. If your teen discloses vaping, seek evaluation and advice from your health-care provider to determine the next steps.

BEHIND THE HEART DOOR

Maybe this is a tough subject because you or someone you love regularly uses some form of tobacco. Every family situation is different. The guidance here is meant for teens who have never used nicotine to help them stay healthy because "safer" isn't the same as "safe." There are also very few program resources ("This Is Quitting" by the Truth Initiative is the first, https://truthinitiative.org/thisisquitting) to help young people quit. Prescriptions and nicotine aids aren't approved for teens.

I said previously that the implications are different for adults. No guilt trips here. It's very difficult to quit. Share your struggle with your teen if you can. Be open and vulnerable and talk honestly about it. Teens respect authenticity.

Devotional

Some of the most sacred moments in Scripture talk about *breath*, a word in the Bible equated with God's Spirit. God created Adam's physical body, but his value came when God breathed into him the very breath of life. This was a personal and direct act. God didn't command the wind to fill Adam's lungs. God animated him with His own breath and spirit.

Scripture specifically notes the moment Jesus breathed His last and, in so doing, gave up His Spirit. Even more miraculously, a resurrected Jesus appeared to His disciples and "He breathed on them" and said, "Receive the Holy Spirit." Perhaps this is why inhaling chemicals into our lungs is so addicting. We were created to be filled with the breath of God, but as humans often do, we exchange the truth of God for a lie and worship created things instead of our Creator.

There is a powerful story filled with mystery and drama in Ezekiel 37 of the prophet in a valley of dry bones. But God breathed life into them, creating an "exceedingly great army," inspiration for Lauren Daigle's song "Come Alive." It's no wonder David closed the book of Psalms with the call to let everything that has breath praise the Lord!

Reflect

What are your honest feelings about vaping?

How can you create a safe space for your teen to come to you comfortably?

As you talk to your teen about healthy choices, what unhealthy choices are in your life that need to be addressed?

Pray

(From James 1) God, You alone are the giver of life and every breath. We know every good and perfect gift comes from You, who never change. Thank You for the gift of life in _____. Help us to continually walk in Your spirit with Your strength. I ask in faith for strength and wisdom to lead courageously, knowing You give generously with compassion. Help me to count it all joy when we face trials, knowing You are faithful to complete the work You started in us. Let me be quick to hear, slow to speak, slow to anger, breathing in the moment You've given us. Breathe strength, courage, and wisdom into _____'s life. Amen.

Act

(Legacy Letter) Take a moment to just breathe. Collect your thoughts.

Slow down. Reflect. Listen.

Write a letter to your teen using the following inspiration prompts:

- Describe the day they were born and how it felt to watch them take their first breath. What were your feelings, hopes, and dreams?
- If you weren't there for their birth, tell them about the first time you met them or about a time you were so impressed or moved by something they did, it took your breath away.

six

SUBSTANCE ABUSE

How to Accept Truth with Grace and Courage

I was nervous. I was about to see my brother for the first time since he returned from rehab. Our relationship suffered for two decades from brokenness, hurt, neglect, and heartbreak. His struggles with substances began in high school as a teen, and they progressively spiraled out of control until arriving at a point of crisis in his marriage and with his children. I had no idea what to expect as I waited for him to arrive.

But God.

The moment I saw the light in his eyes, I knew. God restored my brother from addiction. God restored our relationship from brokenness. God restored his family to be whole again. God restored relationships that seemed unsalvageable. My brother exchanged darkness for light, hurt for healing, destruction for restoration, mourning for laughter, loneliness for companionship.

It's never too late to start again. Healing is messy, but God is working to heal our broken hearts. I'm in awe of my brother's courage, faith, strength, kindness, openness, and compassion. He is such a blessing to me every day! I celebrate answered prayers twenty years in the making. Now we are not only restored siblings, brother and sister in Christ, aunt and uncle to each other's children, and friends, but we are literal neighbors. How amazing is that?

BEHIND THE CLINIC DOOR

Substance abuse is one of the most difficult areas for me to write about because I've lived through its torrential aftermath. Before we discuss signs and symptoms or prevention and treatment, it's essential to see addiction for what it really is: a destructive coping mechanism to deal with the unbearable. Many parenting books will focus on how to stop your teen from using, what to do if you find marijuana in a drawer, and which rehab is most cost-effective. This is not that type of discussion.

Substance abuse is so much more than getting high. It's a symptom of a much more complex and intricate working of the developing teen brain. Using substances is a way to escape that which feels insurmountable, a way to get through one more day and avoid emotional pain, even if only for a few hours.

We have failed to adequately respond with seriousness in committing resources to the mental health crisis. We tell teens they just need to suck it up. But the feelings of loneliness, isolation, pain, and deep guttural hurt are not going away, especially in a post-pandemic world. When you read this chapter, my prayer is that your eyes are opened to the raw pain of young people who so desperately desire connection, peace, and understanding. Using a substance is not the issue, it is the tip of the iceberg, and we are on the *Titanic*.

You see all kinds of teenagers from all walks of life engaging in substance abuse: athletes, band kids, cheerleaders, church kids, and valedictorians. Teens lack coping skills or social support to navigate the crushing pressures of expectations. Substance abuse is easily hidden in families for generations in a cloak of secrecy and a culture of silence.

Looking from the outside, I had an idyllic childhood. My parents were high school sweethearts, and they married right out of high school and had five children, with my being the oldest. We didn't have much money, but we had a modicum of social standing in small town America, with my grandfather serving as the longtime mayor and school board president. He was the only person on both sides of my family to get a university degree—that is, until me. My mother was a walking advertisement for Betty Crocker (the Martha Stewart of the 1950s and 1960s), homemaking and homeschooling. As children we were well-mannered, well-dressed, and well-spoken. We were in church *literally* every time the doors were open. We climbed atop a pedestal to be admired by all, an unsustainable ideal. In that prism of perfection, addiction did *not* spare our family. Addiction runs dark and deep, like a strangling vine winding through our family tree, something I discovered in a genomics course during my master's work. The dangerous combination of bearing the unrelenting burden of propping up our pedestal, our family history, and our home's culture of silence on real issues collided with easy access through friends to substances that gave my brother temporary relief from his pain. As a teen, he may have used substances on Saturday, but he was in church on Sunday without fail. We all *knew*, but no one ever said a word. If he came home drunk, it was nice to see him so "happy," my parents said. On rare occasions when he was caught, my dad would give a half-hearted "don't embarrass us" speech with the unspoken agreement being continued silence.

I once had the courage as a young adult to address my brother's drinking with my parents and was severely chastised for disparaging my brother. I realized the feared danger here was not physical injury or death (very real threats) but the fatal social injuries of falling from our pedestal. The decision of going to rehab in his thirties was fraught with parental hand-wringing over people knowing. "What would people say?" "Wouldn't we be ashamed?" The answer is unequivocally no! My brother found freedom and joy in sharing his testimony from death to life. We should all be so bold. God is doing something new in his life. It's not perfect, but it is divine. Through his courage, relationships with my siblings are being mended as we've found strength and liberty in disclosing and forgiving imperfections. I sincerely pray it will inspire others struggling in the mirage to do the same. I share this story with my brother's permission and blessing, but he is not alone in my family. This story didn't start as instant addiction. So how did we get there?

Health Impacts

Let's start at the beginning. A substance is anything that alters your mood or thoughts. This includes alcohol, nicotine, prescriptions, marijuana, and illicit drugs such as cocaine and heroin. People experiment with substances to deal with social pressure, life transitions, and stress or to dull physical or emotional pain. As parents, we often react to the action of using without considering the pain that drives teens to use. Substances activate the brain's reward system with a flood of dopamine—a neurotransmitter that regulates how you move, feel, and think. Teens are also more easily addicted, with lower thresholds of exposure permanently impacting normal teen brain development, including learning and memory.

Addiction doesn't happen overnight. It starts with substance misuse (not following instructions for prescriptions or over-the-counter medications). Maybe it's taking an extra pain pill if the recommended dose isn't working, or taking an extra pill for attention deficit because it suppresses your appetite. The key is there is *no intent* to get high. No one says, "Hey, I think I'll take a step on the road to addiction today!"

The most commonly misused substance is a psychostimulant that causes neurological arousal and motor activation. In other words, it gets us going in the morning. Yes, I mean caffeine. Surprised? It's socially acceptable and quite marketable to boast about our caffeine dependence (self-finger-pointing at my kitschy T-shirt: "I *do* love Jesus *and* coffee!"). Don't worry, I'm not messing with your morning cup of joe. Caffeine misuse or addiction is mild compared to other substances, but consider the mind-set. Energy drinks are promoted with similar claims as coffee: boost energy and alertness. Energy drinks are like coffee for young people, and almost half of teens regularly consume them. An eight-ounce cup of coffee has about 100mg of caffeine, whereas energy drinks have up to 240mg (and often a boatload of sugar). The American Academy of Pediatrics recommends zero consumption of energy drinks for teens. Escalating risks find teens aged fifteen to twenty-three who combine alcohol with energy drinks are four times more likely to high-intensity binge drink than teens who don't.[1] It's a dangerous and potentially deadly combination. Energy drinks also worsen anxiety, sleep disturbances, and risk-taking.

What's the Problem with Teens Drinking Alcohol?

Addiction is the gritty end of a long and dangerous road, but it starts with the experimentation of easily accessible and socially acceptable substances, most commonly alcohol. There's a myth that alcohol consumption is a natural part of teen experimentation with attitudes of "It's a rite of passage." "We all drank in high school." "They'll be fine." That's all false. Underage drinking is risky and illegal in most cases (in some states teens can legally drink in the presence of a parent or guardian, but legal doesn't mean safe). Why do we insist on seat belts and shrug at drunkenness?

Teens are drinking. You don't need me to tell you that. Nearly one in five get in a car with a drunk driver, and two thousand die in alcohol-related crashes each year. In college, more than one-third of students binge drink.[2] Alcohol causes increased arousal and aggression while lowering inhibition. It increases the risk of falls, car accidents, burns, alcohol poisoning, violence, heart disease, cancer, and sexually transmitted infections. More than half of sexual assault cases on college campuses are linked to alcohol. Up to 15 percent of college freshman girls are sexually assaulted while incapacitated.[3] There are many high-profile cases from which to learn—Duke lacrosse (2005), University of the Pacific basketball (2008), Stanford swimming (2015), and Vanderbilt football (2018)—and all of them involved alcohol. To be clear, alcohol consumption does not *in any way* justify sexual assault. Victimized persons feel distress and self-blame and often tragically don't report for fear of judgment.

What About Marijuana?

The key differential between misuse and abuse is using frequently *with the intent* to get high. Nowhere is this seen more widely in teens than with marijuana. Thirty-six states have legalized medical use. Let me clarify something here: "medical marijuana" is simply marijuana used with a prescription. There isn't enough research to support the medical use of marijuana for teens, although there are narrow recommendations for some effective uses of cannabidiol (CBD) for severe seizures. Eighteen states have legalized recreational use in the form of tea, oils, tinctures, capsules, dried, edibles, you name it. It's an $18.5 billion annual market. However, legal doesn't mean safe. Marijuana is not legal under the age of twenty-one in any state. It negatively impacts judgment and memory. It serves as a gateway to abuse other substances and increases suicide risk. Smoking it causes lung damage. But that doesn't stop teens from trying it. The psychoactive tetrahydrocannabinol (THC) component of marijuana is dangerous for the younger siblings of teens in the home. Packaging isn't required to be kidproof (neither is vaping). It's really hard to see a toddler high in the emergency room because they simply ate a cookie. I've been there and seen torturous guilt. It's not a place you want to be. Marijuana also impairs driving at twice the rate of alcohol, increasing the likelihood of running red lights, driving at high speeds, crossing center lines, hitting pedestrians, and crashing.[4] A dear friend's young adult brother was tragically killed in this way by someone under the influence of marijuana and alcohol. He had just returned safely from a military tour in Iraq only to have his life terribly cut short, and the pain of his loss persists nearly two decades later.

What Does Addiction Look Like?

As substance abuse worsens, your thoughts, attitude, energy, and worldview are increasingly dominated by accessing and using substances. Many people who secretly struggle are high-functioning and keep it together in public. Our biased perception of drug use often pictures a "junkie" on the street, but reality includes students, parents, teachers, even elected officials. It can be *anyone*. I was at a large-scale political event where a prominent speaker was *obviously* and inappropriately under the influence. Everyone knew it, but *no one* said it, other than mutual side-eyed looks. The playbook for all parties is deny, deny, deny. Relationships start to unravel behind closed doors, and family members become codependent to cope. As abuse veers down the road to addiction, the social effects become more prominent.

Relationships crumble. Loved ones experience psychological, physical, and emotional harm. Financial stress arises from seeking supply. Legal consequences emerge. Daily interactions are characterized by deception, manipulation, and fear. Basically, life starts to fall apart.

Substance abuse becomes addiction when a behavioral choice becomes a brain disease with chemical changes and compulsive drug-seeking behaviors, regardless of the consequences. In other words, they're genuinely sick and need professional help. Medical diagnosis of addiction is called substance use disorder, a chronic illness with frequent relapses that pour gasoline on a rapid spiral of other negative health effects. Although any teen can experience addiction, a family history of addiction, mental health conditions, and prior trauma, all impact risk. Abusing on a regular basis creates tolerance (needing more to feel the same) and dependence (your body rebels if you don't have it). Withdrawal is an invisible tether that miserably drives you back to using. There is medication-assisted treatment therapy with counseling that can safely treat some addictions, although inpatient therapy may be a better option.

Symptoms of withdrawal make rational thought impossible. Teens feel violently ill and view their substance(s) of choice as curative (like life-saving medicine) because it quickly relieves the terrifying symptoms that feel like impending death. Intervention requires more than faith or tough love, although those are important elements. I see many families (mine included) desperately more afraid of the impact addiction disclosure will have on their social standing than the threat of death staring them in the face.

**People with substance addiction cannot change
their behavior without outside intervention.**

Parenting Pro Tips

Many parents believe their teen is immune somehow. This just isn't true. Addiction happens across all social spheres and impartially seeks victims. Here are real-life examples I've encountered:

- A seventeen-year-old track star from a wealthy family starts dealing opiates to feed his habit after getting his first opioid prescription at the dentist following the removal of his wisdom teeth.
- Laura Berman, known as Dr. Laura, a popular therapist, shared the heartbreaking story of her sixteen-year-old son's death. He ordered drugs to be delivered to his home from social media. Unbeknownst to him, the pill he took was laced with fentanyl, and he died choking on his vomit in the presence of his parents in what had been his safe space: his own bedroom.[5]
- A fourteen-year-old is at a party for a church youth group when a bowl of "mystery pills" is introduced as a game to "take one and see what happens." They did.

In the first two cases, the parents were shocked. In the third, the teen is now a young adult and their parents still don't know.

So what can you do? First, commit to understanding that *anyone* can experience addiction. Don't adopt the "my kid would never" mentality. It creates a steep barrier for disclosure. If you see the physical signs of drug use—clumsiness, stumbling, slurred words, bloodshot eyes, weight fluctuations, sleeping too little or too much, or trembling—ask *openly* and *plainly*, "Are you drinking or using drugs?" If you're not satisfied with the answer, take them to a health-care provider for assessment and testing. Yes, this may be against their will, but it's for their best. Social reasons for concern include abandoning old friends or hobbies, neglecting personal hygiene, isolating from friends or family, increasing relationship conflict, receiving declining grades, missing school or work, or being uncharacteristically moody or irritable in social situations. Watch their texting and vocabulary lingo for things that look concerning. For example, "Triple V" is Vicodin, valium, and vodka. Kickers, roxy, and M-30 all refer to prescription painkillers. Smarties, A-Train, and study buddies refer to ADD medications. Chicken feed and yellow cake can mean methamphetamines. Inhalants are whippets or huffing high balls. These are just a snippet. The point is to ask about unfamiliar words. Teens know addiction is negatively impacting them, but they cannot stop or accept accountability for their actions even when they know it's dangerous.

What Should I Do If I Suspect My Teen Is Using Drugs?

First, stay calm. If there are signs of withdrawal, this is a crisis situation that needs immediate medical intervention. The Substance Abuse and Mental Health Services Administration (SAMHSA) has a treatment finder to help you, or just go to the emergency room. If there's no immediate health threat, take some time to prepare. Gather facts. Search their room. Recruit support from people in your teen's life. Expect your teen's response will likely be anger and denial. A health-care provider can help mediate this conversation and do a thorough health and risk assessment. If your teen shows up to your conversation under the influence, wait until they're sober—but don't wait too long. Early intervention is biologically important. The longer you wait, the more entrenched their brain becomes in needing and responding to substances. If your teen is chemically dependent on substances, it's not realistic (or safe) to expect them to stop cold turkey on their own. Changing brain responses and behavior is a process, not a switch. Direct your anger at the disease rather than your teen. Avoid further traumatizing teens experiencing addiction with shaming statements. Interventions are glamorized and not often successful. Work with a reputable treatment center to create individual treatment plans. When your teen makes the decision to stop using and enter recovery, be supportive.

Once you're connected to treatment services, you will need a support system for both your teen and you. Create a safe environment by removing or locking up all substances in your home, including over-the-counter and prescription medications and household chemicals. Set specific expectations with clear consequences for breaking them and stick to it. Incentives and positive reinforcement are much more effective than punishments such as humiliation and isolation. Structured schedules and connections through social life, work, and school are helpful. Model healthy coping mechanisms such as prayer, meditation, and mindfulness. Offer an empathetic ear. Join a support group, seek family or individual counseling when needed, and connect to a church with resources to help you. Even if your teen seems as if they're apathetic about therapy, it's still effective.

Recovery is about progress, not perfection.

If your teen in recovery relapses, it shouldn't be seen as failure but as a learning opportunity. It's common and should be treated like other physical disorders such as diabetes. Long-term or repeated treatment might be necessary for severe cases.

According to the Substance Abuse and Mental Health Services Administration, there are four factors that support recovery: (1) empowering teens to make wise choices supporting physical and emotional *health*, (2) having a safe and supportive *home*, (3) participating in daily meaningful activities that give *purpose*, and (4) nurturing a sense of *community* through relationships and social networks that provide support, encouragement, love, and hope.[6]

What Can We Do to Prevent Substance Abuse in Teens?

As a parent, you cannot compete with the way teen brains are wired to minimize risk and feel invincible. Resist the urge to overexaggerate or threaten.

Scare tactics absolutely do not work.

Just be honest and authentic. If nothing else, appeal to their wallet. Addiction is expensive and may present a barrier they can logically see. Illicit (illegal) drug use often starts as prescription misuse. Don't keep old prescriptions in your home. They're more likely to be misused or abused. Participate in a medication take-back or ask your pharmacy about neutralizers to deactivate active components, especially opiates. Flushing medications can compromise water sources. Lock up every over-the-counter medication in your home. It's never safe to share a prescription. Think carefully about the subliminal messages you communicate by giving your teen another family member's medication and unintentionally normalizing taking medications other people give you. Carefully monitor any prescribed pain medications for your teen (especially wisdom tooth removal, in which over-the-counter pain medications are usually effective and sufficient). Prescribed opioid use creates a potential risk for abuse or dependence if not properly educated on the risks and benefits for pain management. At your teen's well visit, your health-care provider will use a CRAFFT screen to assess the risk of substance abuse.[7] Many times I'm able to intervene early for teens who are using substances and whose parents had no idea.

BEHIND THE HOME DOOR

If your teen is struggling with addiction, know that God matched you perfectly as a parent for such a time as this. Seek counseling for support in this journey. God is a perfect Father to us, but we are not perfect children. We are imperfect parents with imperfect children. Meet your teen with empathy and compassion while maintaining safe boundaries.

This is a subject for which there is great pain. I know all too well the crushing discouragement that comes from years of unanswered prayers. I know the pain that accompanies abuse in the form of codependency, triangulation, narcissism, and physical, psychological, and emotional abuse. I know the emotional energy and expense the drama of addiction can eviscerate. If you're living that, you need counseling for healing and healthy boundaries. This was essential for me when I was struggling to help loved ones through addiction. The good news is substance abuse is not an inevitable choice. If this is your teen, *celebrate* their choice.

Conversation Doors
- Explore the resources at onechoiceprevention.org.
- Try the "Talk. They Hear You." SAMHSA app with scenario-based role-play practice.
- Have a movie night (*The Secret Life of Zoey*, *Perfect High*, *Home Run*, or *Overcomer*). Discuss your feelings together afterward.
- Volunteer together at a local recovery center. Options to serve

include administrative tasks, event planning support, community outreach efforts, and food distribution.

- Research the twelve recovery steps for addiction recovery. Discuss how you might be able to support someone in that journey.

Conversation Keys

After you complete your activity together, initiate a conversation. Remember to LOVE your teen.

Listen with your face:

- Say "It's hard to see people make harmful choices."
- Thank them for being open and vulnerable.
- Share one new thing you learned or observed about their decision-making.

Offer open-ended questions:

- "How has addiction impacted you, your friends, or someone you love?"
- "What would it take for you to feel confident about saying no to trying drugs?"
- "What is your biggest fear about drug or alcohol use?"
- "What would you do if you discover a friend or loved one is using drugs or drinking?"
- "What do you wish were different about your school rules for substance use?"
- "What is the most likely way you see yourself being exposed to drugs or alcohol?"
- "What else would you like to share?"

Validate feelings:

- "I can't imagine the pressures and fears you're facing."
- "I'm sure it's hard to see your friends struggling."

- "It's okay to feel sad."
- "You can always tell me anything. I'm here and open for conversation."

Explore next steps together:

Discuss a plan of action for peer pressure, unintentional exposure, substance use by friends, and disclosure of substance abuse. Create a code word your teen can text you in emergencies. The code word means the following:

I'll pick you up from anywhere at any time, no questions asked—until the next morning.

BEHIND THE HEART DOOR

Alarmingly, 25 percent of kids live in a home with someone who abuses substances. This means some of you reading this live with someone who abuses substances or you yourself are personally struggling. Substance abuse takes an emotional and physical toll on *everyone* involved.

If you're struggling with substance addiction, you cannot stop on your own. You need help to repair the ways your brain has been conditioned to respond. There is hope for you.

Devotional

Addiction is a giant, and the most famous giant of all is found in the Bible. Goliath, the Philistine champion, challenged the Israelite army to choose someone to fight him, taunting the Israelites *every* morning *and* evening for forty days. Stop and consider the biblical significance of the number forty. Mentioned 146 times in Scripture, forty represents a time of trial and preparation for great change. God flooded the earth for forty days. The Israelites wandered in the wilderness for forty years. Saul, David, and Solomon each reigned for forty years. Jesus fasted for forty days and nights. There were forty days between Jesus' resurrection and ascension. After Goliath had taunted Israel for forty days with humiliation and fear, God sent David to the battlefield. He was a young shepherd, not even old enough to fight, mocked by the enemy, doubted by his people, and questioned by his own brother. In the face of this giant and armed with only five smooth stones and a slingshot, what did David say?

> You come against me with sword and spear and javelin, but I come against you in the name of the LORD Almighty, the God of the armies of Israel, whom you have defied. This day the LORD will deliver you into my hands. (1 Sam. 17:45–46)

The battle seeking victory over addiction is a giant. It seems impossible, but God loves nothing more than to work in the impossible. You may be in that period of trial. Maybe it's forty days, forty months, or even forty years. Prepare your heart for what the Lord can do. When the giant of addiction taunts you with sword, spear, and javelin, respond in the name of the Lord of hosts, the God of the armies of Israel, and declare the day of your victory, when the Lord will provide deliverance from addiction. Thanks be to God, who gives us victory through Jesus!

Reflect

How has addiction impacted and shaped your life?

In what ways have you avoided a conversation about this with your teen?

How can you support a family experiencing addiction by showing love and empathy?

Pray

(From 1 John 4-5) God, we have absolute confidence in approaching Your throne, knowing if we ask anything in accordance with Your will, You hear us. Help _____ to be an overcomer through You, who are greater than anything in the world. You loved _____ enough to send Your Son. Help us abide in You, obeying Your command to love by carrying the burdens of others. We see teens struggling with addiction. Lead them to life in a mighty and miraculous way. Everyone born of God overcomes the world, the victory upon which we can rest our hearts and our faith. Even when evil seems to win, You are ultimately in control. We can rest in You. Amen.

Act

(Legacy Letter) What's the greatest victory you've seen in your teen's life? Tell their story of victory in defeat, victory in the significant, victory in the mundane. Write the story in a way they can read in the years to come as a historical account of a direct eyewitness. Describe what happened, how you felt, how it impacted others, and how it could potentially change the course of history.

seven

DIVORCE

How to Find Forgiveness and Raise Resilient Kids

His body appeared full-grown, but the worried expression on this sixteen-year-old boy's face was childlike. He casually shared ways he engaged in dangerous, self-damaging, risk-taking behaviors. His demeanor was nonchalant, as if he were recounting what he ate for breakfast. He described engaging in online explicit communication with adult gamers, vaping marijuana, having unprotected sex, and driving under the influence of alcohol. He was also in church every Sunday, he told me, with a fake smile and obligatory head nodding. He was angry but didn't know why. He was lonely. Most of all, he felt undeserving of love.

His parents divorced when he was twelve. Their relationship is tense and conflicted. Each household has different rules. He's not allowed to bring personal items purchased by one parent to the other parent's home. He feels like two different people. He escapes to an online world through gaming, where he builds an alternate, more comfortable reality that transcends separate homes. His mental health screenings suggested depression. His mother is furious with his father for not forcing him to take prescribed medications. Mom demands I call child protective services. Dad threatens to call the police. The teen looks at me with a vacant expression, mentally checking out of this conversation, passively awaiting the verdict.

BEHIND THE CLINIC DOOR

Nearly half of American homes are impacted by divorce. While each family's circumstance is unique and many situations are not nearly as dire as what I've described above, children who experience divorce go through a challenging adjustment period of learning new rules and norms. They experience dramatic lifestyle changes as they adjust to economic loss and single incomes. Financial and relational stressors create physical health risks and academic challenges. Take heart, though. Thriving recovery is possible. Maybe at this point you're thinking, "This doesn't apply to me. I'm happily married." Please read on, because not only can you learn how to support families experiencing divorce, but the principles of building resilience are helpful for all teens.

How Do We Frame the Divorce Experience?

Children who experience divorce are often referred to as coming from a "broken" home. The word *home* is powerful. Home is where the heart is. Dorothy told the Wizard of Oz, "There's no place like home." When you're out somewhere uncomfortable, you just want to go home. Now, imagine your home is labeled as *broken*. Children have absolutely no power to fix that kind of adult brokenness. With the label of a broken home, teachers express pity while other parents skeptically wonder.

Never mind there are homes in which parents aren't divorced but fight like cats and dogs day and night. Never mind there are homes in which a parent is addicted to opiates, abusive at home while serving as a church leader with public admiration. Never mind there are homes experiencing a crippling lack of joy, where children merely exist as holograms capable of disappearing into nothingness during verbal tirades. But we decided to specifically call out divorce as *the* universal brand of a broken home. Can we be real and agree all our homes are broken in some way because we as humans are broken? Although my parents were not divorced, perpetual conflict and dysfunctional relationships made my home feel broken. So let's not frame the totality of someone's childhood through the singular experience of divorce. It's not fair to make the children of divorce feel their experience is a special kind of terrible. It's equally unfair to make other kids feel they should be grateful for a different sort of traumatic experience, because at least they don't have a *broken* home. Having said that, teens experiencing brokenness arising from divorce do have unique needs.

Health Impacts

During the aftermath of divorce, teens feel a wide range of complex emotions for which they are ill-equipped to handle. They might feel angry, not at you as a parent necessarily, but at the fact that life is changing beyond their control. They feel lonely, emotionally insecure, and sad. They might feel relieved at formal separation *and* guilty about that. A teen told me they never wanted to see their dad again, but they felt guilty for not feeling guilty. They might pick sides, directing anger at one parent while blaming another. Try not to take it personally. This reflects normal brain development, especially with younger teens who are concrete thinkers and judge situations not by shades of gray but by absolutes in the frame of a legalistic understanding of justice and fairness.

Coping responses to divorce include being overly introverted and private with their innermost feelings, arguing excessively to justify a personal point of view or adopting risk-taking behaviors to distract from the vulnerability of real feelings. Teens might intentionally provoke conflict, seeking to release emotional tension they don't know how to communicate in a healthy way. It's so hard because, as a parent, you have your own pain to process and new normals to establish, all in a vacuum of loneliness. All of this to say . . .

What if you reframed your teen's behavior? Instead of seeing your teen consciously trying to hurt you, what if you see a subconscious coping strategy to survive?

Instead of feeling angry and hurt, you might find greater compassion in recognizing your child's need for healthy coping skills. Reframing their behaviors uses your emotional energy more efficiently than engaging in every emotional showdown.

How Can We Best Frame Our Response to Trauma?

When a marriage ends, belief in a future you once saw ends too. Teens need to feel confident you believe in *their* future. Our words are so important, because, regardless of how it appears, teens listen carefully to what you say about them, and more importantly, *they believe you.* We get frustrated by repetitive struggles that lead to the same old argument where you push Play on the lecture you've now both memorized. It's a dead end and mutual torture.

Don't let a singular behavioral struggle define the totality of your teen's character.

Their struggle may be *what they do*, but remind them it isn't *who they are*. Don't let one unwise choice hold their entire future hostage. Saying "Why are you always so (fill in the blank: angry, sad, difficult)?" is very different from saying "I can see you're struggling with feeling angry. How can I help?"

For example, if your teen discloses they are watching pornography, saying, "Thank you for sharing this struggle with me. Sometimes people make choices like this to cope with something difficult. What support do you need to help develop better ways to cope?" is more effective than saying, "What were you thinking?! That's disgusting, perverted, and unacceptable!"

Reframing your response to poor decisions and destructive behaviors doesn't mean there isn't further conversation, consequences, or counseling. Discipline should never come from a place of anger and shame but instead be delivered with love and respect in the presence of clear boundaries. The important initial step is offering grace with a clearly defined path to relationship restoration.

What we say:

"I can't believe you did this!"

"You've hurt and disappointed me."

"I don't trust you."

"You've shamed our family with your selfish and destructive choices."

What we should say:

"I'm sorry you're experiencing this."

"I see you're struggling."

"I'm here to support you with healthy boundaries and connection to the resources you need to develop effective coping skills for this season."

"I love you enough to do that."

Parenting Pro Tips

Pediatrician Kenneth Ginsburg offers wise knowledge to help parents nurture resilience.[1] This practical advice is applicable not just in situations of divorce but in all circumstances of stress, trauma, grief, and loss. Every parent, read on.

How Can Families Recover and Thrive?

If your family experiences divorce, emphasize that what happened is not your teen's fault. Tell them and *keep on telling them*, even to the point it feels ridiculous. If possible, find a way to peacefully co-parent with regular communication and consistent rules supporting each other's parenting style. Seek common ground, even if it's just a one-inch square. Each parent should reassure their teens of unconditional love. If your teen experiences loss of love, support, or relationship with one parent, talk to your health-care provider about what to do and ask for coping resources. Shield your teen from as much open conflict as possible. Avoid a situation in which teens feel compelled to play mediator or messenger. Teens with stronger perceptions of family harmony have improved mental health.

Recognize it may be difficult for your teen to be open and honest with you about their true feelings. They may feel the need to shield you from any information they believe might hurt you or they could be afraid of causing more conflict in a contentious relationship. Free them from this burden of protecting you from further hurt by being courageous enough to accept brutally honest thoughts and emotions while also getting help yourself to process this. Make intentional efforts to connect them to other trustworthy adults willing to invest in being a positive influence. Make it clear that you support having a safe space to share confidential concerns. Set boundaries clearly in advance about what can remain confidential and what needs to be shared with you. It's critical for your teen to have a strong relationship with their health-care provider, recognizing them as a confidential and trusted source of support who can identify concerns and intervene early. Connect your teen to a church. Families who engage in spiritual practices together generally have improved coping skills and a greater sense of support.

Practically and logistically speaking, the value of consistency cannot be overemphasized. Keep clear lines of communication open as much as possible with norms on pick-up, vacation, and visitation. Avoid interrogating your teen with questions about the other household. Don't burden teens with money worries. Conversely, don't assuage guilt with lavish gifts. They'd much rather have your time and undivided attention. Commit to your own well-rounded health as a parent. It's scary for your teen when you are sick physically or emotionally if you are their sole caregiver and support system.

How Can We Support Families Experiencing Divorce?

If you haven't experienced divorce but know a family who has, offer support. Just be there. Listen more than you speak. Be trustworthy and keep their confidence. That's worth its weight in gold. Don't ask yes-or-no questions ("Are you okay?" "Can I bring you something?"). Ask instead, "How can I pray for you?" "What night can I bring you dinner?" I've had teens sob on my shoulder about the heartbreak of divorce many times. You don't have to say much. Just be there, hug them, pass the tissues, give them a safe space where they're free to be authentic. Accept them where they are. That means so much!

Offer to host others in your home. It's hard for single parents to have time to themselves without feeling guilty. Offering a fun option for their teen is helpful. If a suddenly single parent is struggling with the tasks the other spouse took care of, such as home maintenance, anticipate that need and offer to arrange to have it done. Be especially sensitive around holidays. These are seasons of new normals with painful reminders of loss. Host a single parent who will be alone for the holidays or offer a fun alternative for a new tradition together.

How Can I Help My Teen to Be Resilient?

Create rules for handling conflict. Determine together what boundaries work best for your family. My husband's family is Italian, so making rules to talk without using hand gestures is out of the question. Sometimes teens need a safe place to be angry, yell, and express anger. I've had teens punch pillows and break pencils to release anger. Make safe, clear boundaries for releasing anger ("You can yell, but you can't hurt anyone or destroy property"). Create a designated safe physical space for tough conversations. In my house it's a cozy corner chair in my office. My kids know it's a safe place to talk and will ask for an appointment in the "counseling chair" (or be told one has been made for them). Give teens a safe space with appropriate guidelines to express emotions with no fear of judgment. Sometimes just sitting calmly with them until intense emotion is spent abates the storm and allows peaceful conversation to follow.

"It's okay to be angry. It's not okay to be disrespectful."

"It's okay to be upset. It's not okay to throw things."

Another way to build resilience is to reframe feelings of power-lessness to strength after experiencing traumatic events beyond their control.

Stop here.

Ask yourself: "What is my teen's greatest strength?"

If you can't answer this question confidently in ten seconds or less, neither can they.

Help craft their sense of self by purposefully identifying strengths and making them feel competent about their unique contribution to your family. They should feel confident about stepping in and serving when there is a need. For example, my daughter's strength is hospital-ity. She always knows how to make anyone feel comfortable, whether it's freshly baked bread, a clean kitchen, or notes on your pillow at night. Thank God she has this, because my idea of hospitality is to go to someone's house who has the gift of hospitality. If someone asks me if my cooking is homemade, I say yes with a secret twinge of guilt. I *made* it *home* from the store with it, didn't I? It's a wonder we didn't all starve when my daughter went to college. My son's strength is comedic humor. He always knows how to make us laugh, especially in serious or difficult situations. (Okay, so maybe he put a hundred paper plates on the wall, *with gum*, for Nerf practice, but still, it's all in how you frame it, and, yes, I'm laughing *now*.) My gift is emotional enemas (you read that right). Uncomfortable but cleansing conversations no one wants but everyone needs to feel better and lighter afterward. (Wait, that's kind of the purpose of this book, so sorry for not better warning you about my gift.)

There is danger here (not in emotional enemas; we're moving on now, although you're free to borrow the term). If one sibling copes in a healthier way than the other, be sure you aren't subconsciously favoring their company because they're easier to be around. Don't say, "Why can't you be like ____?" Demonstrate equal value for different strengths.

In challenging times, it's important to celebrate small victories, especially in days plagued by setbacks and struggles. Praise your teen authentically for *specific* accomplishments. Saying "I'm proud of you" is different from saying "You handled that difficult situation with grace and maturity. I'm proud of you."

Most importantly, find forgiveness. One of my favorite stories comes from Clara Barton, the Civil War nurse hero who founded the American Red Cross. She was reminded by a friend of a cruel deed she experienced. When Clara didn't seem upset, the friend asked if perhaps she'd forgotten. "No," she replied, "I distinctly remember forgetting that."[2] Chronic anger from unforgiveness increases your risk of heart disease, pain, sleep disturbance, depression, anxiety, and stress while compromising your immune system. Lysa TerKheurst's book *Forgiving What You Can't Forget* is an excellent resource.[3]

Most children who experience divorce or loss are resilient and experience meaningful recovery. Divorce is a process and not a one-time event. There's ebb and flow, gifts and losses, heartbreak and healing on a messy back-and-forth looping path, not a straight-line journey.

BEHIND THE HOME DOOR

Your divorce may be something you've never had a conversation with your teen about outside the boundaries of anger, hurt, bitterness, or maybe just emotionless logistics of who is picking up whom where and when. Your teen longs for an honest conversation to ask genuine questions without feeling as if there is an image-crafting agenda. This is difficult in contentious divorces, where parents are guarded about what they say, afraid of the other parent weaponizing vulnerability. That's why it can be helpful for your teen to have another trusted adult to talk with in a more unguarded manner. Set some ground rules in what they can and cannot ask. If they ask something outside those bounds, be firm but honest in saying, "I can't answer that for you right now. I may revisit my decision later." Every situation is different. There are some things it's not appropriate for teens to know. There are some things it would hurt them to know, and they don't realize they aren't yet equipped to handle that hurt. I can't help but think of the scene in the movie *Hope Floats* in which Birdee sits on the front porch, waiting to pick up the pieces of her daughter Bernice's heartbreak after her parents' divorce. Bernice wants so badly to go with her father and has an idealized view of his devotion to her. Birdee steps back and allows him to reject her, knowing the hurt of that moment is inevitable and will be better served now than down the road. The strength Birdee displays in that moment, carrying her screaming, heartbroken daughter, makes me cry every time.

Maybe you divorced long ago, when your teens were babies, and you've put it behind you and moved on. Maybe you had a divorce your teens don't know about. It's never too late to revisit those experiences and create opportunities for conversation. You never know what wounds you may be able to heal and what lessons you'll be able to appreciate in retrospect.

Conversation Doors

- If you experienced divorce, invite your teen to ask questions. It might help to have them write out their questions in advance, choosing which ones to answer as circumstances dictate.

- Ask your teen to share their perceptions of divorce and how it impacts them or their friends. Make a list of friends struggling with divorce and commit to pray for and encourage them regularly together.
- Share your wedding photos/video. Tell them the story of your courtship and what you learned about God's unconditional love, even through love and loss.
- Share mementos from your courtship or wedding. It may be a wedding dress, special gift you received, love letters, or keepsakes from the era in which you were married. Tell the story of how you met.
- Take your teen to a place that is/was special in your marriage. It might be where you were engaged, a place you ate together frequently while dating, a previous home you shared, a place you shared the news of a coming baby, or another momentous occasion.
- Create a family time capsule together. If you're experiencing divorce, things seem hard right now but won't always be that way. Include a letter to your future selves. When you open the time capsule at a time of your choosing, you'll likely be encouraged to see how you've grown.

Conversation Keys

After you complete your activity together, initiate a conversation. Remember to LOVE your teen.

Listen with your face:
- Say, "I know this is a complicated subject with a lot of emotions."
- Thank them for being willing to share their thoughts and feelings.

- Share one new thing you learned or observed about their future hopes.

Offer open-ended questions:

- "How has divorce impacted you personally?"
- "How do you want your marriage to be different from what you've seen or experienced?"
- "What emotions do you have about this that are difficult to face? What scares you?"
- "What lessons about love have you learned that you will carry into your future?"
- "When you think about your future, how do you envision it?"
- "What do you wish you could change about your situation?"
- "What else would you like to share?"

Validate feelings:

- "This is really hard."
- "I wish our situation were different. I wish things could be like you want them to be."
- "It's okay to be (fill in the blank: confused, hurt, angry) about this."
- "No matter what happens, I will always love you unconditionally."

Explore next steps together:

Answer the following questions together:

Did you uncover emotions hiding under the surface? Are these struggles impacting daily life? If so, consider counseling to help process your teen's feelings (*and* yours) in a healthy way that moves toward restoration. Is it time to set new ground rules between the two households? Do you need a conversation (possibly mediated by a neutral party) with both families to revisit boundaries and norms to help your teen?

If you're in a blended family, are there conversations that need to be had? Is your teen at peace with their new bonus family? Many churches offer support groups for children experiencing divorce and blended families. Explore resources to develop healthy coping skills. Sometimes families feel guilty seeking support, as if acknowledging the need for mental health validates the guilt you feel for things that aren't under your control. There is no condemnation here. Validating feelings goes a long way on the road to recovery.

Maybe you're not divorced, but that's a constant sort of maybe question each time you argue. If your relationship is rocky, maybe couples therapy is needed to bring peace to your family. Are there boundaries needed surrounding unhealthy patterns of communication?

If you're blessed with a happy marriage, think of some ways you can provide support, encouragement, and hospitality to teens experiencing divorce or family conflict.

BEHIND THE HEART DOOR

Dear friend, you are beloved always by God. This may be an incredibly tender place for you. If you were hurt unfairly in a divorce or were betrayed or abandoned, I'm so sorry. I can't imagine how hard that must be. If there's any sort of emotional, physical, psychological, or mental abuse, it's essential for you to carefully construct healthy, guilt-free boundaries to protect both you and your kids. I haven't personally experienced divorce, but I have had a front-row seat to closest friends and family who have. I'm amazed and inspired by their strength and resilience in the middle of incredible pain.

You may feel frustrated and angry that it still hurts. But God has compassion for the hurt you're enduring. Have compassion for yourself. *The most important thing you can do to help your teen heal is to seek your own personal healing journey.* Share your struggles, fears, and progress. Don't feel guilty taking alone time for self-care.

While your teen may demand your time today, prioritizing personal healing assures they'll have your time tomorrow.

Devotional

Maybe you experienced unimaginable betrayal and abandonment in divorce by someone you loved and trusted. Jesus was betrayed to death by a kiss and a few coins. His closest companions abandoned Him at His most vulnerable in the garden of Gethsemane. His hurt and anguish were so great He sweated drops of blood. He forgave this betrayal, personally restored one of His closest friends, Peter, and instructed us to forgive as well.

Unforgiveness is a state of chronic stress that literally destroys your physical heart and health while devouring your soul. We see this in the story of Ruth, when her mother-in-law, Naomi, experienced the loss of her husband and chose bitterness to the point of changing her name to Mara, literally meaning "bitter." Her daughter-in-law Ruth experienced similar loss but chose blessing over bitterness and was given, through her kinsman-redeemer, a baby in the line of Jesus. When the baby was born, a beautiful picture of restoration illustrated Mara choosing blessing over bitterness and responding once again to the name Naomi.

Reflect

How has divorce impacted and shaped your life?

With honest reflection, are you harboring unforgiveness toward someone because of divorce?

What steps do you need to take to continue your healing journey?

Pray

(From Romans 8 and 12) God, there is no condemnation for those who are in Christ Jesus. You gave us the gift of adoption. We are heirs of God and joint heirs with Christ. Your Spirit helps us in our weakness. Even when we don't know what to pray, You speak over us with emotion too deep for words. All things work together for good for those who love You and are called according to Your purpose. If You are for us, then who can be against us? Help us to be joyful in hope, patient in affliction, and faithful in prayer, surrendering our fears for today and our worries for tomorrow. Give me the courage to choose blessing over bitterness. Empower me to be a living reflection of Your unconditional love and forgiveness. Amen.

Act

(Legacy Letter) Choose an option that best fits your circumstances and the state of your heart.

- For parents experiencing divorce, write a letter to your teen praising the positive qualities they inherited from their other parent. Tell them, no matter how the relationship ended, they are a gift to cherish with no regrets.
- Write a letter affirming unconditional love for your teen.

Reaffirm your commitment to pursuing a healthy relationship. Even in times of conflict, your love will never stop.

- If you're married or remarried, share the story of a time of conflict in your relationship, how you navigated, what you learned, and how you experienced forgiveness and grace.
- Write a letter to your teen's future spouse with the lessons you've learned and the hopes and prayers for their future relationship.

e i g h t

SEX AND SEXTING

How to Be Naked and Unafraid

A girl in a soccer uniform with a ponytail sat quietly on the exam table. She nodded politely, greeting me with a half-smile. She had a headache but couldn't tell me when it started, what triggered it, how it felt, or where it hurt. She couldn't tell me much of anything, really. Her mom was at a loss and said she'd been called by the school nurse. After a careful physical exam, I decided to use a behavior rating scale for depression. Bingo. It was off the chart. I spoke with her alone, and she expressed active thoughts of suicide. "No," she said, her mother didn't know. I pulled up my stool to sit at eye level with her. "You are safe here to share what happened to you." She hesitated, took a deep breath, and cried as her story spilled out.

An older boy at school noticed her. She was flattered. They connected on social media. She felt pretty for the first time. They exchanged explicit texts. The feedback was instant and intoxicating. He asked for pictures. "No," she said. "Please," he begged. "I'm afraid," she pleaded. "I love you," he assured her. "What if someone else sees," she wondered. "I won't share," he promised, adding, "You're just so beautiful." She relented just enough to test the waters. He showered her with praise. Soon the photos were nude. She felt safe because she trusted him. He loved her. But he showed the photos to classmates and word got around lightning fast. An anonymous report led her to the school administrators. She was asked, "Did you do this?" "Yes," she said, but she felt guilty and deleted everything. He was questioned. "Did you ask for these?" "No way," he said. "She sent those on her own. I deleted them. I don't have them." She was kicked off her soccer team. He was excused.

And here she was sitting in my clinic devastated.

BEHIND THE CLINIC DOOR

Sexting is a modern-day reality. Your teen has either sent a sext, received a sext, or knows someone who has. This story portrays a girl sexting a boy, but it's happening in all ways and in all contexts, so no assumptions should be made on gender. It's awkward and even terrifying for parents to discuss their child's sexuality. Yikes! You may be afraid you'll give them ideas. News flash: God created us as sexual beings, and they already have ideas (plenty, actually). I would much rather *you* give them ideas than let their peers fill that void.

How Do I Talk About Sex?

Recently, my husband and I both got reading glasses and exchanged humorous photos. I was asked by my child (who will remain unnamed) if that was "old-people sexting." But really, if you have biological kids, you obviously know about the birds and the bees.

So let's start at the beginning and get comfy talking about sex before we talk about sexting. Just remember, you're talking to the girl who got her education while sneaking down certain aisles at Walmart. If I can talk about it, you can too.

God designed our sexuality, and we need to be comfortable discussing sexual health in a developmentally appropriate way. This starts with toddlers being able to name their body parts. Preschoolers understand their body is private and know the boundaries of appropriate touch. School-aged children should know puberty basics and the importance of hygiene and self-care. Preteens should know the basic physical functions of reproduction. Teens should know the details about sexual and reproductive functions, including menstruation, erections, nocturnal emissions, pregnancy, and sexually transmitted infections. We should approach conversation with normalcy and body positivity.

Sex is not a secret thing, but it is a sacred thing.

Many times, kids (especially church kids) are given messages such as the following:

"Modest is hottest!"

"Save yourself for marriage!"

"Keep your eyes and heart clean!"

"Be responsible with what you wear so you won't tempt impure thoughts."

Let's think about this. These messages convey that we expect our teens to be basically asexual until their wedding night, when they're supposed to instantly rip their clothes off and transform into sex kittens right after the preacher says, "I *now* pronounce you," because suddenly sex is *now* good? Of course we don't consciously think this, but those are the subconscious messages we absolutely give. We give teens the totally unfair and unrealistic impression that waiting until marriage guarantees a good sex life. That is so far from the truth. (I mean, let's be real. It takes time and practice.) Even worse, young couples saving sex for marriage often are unprepared in practical terms for what's ahead. Then you have marriages where women feel dirty and used, but they don't know why, and men feel perverted and shamed over their sexual desire for their wives. They have questions like, "We saved ourselves for this?" "What are we doing wrong?" "Shouldn't we be having sex all day every day?"

We desperately need to talk about sex in a healthy context within appropriate boundaries. Listen, your kids won't love it. They will complain and groan and protest *the whole time*. I still get so much grief for that one time I drew a uterus on a napkin at Chili's while answering my daughter's question about menstruation. (Yes, I really did that.) Did they remember what I taught them? Why, yes, indeed they did, thank you very much. Another time we bought large volumes of menstruation products for a house of three females, and as they went down the grocery store conveyor belt, the clerk asked my husband, "How's it going?" He replied, "From the looks of it, not so good!" This led to a conversation with my son to correct his (hilarious) misconceptions about female reproduction. He put up his hoodie as I was talking and kept pulling it tighter and tighter until only his nose was sticking out of a tiny hole. His response to my expertly delivered explanation was, "We shall *never* speak of this again."

Talking to your teens about sex shouldn't be "the talk" but rather a series of talks. Give information in small, bite-sized pieces as opportunities present themselves and the need arises. Normalize conversation and you'll be amazed at how many questions you'll get, which makes your job much easier, as you simply serve as a guide on the side. Connecting them to a health-care provider you trust also gives them an outlet for sensitive conversations and appropriate guidance they can discuss with you. For example, boys should begin self-testicular exams at age fifteen. It's important to normalize this and be comfortable with their body. Confidential conversations with health-care providers should begin (without parents present) around age twelve to fourteen. This is not to shut parents out in any way, but to help teens begin to assume accountability for their own care and to give them a confidential outlet to express safety or health concerns. Pediatric care providers desire to build partnerships with parents and teens whenever we can, especially through annual checkups. Again, this is why someone you trust can be very reassuring. Different pediatric care providers have different levels of comfort in providing gynecologic care to teens in the primary care office. The American College of Obstetricians and Gynecologists recommends a first gynecology visit for girls between the ages of thirteen to fifteen.[1] But this doesn't mean pelvic exams or pap smears; those aren't recommended until a person is sexually active or age twenty-one, whichever comes first. In fact, the whole point of going early is to be comfortable, so your first visit is *not* a pelvic exam. Gynecologists can provide introductory support through puberty, menstruation, the dimensions of sexual health, and eventually childbirth.

What About Sexually Transmitted Infections?

Sexually transmitted infections (STIs) are a real and present danger. A common misconception among teens is that you can only get an STI from vaginal intercourse, but that's not true. Herpes and human papillomavirus (HPV) can be transmitted by skin-to-skin contact.

Oral and throat cancers from HPV arising from oral sex encounters (commonly perceived as safe by teens) are increasing significantly. This might make some of you uncomfortable, but anal intercourse is often perceived as safe (not getting pregnant), although it carries the risk of STIs regardless of gender. Many STIs have minor, fleeting, or even no symptoms until later, when they cause problems in pregnancy or show up as reproductive cancers.

How Do We Talk About Abstinence and Preparing for Sex?

The only sure way to protect yourself from pregnancy and STI exposure is abstinence. This is true no matter your age or relationship status, but it is especially relevant for teens more inexperienced in sex and more likely to engage in risk-taking behaviors such as unprotected sex, sex under the influence of drugs or alcohol, or sex with strangers. According to the American Academy of Pediatrics, a positive approach to abstinence, combined with developmentally appropriate education, can be helpful, as more than half of young adult women surveyed wished they'd waited longer to have sex, and nearly 70 percent who initiated sex at the age of fifteen or younger wished they had waited.[2] An estimated 55 percent of teens have sex before the age of eighteen.[3]

Empower your teen to say no with confidence and self-boundaries. This requires thought, conversation, and planning. Often parents simply tell their teens not to have sex, end of story, or teens just *know* their parents' expectations of abstinence with no further discussion. I disagree with this approach. Talking to teens about sex will not give them ideas (they already have those), but it *will* give them second thoughts. Teens who talk to their parents about sex are more likely to delay sexual initiation and to avoid risk-taking behaviors.[4] Consider this health guidance for teens considering having sex. First, they should get baseline STI testing, including HIV (genital swabs and blood work). They need to know where to get vaginal, anal, and oral condoms and how to use them correctly from start to finish for protection. They need to talk with their partner about their STI history, past partners, and pregnancy planning. They have to talk about consent and sexual boundaries in terms of what you will and will not do and your safe word. They need to talk to their health-care provider about vaccines for HPV and Hepatitis B. Females should see a gynecologist and begin pap smears. They need to know where to get STI screenings should they become aware of an exposure or symptoms. Whew! Let's take a step back. Remember when your teen was about four or five and told you they wanted to run away? Were you ever that parent who helped them pack a suitcase as you walked them through the dangers ahead? Now, by the time you lay out all the sexual pitfalls and precautions, a fifteen-year-old will likely be wide-eyed and second-guessing their readiness.

Health Impacts of Sexting

As we consider the messages our teens get from us about sex, think about the messages they get from the popular culture around them. Teen magazines and social influencers coach teens on how/when/where/what to sext as well as how to feel *confident* about it. It's a normalized form of digital communication and a social norm in relationships. On the other hand, it's potentially a criminal offense. How can we expect teens to navigate this kind of conflicting nuance?

What Does It Mean to Send a Nude?

Sexting (which became an official word in 2009 as a combination of *sex* and *texting*) is a form of digital communication ranging from explicit texts (just words), suggestive or explicit audio messages, to partially or fully nude photos or videos. Wait, did you catch that? Sexting is *not* just photos. Teens often start with explicit audio or written messages. It can be deliberate or accidental, consensual or non-consensual, legal or illegal. About 10 to 25 percent of teens say they've sexted. You can explore credible research by criminal justice professors Sameer Hinduja and Justin W. Patchin at cyberbullying.org. You'll find sexting rates specific to your state and see the numbers broken down by age, gender, and other demographics.

In some states, outdated child pornography laws create severe and unintended criminal consequences. These laws were originally created to protect teens from adult predators. Some states updated their laws to reflect modern contexts while others include stringent criminal charges and requirements to register as a sex offender. All states are different, but let's look at my home state of Texas as an example.[5] For the first sexting offense, it's a Class C misdemeanor. A second offense is a Class B misdemeanor with up to 180 days in jail and up to a $2,000 fine. There are harsher punishments for malicious intent, harassment, or threat of harm. For adults over eighteen, it's a felony. There are some protections. *If* the images were only of the recipient and the sender *and if* the images were sent in the context of a dating relationship *and if* both parties are no more than two years apart in age (including one party being over eighteen), then it *might* be okay. That's a lot of *ifs* for a *might*.

It's critically important that you as a parent understand the potential criminal implications of sexting. Once explicit images of a minor are on *any* personal digital device, you possess intimate visual material that could be considered child pornography and be criminally liable. Before we even talk about how to handle this from a relational perspective, we need to understand the legal context. Sharing or forwarding explicit material can potentially move the offense from *possession* to *distribution* of child pornography. Having said that, threatening teens with criminal prosecution is not in any way a successful deterrent.

Social media disadvantages teens who haven't yet achieved cognitive development progressing from concrete to abstract thinking, which allows reasoning through complex situations. Wait, what? This means kids think concretely (black and white) and progress to formal reasoning (shades of gray). For some social media apps, notifications say a shared image will disappear, giving teens a false sense of safety when experimenting with sexting. When it says the image will disappear, it disappears from everywhere including screen shots, right? Wrong.

Helping your teen to think abstractly is helpful. Maybe you trust someone in a relationship, but what if a friend uses their phone? What if they lose their phone? What if they accidentally forward something? What if a teacher sees something? What if they break up with someone? It's important for teens to understand the moment they *take* (not *send*) a photo, they lose control of that image. Look to Hunger Games star Jennifer Lawrence, the victim of a photo hack dubbed the "snappening,"[6] in which explicit images were stolen from her cloud storage. Maybe your teen hasn't sent images but experiments with taking them. There is vulnerability there, as teens often share phones. Also, recipients can decide at any time to share images despite prior promises. Sometimes it's boasting about sexual exploits. Sometimes it's used as blackmail (sextortion) or posted on a revenge porn website (yes, that's a real thing).

What Are the Risks of Sexting?

While some health experts take the stance that sexting should be a normalized behavior, and there is some reasonable dialogue to be had around safer sexting, science suggests there is a correlation of sexting and sexual risk behaviors (unprotected sex, increased number of sexual partners, and lack of contraception use).[7] Teens engaging in sexting are at increased risk for anxiety and depression. The younger the teen, the greater the risk. Other risks include cyberbullying, dating violence, and sextortion. Most concerning is the increase in suicide behaviors related to sexting.

One high-profile case was that of fifteen-year-old Amanda Todd.[8] After meeting a man online and chatting awhile, she impulsively flashed her breasts on camera. He stalked her on the internet, demanding more photos. When she refused, he sent the photo to her classmates via social media messaging. Ashamed and bullied, she struggled in isolation with severe anxiety and depression. Without an effective coping mechanism for post-traumatic stress, she self-medicated with substances and self-harming behaviors. Tragically, Amanda died by suicide in 2012. Her story is perhaps more prominent because she shared it in a viral YouTube video before her death. Sadly, this is not unique.

You cannot underestimate the power of sexuality. Your teens are watching once "wholesome" child stars use it to transform their careers. Do you know why? Because it works (like a wrecking ball—Oops, did I do it again? Give you an earworm?). You get the point. When your teen sexts, messages they hear are "You're desirable, beautiful, confident, and strong." Contrast that with messages we as parents give about sexting: "Ew!" "It's trashy." "That's nasty." "I'm glad you're too smart to do that." Which message do you think will win in the decision-making process? We have to leave a door open for grace. No one wants their teen to sext, but our kids aren't perfect and neither are we. Leaving a door open encourages early disclosure before great harm. About a quarter of teens report feeling extremely upset, ashamed, or fearful after generating and exchanging sexts. Sexting can prompt symptoms of mental health concerns, especially when coercion, force, or nonconsensual behavior is involved. In my experience, most teens engaged in sexting aren't talking to their parents or getting credible information, leaving them vulnerable, and by the time they disclose to an adult, harm has already occurred. As parents, we all want our kids to be safe.

When your child was young, did you ever lose them in a public place? That feeling of panic is awful. On my first outing alone with all four kids (all ages seven and under at the time), I turned my back for an instant at a museum and my three-year-old was gone. To say I lost my mind is an understatement. It turns out he wandered away with a tour group, and a museum worker had him in her office. They were trying to get him to say my name to verify my identity. He just kept wailing "Mama!" They asked, "What is her *real* name?" He replied, "Mom!" Was my emotion relief in that moment of finding him? For a nanosecond. But irrational anger at a three-year-old quickly followed. I *told* him not to let go of the stroller. *Why* did he do that?! That same anger applies to feelings about your teen's safety risk in the moment of discovery or disclosure. When you step into your teen's world and see what they're facing, you can cultivate empathy and be prepared with a response seasoned with grace. Anytime a teen discloses sexting to you, they're coming to you from a place of hurt. They need comfort first.

Parenting Pro Tips

Let's go to that moment. Your teen comes to you and intentionally discloses sex or sexting or you unintentionally discover it. Your heart drops. You get tunnel vision. What will you say? Your decision in that instant could change the course of your teen's life. If you don't think about it beforehand, you'll be at the mercy of your emotions. Guaranteed. Most parents feel anger. They're not angry *at* their teen really, they're angry *for* their teen. Let's walk through some scenarios together.

Having Sex

You need to first make sure they're healthy and safe. Get health counseling and an evaluation for pregnancy (for females) and STIs. Your health-care provider can help initiate a discussion and connection to resources. Affirm your unconditional love for your teen in this moment. Open communication for future discussions in setting expectations and establishing boundaries.

Receiving Unsolicited Images

If your teen receives an unsolicited image, it should generally be deleted immediately. Determine the potential criminality of the situation. Don't forward or share the image. Contact the school and/or police. Parents of any other teens involved should be informed, whether by you, the school, or law enforcement. If the image is from an adult, *immediately* contact the police. My teens have occasionally received explicit photos from strangers' social media contact requests. They immediately bring me their phone, knowing there is safe disclosure, and we decide what to do together (usually delete and report).

Unintentional Discovery

If you discover your teen is sending and/or receiving sexually explicit digital media, respond with compassion and kindness. Don't generalize unwise behaviors into character traits. Saying, "Sending these messages puts you at risk for bullying, abuse, and even legal consequences" is very different from saying "How could you be so dumb?" or "Do you want everyone to know you have no morals?" or "You've just ruined your whole life!" Preserve their dignity. This isn't something grandma, siblings, the grocery store clerk, or your social media needs to know.

After you've created a safe space and opened a door for grace, explore the details.

- Were images sent to or received by an adult who is targeting, abusing, or exploiting your teen? If so, call the police.
- Was it consensual? If not, call the police. If so, consider the legal implications in your state's sexting laws.
- Were images shared outside a consensual relationship? If so, contact the platforms where the images are posted to have them removed as soon as possible. If other students are involved, contact the school. Make sure you know the school's policy on sexting and consider potentially unintended negative disciplinary action. Consult an attorney if you have the means or access to do so in considering the criminal implications.

Intentional Disclosure

First, think carefully. Why is your teen sharing this with you right now? Overwhelmingly the odds say they're distressed and at a tipping point. They're scared, terrified probably. It's risky to disclose. In that moment, practice saying first, "I'm sorry you experienced this." Does this mean there won't be further consequences or action taken? Of course not. But in that moment, validate their feelings and offer a safe emotional haven for further discussion. If you don't know what to say or how to respond, tell them you need some time to think it over, but reassure them of your unconditional love. Lastly, acknowledge the reality of their trauma. Seek professional mental health services early to promote effective coping and resilience. This experience doesn't have to define their character forever. Offer a path to grace and restoration with dignity.

Encourage your teen to refrain from sending nudes to avoid legal, psychological, and emotional consequences. Have an open discussion about the boundaries of healthy digital communication. Keep phones out of bedroom spaces, where it's easier to experiment with photos in privacy. Where is the line between flirting and sexting? Does your teen feel empowered to say no if asked for images? It's harder than it seems. Practicing confidently beforehand can help.

Investigate the policies at your teen's school. Do they clearly state possession of explicit material is prohibited? Do they outline disciplinary measures on a case-by-case basis? Do they inform students that their parents and the police may be notified? Do they have zero tolerance for harassment, threats, or bullying related to shared images? Do they protect teens experiencing trauma from further humiliation and victimization?

BEHIND THE HOME DOOR

I've talked to many teens who grew up in church and engaged in sexting, and their parents still don't know! I've also spoken at conferences about this, and during the Q&A, inevitably a parent tearfully shares a personal experience. The story is always the same: "My kid grew up in church and they started sexting and I didn't know." The most compelling moment is always when a parent says, "Don't say this couldn't happen to my kid!" We need grace and kindness with more open communication. This might feel very awkward to discuss. Maybe you need to go back to the basics of reproduction if these are things you haven't discussed freely. It's okay to say, "I know we haven't talked much about this in the past, but it's important and I'm working to learn better ways to have a conversation about it."

Conversation Doors
- Explore Amanda Todd's story together. Have an open discussion about the lessons that can be learned from her tragic death.
- Visit coolnotcoolquiz.org and take the Cool, Not Cool quiz. Alternatively, take the Respect Effect Challenges together.

- Explore cyberbullying.org to find the laws governing sexting in your state and discuss them.
- Visit thatsnotcool.com and look at the Callout Cards, ready-made responses if your teen gets a request for an explicit photo. Get a group of friends together to make their own responses using photo software. Host a contest.
- Explore articles in teen magazines about sexting and discuss the conflicting messages.

Conversation Keys

After you complete your activity together, initiate a conversation. Remember to LOVE your teen.

Listen with your face:
- Say, "The pressure you face must feel overwhelming."
- Thank them for being willing to share their thoughts and feelings.
- Share one new thing you learned or observed about their values.

Offer open-ended questions:
- "How have you experienced sexting in your peer group?"
- "What are your personal boundaries for sexting?"
- "Tell me about the times you felt your behaviors didn't match your values."
- "What would you do if someone sent you a nude without you asking for it?"
- "What fears do you have about what could happen?"
- "How can you plan now for the best choices to support what you'd like your future to look like?"
- "What else would you like to share?"

Validate feelings:
- "I'm sure this feels overwhelming."
- "I always have an open door to talk about this."
- "It's okay to be confused."
- "No matter what happens, I love you and we will find a way forward together."

Explore next steps together:

Answer the following questions together:
- What will your teen do if they receive an unsolicited sext and how will you respond?
- How will your teen respond if they get a request for nudes and how can they talk to you about it in a safe way?
- How and when would you notify the school or law enforcement of sexting?

BEHIND THE HEART DOOR

Parents, if you have teens who have sexted or had prior sexual relationships in their teen years and your heart hurts for something they experienced in the course of that, put down this book, go find them, and tell them they're amazing and wonderful and you're confident in the optimism of their future. They need you to see them outside the singular lens of their sexual experience. Many will have lifetime consequences they already have to live with, like a nude photo popping up at some point in the future or an STI that could impact fertility. They need grace and help reclaiming their dignity and self-worth if they feel it's lost. Speak up on their behalf when needed. Affirm your unconditional love.

In a world where teens are constantly bombarded with sexual

images and messages, it's hard to cut through the noise to shape a healthy view of sexuality. Despite the pull of popular culture, teens are getting powerful subliminal messages about sex at home. This may be a sensitive subject for you. Maybe you never thought about your sex life through the eyes of your teen. Maybe that's really uncomfortable. Maybe you have abuse or trauma you haven't addressed and you know it's time.

Devotional

Adam and Eve were naked and unashamed, and God called it good. If you're married, it might be a vulnerable moment to thoughtfully take a step back and consider how your teen views your physical relationship. Obviously, they don't need the details or for you to put a sock on the doorknob (you'll assuredly scar them for life), but what is their perception of how you view sexual intimacy? You think your teens are oblivious to your sex life, but I promise they know more than you think. This plays a powerful role in framing your teen's view of sex in the context of Christlike love.

The Song of Solomon provides vivid imagery of sexuality that is definitely not G-rated. This *eros* (erotic, sensual) expression of love must be balanced with *agape* (pure, sacrificial, unconditional) and *phileo* (friendship) love for healthy relationships that embrace but don't worship sexuality.

Reflect

Do your teens see physical affection or intimacy in your home as frosty, obligatory, or nonexistent?

Do they see respect? Affection? Joy? Prioritizing private time together?

How can your marriage convey healthy sexuality to your teens?

Pray

(1 Corinthians 10 and 13) God, help me to speak with love that is patient and kind. Love does not envy or boast, and it is not arrogant or rude. Love does not demand its own way. It doesn't rejoice with wrongdoing but rejoices with truth. Help me to love my teen in these ways. Help them to clearly see Christlike love in a healthy relationship. When they're tempted to follow a path to unhealthy relationships, You are faithful to not let them be tempted beyond what they can bear. Provide a clear path of escape. Help me to bear all things, believe all things, hope all things, and endure all things in love for my teen. Amen.

Act

(Legacy Letter) Teens take a lot of selfies, looking for that perfect angle. Sexting is tempting because adoring praise activates feel-good chemicals in our brains. Your teen wants to feel attractive and appealing. Honestly, we do too! I'm sure you examine photos critically (bad angle, love handles, wrong side, wrinkles), but if someone looks at your photo and says, "You look stunning in this photo!" you will look at that photo ten times with a big smile. Your teen is no different.

Choose your favorite current photo of your teen. Write a letter describing everything you love about the photo. Is it a fashion choice or a facial expression? If you're not in the habit of verbally complimenting your teen, this will feel awkward. Push through it. Their peers do it all the time. What about their personality shines through? Reaffirm your unconditional love for their uniqueness.

nine

PORNOGRAPHY

How to Find Freedom from Secrets

I didn't know him before this moment. I was speaking to a group of health professionals about human trafficking, as I often do. I fully expect people to approach me afterward with questions on clinical protocols, but I didn't expect his question.

"What do I do if I've seen really, I mean really, bad stuff in porn?"

He watched porn frequently, as "any red-blooded American male would," he said. But lately he'd seen disturbing things. Gratuitous violence. Gut-wrenching abuse. He wondered about criminality. And he was pretty sure they were children. He'd tried to find some sort of reporting mechanism but couldn't. He felt torn between opposing cultural paradigms. He viewed porn as a healthy outlet for sexuality, but as a health-care professional he's a mandated reporter of abuse. Now I presented another layer of complexity: the intersection of pornography and trafficking.

We were both distressed.

BEHIND THE CLINIC DOOR

Growing up in the seventies, eighties, or nineties, your first pornography exposure was likely a "dirty magazine" or maybe a video tape someone had somehow gotten from somewhere. That is nowhere near what teens experience today. The internet completely transformed the pornography industry. Digital content is largely unregulated, creating endless possibilities for content and delivery. Nearly half of teens aged nine to sixteen years regularly encounter sexual material online.[1] Early exposure causes health risks, and even more concerning, repeated exposure actually changes the way the brain responds to sexual stimulus.

What Is Porn, Really?

The word *pornography* originates from two Greek words: *porniea* (a broad term to describe sexual immorality) and *graphe* (written word). Pornography is written or visual media that elicits a sexual response of the consumer. The Oxford Dictionary further states pornography is "intended to stimulate *erotic* rather than *aesthetic* [appreciation of beauty] or *emotional* feelings."[2] In other words, it's all sex and only sex. There are some significant intricacies of the legal definitions I won't delve into, but know that, like sexting, pornography intersects criminality, especially when it involves the exploitation of minors and persons in human trafficking who are often forced or coerced.

To quote Solomon in Ecclesiastes 1:9, "What has been done will be done again; there is nothing new under the sun." In the 1980s an archaeologist discovered ancient pornographic petroglyphs in China.[3] A brothel in Pompeii (covered by volcanic ash in AD 70) displays erotic wall paintings.[4] The earliest known pornographic films were produced in the 1890s (not 1980s). However, modern pornography consumption is exploding with the triple-A engine: accessibility, affordability, and anonymity. No more sneaking home a brown-paper-covered magazine from the gas station.

Teens have endless access to free materials of mind-boggling variety as porn production shifts from professionally generated to consumer-generated media. We discussed the rise of social media earlier; the pornography industry is equally empowered, as anyone can upload any content at any moment, and this expands the pornography industry with the rise of sites such as OnlyFans, or Pornhub, which boast nearly 42 billion visitors per year. With 50,000 searches per minute and 81 million daily average visits, it's estimated one year of uploads to Pornhub could fill the memory of every smartphone on earth.[5] Looking at Pornhub in an internet search engine yields this advertisement: "The world's leading free porn site. Choose from millions of hardcore videos that stream quickly and high quality, including amazing VR (virtual reality) porn." The first option listed as a suggestion to explore? Stepmom and stepsister porn. Yes, seriously.

Parents, that's amazingly tame, entry-level stuff. Porn today is not people having sex when the pizza delivery guy rings the doorbell. That's not even close. We are talking way more disturbing things. Pornography today is broadly unregulated. Of greater concern is that it's disturbingly more violent in terms of pushing the boundaries of physical, psychological, and sexual abuse. Five of the top ten most-searched terms in porn encompass people of color, who are disproportionately exploited.[6] And there are many other search terms (mostly abbreviations) you wouldn't be familiar with if you don't watch porn. Your teens, however, are likely familiar with these search terms even if they don't watch porn. This is lunchroom table talk. The point is this: we need to be open to unfamiliar narratives and empower teens to confidently dismiss feelings of embarrassment or exclusion prompted by a lack of knowledge by saying confidently, "This is not a conversation I need to be a part of. See you later!"

Porn consumption can be passive (reading an erotic book, which is enormously popular among high school girls) or active (watching a video), but it is becoming increasingly interactive through online chats, blogs, on-demand live performances, custom requests, and virtual reality. Viewers increasingly desire a physical outlet, but it often doesn't live up to online experiences.

Health Impacts

Researchers are still collecting reliable information, but consider the following statistics:

- 84.4 percent of males and 57 percent of females ages fourteen to eighteen report pornography exposure[7]
- 22 percent of underage pornography consumers are less than ten years old; 36 percent are ten to fourteen years old[8]
- Pornography use is associated with more risk-taking sexual behaviors and increased sexual aggression (both as perpetrator and victim)[9]
- 75 percent of parents surveyed in Britain reported their child had no pornography exposure while only 53 percent of their children reported the same[10]
- The COVID-19 pandemic prompted an unprecedented spike in pornography access on the internet[11]
- Violent and sexualized video games impact teen attitudes about dating and sexual violence[12]

These statistics are gathered from studies where teens mostly self-report, so the actual percentages could be much higher. In a study surveying relationship partners, 50 percent of males admitted to pornography consumption while only 4 percent of their partners reported their knowledge of it.[13]

How Does Pornography Impact Teen Health?

Pornography features staged lighting, scripting, and surgical and cosmetic enhancements. People in pornographic media are paid to perform or are forced, coerced, or abused. There is no portrayal of a healthy, realistic, consensual relationship. However, 53 percent of boys and 39 percent of girls believe porn is a realistic portrayal of sex, although it introduces rape, incest, violence, and racism as normative.[14] Porn doesn't educate consumers about pregnancy, sexually transmitted infections, and emotional and physical trauma.[15]

Frequent pornography exposure negatively impacts relationship satisfaction and quality, relational trust, effective communication, conflict resolution, and sexual gratification in real-life relationships. Teens with frequent pornography exposure are more likely to criticize their partner's body and accept infidelity, violence, sextortion, revenge porn, and image-based abuse. This has a dose-graded effect, meaning the more pornography engagement, the greater these impacts. Ultimately, pornography contributes to aggressive behaviors, distorted gender roles, objectification of women, unrealistic expectations of sexual relationships, and high-risk sexual behaviors such as not using protection or having multiple partners. Pornography use increases feelings of loneliness, isolation, anxiety, and depression.[16]

Teens are especially vulnerable to chemical reactions and brain changes associated with repeated pornography exposure.[17] Teen brains are neuroplastic, meaning they grow and adapt by creating new pathways based on chemical influences (hormones), environmental influences (pornography), time spent, and energy expended. Initially, the brain responds to pornographic exposure with significant sexual stimulus (arousal). The brain's reward center releases dopamine and rewires with a preference for that particular stimulus using a feedback loop. The longer and more often the neural pathway is used, the more it's reinforced. Basically, the brain is trained for porn. Teens who frequently consume pornography experience chronic stress that drives them to their stimulus for a temporary release of dopamine. Over time, that pathway becomes desensitized with decreased pleasure response. It quiets the prefrontal cortex that helps us make good decisions. If they're cut off from accessing this pathway through pornography, it causes anxiety.

The override to this in the brain is not *more* porn but *new* porn with novelty escalation: new situations and partners with different elements including gender, race or ethnicity, violence, or abuse. The good news is that brains can heal over time, creating alternative, healthier pathways, but the older you are and the longer and more frequent pornography consumption is, the harder it is to rewire.

Niko Tinbergen, a Nobel Prize–winning researcher, conducted some fascinating research on how natural behaviors were influenced by visual stimuli (supernormal stimuli).[18] Scientists created cardboard female butterflies (a superstimulus) with more vibrant colors and exaggerated features. Predictably, male butterflies attempted to mate with these paper cutouts. Unpredictably, when female butterflies were reintroduced, males overwhelmingly preferred the cardboard version over the real butterflies for "mating." This phenomenon is seen when people prefer sexual stimulus through pornography over real life. Researchers are currently exploring porn-induced erectile dysfunction in college-aged males related to difficulty achieving sexual stimulus in real-life relationships after being accustomed to online arousal.[19] Yes, we are talking about young men and the little blue pill.[20] Although there is no official diagnosis of pornography addiction, specialists and researchers are continuing to investigate and address the symptoms of internet addictions, including gaming, sexual addiction, and online gambling.

How Does Consent Relate to Pornography?

Pornography depicts sexual violence without consent. Teens who frequently view pornography are more likely to engage in violence[21] and image-based abuse (revenge porn, that is, sharing explicit images or videos without consent). A recent study found one in three young adults experienced image-based abuse while one in six perpetrated abuse.[22] Females, gender diverse youth, and ethnic and racial minorities are disproportionately impacted negatively.

Because teens see pornography as a realistic depiction of sex, they seek to mimic it in real life. Here is where criminality complicates sex. Consent is a difficult thing to define and has some complex legal implications. In practice, consent is a verbal agreement between two parties to engage in sexual activity. Consent cannot be given by someone who is underage, under the influence of drugs or alcohol, asleep or unconscious, or otherwise forced. Some persons appearing on pornographic media are being trafficked and forced to perform. Talking with your teen about personal boundaries and consent for personal touch of any kind is important to protect them from the vulnerability of violating someone, being violated, or being falsely accused. Consent is complicated for teens in a world caught between the MeToo movement and normalization of pornography with a romanticization of male dominance and abusive sexual behaviors in popular media such as *Fifty Shades of Grey* and *365 Days.*

Your teens need you to lead them well in this space of uncomfortable conversation.

Maybe you're thinking you don't want to expose your teen to a conversation about something they haven't been exposed to yet. The truth is that they will be exposed to many of these things at some point.

You can choose to expose them proactively in a healthy way in a controlled environment while empowering them to respond or you can let fate take its course and respond retroactively.

My daughter was in the fifth grade when a female classmate described to her in graphic detail a pornographic video she stumbled across on YouTube. My son was twelve when I picked up his phone to see a group chat challenging each other to "No Nut November," using emojis I'll leave to your imagination. This was a group of twelve-year-old boys taking a challenge to refrain from masturbating for a month because it's "good for their health" (thank you previously referenced reliable teen internet searches). They discussed attractive girls in detail to up the ante on temptation. My son knew the chat wasn't appropriate, so he just ignored it, but it was still on his phone and he didn't recognize the risk. My husband promptly got on the chat and reminded the boys that anyone can see any text chats at any time, and we reported it to their coach. Needless to say, my son was kicked out of the group chat and excluded from further conversations, much to his relief. Here's the thing. He wasn't angry about our intervention; he was grateful for a way out of a situation that was over his head.

Parenting Pro Tips

Take a when-not-if approach in talking to your teens about pornography. And it's not just boys. Girls watch porn too. And teens often watch porn together. If teens know they will likely be exposed to pornography at some point, instead of feeling ashamed and unprepared, it will empower them to be ready with a response and to share that experience with you. Instead of asking, "Have you been watching porn?" try, "Have you seen anything that makes you uncomfortable?"

Preventing Exposure

The fact is that pornographic images stay in our minds forever. The less exposure, the less intrusion in unwelcome moments. Limit your teen's opportunity for private screen use. Encourage a culture of accountability in your family. Place home computers in an open area, such as the dining or living room. Check-in phones to a central location at night, because temptation can be strong in the wee hours of the quiet night in the privacy of your bedroom.

Teens with strong parental attachment are less likely to intentionally seek pornography. Invest in your relationship by spending time together and doing things that are enjoyable and fun. It doesn't always have to be a serious conversation. (This is me looking super-guilty right here, and all my kids saying, "Yeah, Mom!" Duly noted by the family buzzkill.) Go to church. Teens with strong spiritual connections are less likely to struggle with porn. The flip side of this is that kids who go to church and struggle with porn may feel more shame and be less likely to disclose. Lower the barrier created by the not-my-kid mind-set. Help teens to recognize the signs of unhealthy relationships, including jealousy, manipulation, bullying, threats of violence or self-harm, or pressure to engage in pornography with statements such as "If you love me, you'd do it." Create a plan for walking away from that relationship. If an adult initiates pornography exposure, teens need to report it *immediately*, as this falls under the legal definition of abuse in most states. Abusers frequently use pornography to groom victims.

Responding to Unintentional Exposure

Before it happens, make it clear to your teen that you understand unintentional exposure can happen and any such disclosure won't result in anger or punishment. Normalize disclosure by discussing possible ways accidental exposure can happen (errors typing a website URL, unsolicited video or URL from a friend, connection request from an unknown social media account with an explicit profile photo, spam email, others showing something on their phone, exposure to another friend or family member consuming pornography). Bringing these up makes it easier to say, "Hey, you know that thing you warned me about? It happened today." Empower your teen to walk away from social pressure. Teach them how to block phone contacts, mark email as spam, and report explicit material on social media platforms.

Listen up and pay close attention here. This is really important. Tell your teen that sexual arousal during unintentional exposure to pornography is a *normal physical response*. Teens feel significant shame about bodily reactions they cannot control, especially when they internalize subconscious messages such as "sex is bad" or they should "wait until marriage." They might feel any sexual response is a violation. They won't ask you but struggle with inner guilt. Lead confidently with reassurance. You can say something like the following:

God created your sexuality. Your body had the
right response in the wrong circumstance. You
shouldn't feel embarrassed or ashamed.

Responding to Discovery

Plan for disclosure should your teen be persuaded to watch something by a peer or on their own. How and when should they tell you and what will be the course of action? If you discover pornography use, stay calm. Don't go charging in, yelling off the cuff. Consult a primary health-care provider, mentor, trusted friend, or minister and ask for advice and support. Choose your timing for a conversation and lead with the facts of what you know. Don't set them up to lie by asking something for which you already have the answer ("Are you watching porn?!"). Ask them to share their perspective and add any further facts for consideration. Be ready to talk about risks and health impacts. Depending on their response, tell them you'll take some time to think about the events and follow up with actions to give accountability and restore trust.

Responding to Disclosure

Most importantly, express your unconditional love. ("I will always love you no matter what happens." "I'm upset and I have questions, but we'll get through this together.") If your child is under the age of twelve and discloses intentional pornography consumption, make an appointment with a health-care provider to guide the decision-making about evaluation and therapy, as this can be an indication of experiencing abuse or other serious underlying mental health concerns.[23] Traumatic exposures to violence in pornography also can be damaging. If your child is over the age of twelve, the need for a medical evaluation depends on how often they're watching and how much distress it's causing. If the exposure was relatively short-term and infrequent, dragging them to confession or therapy will be shaming and likely do more harm than good. Seek guidance from a trusted friend or mentor on setting up accountability moving forward. If there are signs of mental health concerns, call your health-care provider.

BEHIND THE HEART DOOR

Guilt is a healthy emotion. When we touch a hot stove, our brain signals danger and we remove our hand quickly. Guilt warns us to leave a situation causing harm.

Guilt tells us what we did was wrong.
Shame tells us who we are is wrong.

Guilt helps you to understand how your actions impact your future and other people, but shame says you are deeply flawed and unworthy of love. Shame leads to self-harm, addiction, and depression. When teens express guilt about pornography habits, we as parents should harness that as a helpful, healthy prompt to change behavior. Actively speak against feelings of shame by expressing messages of hope and worthiness of love.

Conversation Doors

- Watch the three-part documentary series titled *Brain, Heart, World* from Fight the New Drug. Discuss your reactions.

- Read about Terry Crews, actor and former professional football player, who openly shares his struggles with pornography.
- Watch the movie *Fireproof* by the Kendrick brothers. Discuss your reactions. From this movie came the book *The Love Dare*.[24] (There also is a *Love Dare for Parents*.)[25] You also can take a free parenting assessment at lovedaretest.com. This may be a forty-day side journey for you to convey parental love in a meaningful way.
- Arrange to have Fight the New Drug give a presentation at your teen's school.

Conversation Keys

After you complete your activity together, initiate a conversation. Remember to LOVE your teen.

Listen with your face:
- Say, "It sounds like you _____," and then reflect back what you heard.
- Thank them for a conversation about an uncomfortable topic.
- Share one new thing you learned or observed about how they think.

Offer open-ended questions:
- "What kinds of exposure have you had to pornography?"
- "How has pornography impacted your relationships?"
- "What would you do if you accidentally came across pornography?"
- "How can I help you feel safe about disclosing your struggles in the future?"
- "What else would you like to share?"

Validate feelings:
- "I'm sorry you were hurt by _____."

CLOSED DOORS

- "I imagine it's hard to go against what seems like the norm."
- "It's okay to be worried about this."
- "I will always love you, no matter what, and I want you to feel safe to share your feelings."

Explore next steps together:

Plan for a response to unintentional exposure, peer pressure, or individual consumption. Tell your teen what the consequences may look like and how the road of grace will restore trust and right relationships. Parents, this is hard to hear, but your teen might have already experienced negative exposures they are terrified to share with you. Creating expectations for your response and consequences gives them the courage to share and take the first steps toward freedom.

BEHIND THE HEART DOOR

Many of you regularly consume pornography. You're wondering how in the world you can walk your teen through this issue without feeling like a hypocrite. The emphasis in this chapter is on the detrimental effects pornography has on teen brains, but the darkness that engulfs adults here is secrecy. I've seen professionally and personally the crushing weight of this weary load destroy families. Every time, the story is the same, and it always involves deception until the excruciating moment of discovery, when the grenade explodes. There is freedom and hope for you.

Devotional

King David had it all. He was glowing with health and had a fine appearance with handsome features. He was a musician, a singer/

songwriter, and an instrumentalist. He slayed giants and killed lions and bears with his bare hands. He was an adored and celebrated king of Israel. Women loved him.

But a secret destroyed him as well as innocent lives around him.

As he was walking on his palace roof, he saw a beautiful woman bathing. He could have walked away, but he lusted after her and abused his power to take her, regardless of the cost. This reads much like modern pornography. There was no consent here. Secrets spin complicated webs until you're consumed by your efforts to keep your secret *at all costs, even death*. But God knows every secret of our hearts. *Every* secret will come to light. God demands an account, naked and exposed. David described this feeling as groaning while his body wasted away, vitality drained like a fever. After confessing his sin, David described God as his hiding place, *surrounding* him with *shouts* of deliverance and freedom.

Reflect

What secrets are you hiding that are preventing you from walking in truth and light with others?

How have someone else's secrets negatively impacted or hurt you?

What steps can you take today toward healing and forgiveness?

Pray

(From Galatians 5–6) Thank You for the freedom we have in Christ. Help _____ to stand fast in the liberty Christ has freely gifted them. Save _____ from being entangled and burdened by the weight of pornography. Call them to freedom. Help us to see freedom as You intended— not as freedom to sin, but as freedom from sin. If _____ is ensnared by temptation, help me restore them with a spirit of gentleness and compassion, carrying the burden together. Help _____ to daily walk by Your Spirit. Let love, joy, peace, patience, kindness, goodness, faithfulness, gentleness, and self-control be the fruits of the freedom in our lives. Peace and mercy be upon us, and may the grace of the Lord Jesus Christ be with us forever. Amen.

Act

(Legacy Letter) Think of a healthy, edifying relationship your teen has with someone. It could be a friend, family member, coach, teacher, younger child, elderly person, or someone else. Who do you love your teen to be with because it brings out the best in their personality? Who is spurring your teen to good works? Who makes you at ease because you know your teen is safe, loved, and supported? Who makes your teen's personality shine through with confidence?

Find (or take) a photo of your teen and that person. Write a letter detailing what you admire and appreciate about that healthy relationship. Specify ways that person brings out the best in your teen.

t e n

SOCIAL JUSTICE

How to Talk to Your Teens About Racism

She worked for three years to arrive at this moment. She was nervous, petrified really. The doctoral student I advised was about to present her project on implicit bias (unintentionally expressing racist thoughts or actions) in health care to a large group of nurses. I wasn't nervous, not a bit. I was excited. I'd been advising these projects for more than a decade, and I knew this was a good one. The student had little experience with public speaking. "Not to worry," I said. "I've got you." We rehearsed religiously. She moved me to tears. It was exceptional.

She knocked the presentation out of the park.

My heart swelled.

Then it stopped.

I read the comments.

They accused her of being biased. They questioned her credibility. They criticized the organization for allowing her to speak. They accused her of being racist and unprofessional. There were also affirmations, but these harsh words stopped me in my tracks.

It never occurred to me that her fear wasn't public speaking but, instead, the vulnerability of sharing her perspective.

I was broken and humbled.

BEHIND THE CLINIC DOOR

Social justice is a polarizing buzzword that can turn the most well-intentioned family gatherings into WWE, but today's teens are deeply passionate about it. One in twelve parents report their teen attended some sort of social demonstration in 2020.[1] Generally speaking, teens view social justice as simply wanting all people to be fairly treated in society. I know, I know. We all have very different ideas about *how* that should be accomplished. Let's work together to push aside political rhetoric for a moment and reframe this as a relationship issue. How can we effectively meet our teens in this space and seek to understand their perspective? This is a teaching moment to engage in civil dialogue, even about things on which you may disagree. The first step is listening and seeking to understand the heart of your teen.

Nowhere has dialogue on social justice been more prominent than conversations surrounding race. In a recent survey, 83 percent of teens reported systemic racism as a serious issue, and 86 percent felt proud for taking a stand.[2] The word *racism* stirs deeply felt emotion. It's difficult to discuss, but our teens are not only having conversations, they're engaging in self-reflection and open dialogue. We can learn from their compassionate strength with a gentle reminder from 1 Timothy 4:12: "Don't let anyone look down on you because you are young, but set an example for the believers in speech, in conduct, in love, in faith and in purity."

Listen, I am not a racial relations expert. I'm a nurse who deeply cares about the well-being of all children. I'm a professor who wants to support my students. I'm a Christian who believes every person is beautifully created in the image of God. I'm a White woman, sharing my perspective through that lens. Most of all, I'm a parent, just like you, trying my best to lead conversations with my teens. Join me as we seek to understand why this topic is so important to our teens and how we can love others well in this space.

Health Impacts

I haven't personally experienced racism, but I've witnessed it. A relative tells offensive jokes or uses slurs at a family event. Families refuse to allow a student of color to care for their child. Faculty ask if a student "played the Black card" in an academic appeal. A patient refuses care from an Asian nurse, afraid of contracting COVID-19. A physician tells me they're working with a "really nice Black nurse today." (I've never heard anyone say, "I worked with a really nice White nurse today.") A physician laughingly tells a teen he knows can't speak English, "Go back to Mexico." A student rolls their eyes at the dress of an Orthodox Jew, making an offhand joke about money. An Asian student asks a Pacific Islander student, "Are you al-Qaeda?" A clinician colleague from India is terrified to take her children out in public where people assume they're Muslim simply because of their skin color, targeting them with slurs and aggression. Similar assumptions are made of a physician who wears a Punjabi Pagdi, a turban representing respect and honor. I've seen worse, but these are everyday things.

Recently, I had an unexpectedly emotional encounter. When meeting a student, I noticed her stated name didn't match her name of record. I asked for clarification. She said her real name was difficult to pronounce, and people started using a nickname for her, so she went with it. I asked her to teach me how to say her real name. It took me a couple of tries, but I got it. She was teary. I was stunned. I remembered a study that found a unique brain activation when we hear our own name, which causes a burst of feel-good hormones.[3] This reaction is so powerful, patients in a coma have brain responses to hearing their name.[4] When we dismiss someone's name as too hard to say, we unintentionally communicate they need to conform to our culture for our comfort.

What's the Difference Between Race and Ethnicity?

Race was previously viewed as a social construct based on where people lived geographically or visible differences in physical characteristics (phenotype) such as height, eye color, hair color, and blood type. Advances in genomic science help us to reexamine relationships between genetic differences and the physical expressions of race. Humans are actually 99.9 percent identical at the genome level, meaning that our biological differences are extremely small.[5] Race categories include White, Black or African American, American Indian or Alaska Native, Asian, and Native Hawaiian or other Pacific Islander. The term BIPOC is used to describe Black, indigenous, and people of color.

Ethnicity, by comparison, is simply a shared cultural heritage, which includes language, religion, and other national or tribal practices. For example, a person might identify their race as Black and their ethnicity as Hispanic. One person might identify as Japanese and another as Vietnamese ethnicity, but both are Asian in terms of race. Hispanic is a describing word for ethnicity for persons whose heritage originates in a Spanish-speaking country. Latina and Latino, on the other hand, are feminine and masculine terms indicating heritage from nations south of the United States (Mexico, South America, and the Caribbean). Latinx is a much-debated gender-neutral version. Conversationally, people may refer to themselves as Cuban, Mexican, or Latin American as their ethnic origin. In very simplistic terms, race is how you look, ethnicity is where you're from.

What Is Racism?

Let's walk respectfully together through some more difficult concepts to inform our conversation with our teens, starting with a simple definition of racism. Racism is a system of assigning social value based on physical appearance and using structure to create opportunities to unfairly disadvantage some and unfairly advantage others.

Institutional racism creates barriers through laws and societal regulations. There are many examples of this in American history, including the internment of nearly 120,000 Japanese Americans during World War II and a litany of injustices toward Native Americans. Before the Civil War, the United States recorded nearly four million enslaved Black people, after which Black code laws were enacted to limit the freedom of former slaves and ensure cheap labor during the Reconstruction era. By the 1880s, big cities that did not fully enforce or adopt discriminatory laws attracted Black families. When this happened, city leaders demanded more restrictions, leading to Jim Crow laws and the rise of segregation. Black people had separate buses, water fountains, restrooms, entrances, public pools, elevators, cemeteries, churches, schools, and even duties within the various branches of the armed forces. Some states outlawed marriages between White and Black persons, with social or legal adoption of the "one-drop rule," meaning a single drop of "Black blood" makes a person Black, before these laws were struck down by the Supreme Court in 1967.

President Lyndon B. Johnson signed the 1964 Civil Rights Act that legally ended segregation and recognized the equal rights of Black Americans to public spaces and banned employment discrimination. Social acceptance resisted, however. History gives us context to understand the concerns expressed by teens today about systemic racism. The civil rights movement was in our lifetime. This is not-so-distant history. I work with nurses who attended segregated colleges. Today's teens are being raised by parents and grandparents who witnessed these events firsthand.

In actuality, things still happen today. Recently my family was driving through Arkansas when we were shocked to see billboards advertising "White Pride Radio." This was indeed real, with a ferocious legal battle at the time. The last billboard has since been removed, but it certainly made an impression. In these historical considerations, it's important to not only recognize the pain that was experienced but to celebrate the courage and resilience of the people who endured.

Person-mediated racism is what most people think of when the word *racism* is used. This simply means we make assumptions about other people based on how they look and knowingly (*explicit bias*) or unknowingly (*implicit bias*) act on those assumptions. Explicit bias is exemplified in historic events such as Rosa Parks, Emmett Till, and the Ku Klux Klan. Implicit bias comes from ingrained ways of thinking because of how we were raised or what we fear when we face unfamiliar situations. It's avoiding, disrespecting, giving differential treatment, or making assumptions about a person's motives or abilities based on the color of their skin.

Let me give you a personal example. When I was a nursing student, I was assigned in labor and delivery to care for an Asian woman after childbirth. I wasn't allowed to do much except make sure her ice water pitcher was full. I took that responsibility way too seriously. She refused to drink, and I *scolded* her (politely and professionally, of course, based on my forty-seven minutes of expert knowledge acquired from the previous day's lecture). I told her if she wasn't hydrated, she couldn't breastfeed, and her baby might starve. (Wouldn't you want me to be your nurse?) Finally, another nurse pulled me (by my ear) to the linen closet and plainly educated me about yin-and-yang cultural practices after birth. Bottom line, this woman was desperate for a hot drink and a warm blanket. I offered cold water, ice packs, and an even frostier attitude. I saw her birthing experience only through the bias of my own cultural experience and I *judged* her.

Internalized racism happens when people experience significant discriminatory behaviors to the point of accepting limitations and losing self-worth. It means self-restricting from certain places or activities, thinking, "I don't belong there."

How Does Racism Impact Teen Health?

In an increasingly diverse society, Gen Z is emerging as the most racially diverse generation, where almost half identify as diverse or biracial. Today's teens are especially perceptive of microaggressions, that is, subtle comments that convey explicit or implicit bias. Common questions or comments to teens with different skin color received as off-putting include the following: "Where are you from?" "What are you exactly?" "You speak good English." "You're a credit to your race." Teens overwhelmingly report more blatant personal experiences. Teens also witness racism vicariously by sharing experiences through social media and news reports. These are deeply upsetting to many teens, along with the distress caused by heated conversations among peers, online, or in person.

Immigrant teens live with an intense fear of deportation or arrest of themselves or their loved ones. The Deferred Action for Childhood Arrivals (DACA) program was created in 2012 by President Barack Obama to allow young people brought illegally to the United States by their parents to have temporary protection from deportation. They received permission to work, go to school, and obtain driver's licenses if they met a strict set of rules and standards, which also required renewal every two years. There are about 800,000 DREAMers, as they are called, and I've taught many. It's easy to argue about policy in the abstract, but when a student is weeping in your office in the last semester of their nursing program, terrified of being deported because they were brought to the United States as a baby and they have no memory of their country of origin and can't even speak that country's language, the situation becomes much more complicated and personal.

Racism negatively impacts health outcomes from birth and contributes to mental health conditions.[6] I regularly encounter this in practice. Teens who personally experience racism or discrimination have harmful health impacts, especially youth of color who have experienced prejudice and oppression. However, simply witnessing this treatment of others can also be traumatizing.[7] Exposure to racism creates a state of chronic stress for teens, which kick-starts a negative physiologic cascade that impacts every organ system. However, we need a strengths-based approach to see teens through more than the singular lens of the hardships they've endured. Seeking opportunities to celebrate strength and resilience is empowering and uplifting.

Parenting Pro Tips

I often hear my White friends and colleagues say, "I'm color-blind. I treat everyone equally, no matter the color of their skin." Although well-intentioned, this causes us to miss out on the wonderful differences God created in all of us. We need to celebrate the unique elements of our cultural heritage and use opportunities such as celebration months to learn more and practice empathy and kindness.

I've also heard it said that racism isn't caught, it's taught. Babies as young as three months old show a preference for faces similar to theirs.[8] Toddlers can easily mimic racist behaviors. When this happens, we, as parents, often panic and tell them to shush and vaguely admonish, "Don't say things *like that!*" This sends the message that race is a taboo subject and not to be discussed. Most kids are genuinely curious. Having plainspoken conversations with teens about race decreases racist behaviors more than giving only general kinds of messages such as "We should all love everyone no matter what."

Racially Diverse Families

Writer Torrie Sorge lifted my eyes to the unique needs of interracial and mixed-race families, which are growing in number. She told me that teens who are mixed-race are often high achievers and embrace diversity. Their experiences, while similar, are often more layered and complex while being overlooked and dismissed. While other groups find safety and acceptance among their family and/or community, mixed-race individuals feel alone. They don't fit anywhere, from friend groups to social groups to even within their own family. When both of your parents are each from a different race and neither understands the tension of living between worlds, it can be difficult to relate to the daily realities facing their teens. Allowing a safe space for conversation and embracing multicultural role models are helpful.

Transracial Adoption

I want to give a special shout-out to families who have chosen to love a child through transracial or transcultural adoption. The act of adoption is beautiful and mirrors God's adoption of us as His children. Adoptive parents, however, will tell you this road is not easy. It requires patience, kindness, empathy, and sitting through painful grieving and longing. These families need community support. It may be something as simple as hair styling or as complex as identifying with experiences of racial injustice.

There are things you can do to help these teens thrive. First, make it clear, as adopted parents, you are not the rescuer/savior/hero of their story. Engage "racial mirrors," a support person who looks like your teen, to serve as a role model. Give your child permission not to answer intrusive and offensive questions from others. Thoughtfully consider all aspects of school experiences, including students, teachers, and curriculum. Fill your home with positive images and stories of people from different cultural backgrounds, especially their own. Intentionally celebrate cultural events and embrace new traditions as a family. Engage in a community that reflects and supports your adopted child's cultural heritage. Acknowledge you can't always make things better. Sometimes you just need to embrace their grief over the loss of their biological parents, their culture, and "what could have been."

For White Families

From my family to yours, there are simple but meaningful practices you can adopt together to demonstrate welcomeness and inclusion. Intentionally model publicly the behavior you want to see in your teen. Seek to learn from the experiences of others. Diversify your social network and intentionally invite families or friends of other ethnicities or races. Participate in culturally diverse community events. Teach your teen to speak up on behalf of others when racist speech or action occurs. Apologize sincerely when you misstep or misspeak. Take this self-assessment as a family:

- Do you have a selection of books by a wide variety of authors on your shelves?
- Do you follow people on social media who look different from you?

- Do you interact with diverse people in your neighborhood?
- Do you have friendships with families who are different from you?
- Do you try foods from different cultures with an open mind and positive attitude?
- Do you watch movies or TV shows with diverse characters?
- Do you patronize businesses owned and operated by persons of a racial minority?
- Do you openly talk about racist behaviors when you see them happen?
- How can you make your home a welcoming haven to all who visit?

BEHIND THE HOME DOOR

In preparing to write this chapter, I learned my BIPOC friends are remarkably comfortable and gracious with these conversations. If this is you, you're likely nodding your head and saying this simply reflects your everyday lived experience and I've told you absolutely nothing you don't already know. You've welcomed me to your conversation table. Thank you.

If this isn't something you've had a meaningful conversation about with your teen before, you may be genuinely surprised to hear their feelings and experiences. This is a hard topic to bring up at the dinner table. Imagine your teen saying over a bite of green beans, "Hey, everybody, I'd like to share my deepest thoughts about racism." Not happening. But if we don't frame these conversations, other forces will. People are genuinely afraid of saying the wrong thing. A good strategy is to listen more than you talk and to keep an open mind and heart. If you don't agree on something with your teen, look past the details and ask yourself, "Where is their heart on this?" Can you find a starting space of agreement and empathy there?

Conversation Doors

- Have a movie night: *The Perfect Game, Blue Miracle, Black Panther, Crazy Rich Asians, The Farewell, To Kill a Mockingbird, Te Ata, Remember the Titans, Million Dollar Arm, The Hate U Give, In the Heights, Hamilton, Moana, Same Kind of Different as Me, The Help, Hidden Figures, 42, Just Mercy, Magic of Ordinary Days, The Courageous Heart of Irena Sendler.*
- Read a book together: *Just Mercy, Reaching for the Moon, To Kill a Mockingbird, Claudette Colvin, The Boy in the Striped Pajamas, The Book Thief, My Family Divided, Same Kind of Different as Me, Warriors Don't Cry, The Hiding Place.*
- Watch the documentary *A Class Divided*, the story of an elementary school teacher in small-town Iowa. The day after Martin Luther King Jr. was assassinated, she divided her third-grade class into blue-eyed and brown-eyed groups to teach a lesson on discrimination.
- If you know someone who has experienced racism and is willing to share, plan a time to get together.
- Take the Harvard Implicit Association Test for race (find this online), a photo test that assesses your preference for different facial features. Discuss your results as a family.

Conversation Keys

After you complete your activity together, initiate a conversation. Remember to LOVE your teen.

Listen with your face:
- Say, "What I'm hearing you say is _____."
- Thank them for being willing to share their thoughts and feelings.
- Share one new thing you learned or observed about their convictions.

Offer open-ended questions:
- "How have you experienced bias or racism?"
- "How have conversations about racism personally impacted you?"
- "What do you wish you could say to your friends about how you feel?"
- "What would you do if you saw someone experiencing racism?"
- "What fears do you have about what could happen?"
- "How can I help you feel safe?"
- "What else would you like to share?"

Validate feelings:
- "I'm sorry you experienced this."
- "I believe you can be a positive influence."
- "It's okay to be (fill in the blank: confused, hurt, angry) about this."
- "I am here for you and want to be a safe space for you to talk about your feelings."

Explore next steps together:

As individual families, we don't have much control about things that go on in the world unless you're a legislator, celebrity, or someone with a great deal of power. However, we can influence our own families and our homes. Plan together to make your home a safe space. Discuss together anti-racist behaviors you can adopt as a family.

BEHIND THE HEART DOOR

Maybe this is a painful topic for you. If you are a person of color and have personally experienced racism, my heart hurts with you. I sincerely thank you for every courteous conversation you've had to share your experience and perspective, even perhaps at great personal cost.

Maybe you don't want to have these conversations. You fear saying something insensitive and resent being labeled as "racist" when that's not your heart or intent. Listen to your teen with empathy. Avoid interruption or domination of the conversation. Reflect back your understanding, demonstrating acceptance if someone is not ready to share their experiences. Building trust takes time. Be honest and open about your thoughts, presenting them in a considerate way. Learn to sit comfortably in uncomfortable spaces.

Instead of focusing on defending your view in moments of disagreement, consciously work toward finding common ground, even if it's just a tiny square.

Maybe you've never experienced racism and are struggling to come to a settled place in your spirit. I welcome you to this conversation table. Maybe you're thinking, "There's not a racist bone in my body!" As a health professional, I assure you in my careful study of 206 human bones, none of them are racist. Racism isn't in our bones; it's in our DNA.

I present you with this thought:

If you're asking yourself, "Am I racist?" I gently propose you are asking the right question of the wrong person.

We all (*every single one of us*) have implicit bias, meaning we don't see it easily in ourselves. We need to listen to the experiences of others and thoughtfully examine our own lives for unintentionally hurtful words or behaviors.

Imagine buying your teen some new clothes with generous intentions. But they're very hurt by your purchase. You're caught off guard. It's not the reaction you expected. Your teen believes you just don't like their style. It's too provocative. It's sloppy. They've gained weight. Their perception is you want them to project the image *you* prefer as a self-reflection of your parenting. You're immediately defensive, thinking, "That's not what I meant at all!"

Stop. Think.

That's not what I meant . . . *or was it?*

Do you subtly wish they would dress more to your taste? More modestly? More neatly? More flattering to their body type? If you're *really* honest, is there any grain of truth in this? Maybe not, but *maybe so.* This is the work of searching our hearts, asking hard questions, adopting a posture of openness. Now, relate this back to implicit bias. See it? Search your heart. I'm right there with you.

Devotional

At the heart of the matter, racism is not a social issue as much as it is a spiritual issue. We are *all* created in God's image. The New

Testament consistently amplifies marginalized persons and ethnicities. When Jesus was born, the good news went to shepherds, hardly the elite in ancient society. The Magi who followed the star to Bethlehem came from another country, likely viewed as pagan by Jewish society, but invited into the story of the birth of Christ. Jesus spent part of His childhood in Egypt, a political refugee in a foreign country. In the parable of the good Samaritan, Jesus flipped the cultural script and made the ethnic minority Samaritan the protagonist while chastising religious leaders. Although Jesus was Jewish, He healed the daughter of a Gentile. Jesus gave the Great Commission, sending the gospel to *all* nations.

But God gave *us* a ministry of reconciliation. This is beautifully illustrated through vivid imagery in the book of Revelation's depiction of a great multitude from *every* nation, tribe, people, and language, *all* standing before God's throne and worshiping as *one*.

Reflect

How do you really feel about what we've discussed together?

Think about the times you've experienced or witnessed acts of discrimination or bias but haven't acted. What do you wish you'd done differently?

How can you be more welcoming of those who look, think, act, or even vote differently than you do?

Pray

(From 2 Corinthians 13 and Philippians 2) God, examine our hearts. Help us to do what is right even when we feel powerless. Help us to rejoice in our weaknesses and to rely on Your perfect strength. We pray for Your restoration. Help us to use authority to build others up and not tear them down. Help us to comfort our brothers and sisters who are hurting. We pray for peace and unity in our communities. Will You send the grace of Jesus and the love of God and the fellowship of the Holy Spirit to be in these conversations? Help us to be of the same mind with the same love, in full accord with united hearts. Help us to do nothing from selfish ambition or conceit but, in humility, to count others as more significant than ourselves. Help us to look to the interests of others and to shine as lights in the world as a beacon of hope for Your glory. Amen.

Act

(Legacy Letter) Think about a person of color who has inspired you or deeply impacted your life, your teen's life, or the life of someone you know. How has that changed you? Write a letter sharing that story.

In what ways have you experienced or witnessed racism or bias? How can you share that experience with a meaningful perspective and a word of encouragement?

eleven

GENDER IDENTITY

How to Respond with Compassion and Kindness

The first time I saw Jacob, he was distressed. Although he had come for a checkup, I quickly uncovered risk-taking behaviors, and his mental health screening concerned me. His relationship with his parents was contentious. They were frustrated with his seeming disregard for rules. I carefully approached my concern about his mental health but was met with resistance. I referred him for a mental health evaluation but wasn't optimistic he'd go.

A few months later I was relieved to see Jacob on my schedule. I walked into the exam room and quickly realized I had made a mistake and was in the wrong room. As I stood there, looking puzzled and double-checking the chart, the girl on the table laughed at my flustered state. I apologized and turned to leave when I heard a familiar voice say, "No, it's me! I'm Elizabeth now." I turned back, beginning to comprehend a radical visual transformation into a completely different teen.

As we talked, I learned the parents had moved, leaving their teen (now eighteen) in the care of friends to complete the senior year of high school. The accompanying social worker disclosed serious suicide behaviors requiring hospitalization and the need to access follow-up counseling services. At this point the father arrived, visibly angry and bellowing, "Don't anyone dare call my boy Elizabeth!"

BEHIND THE CLINIC DOOR

Conversations surrounding issues of gender are absolutely everywhere. We hear heated rhetoric on television, during school forums, at the grocery store, and even in our living rooms. I don't blame you for feeling tempted to head for the hills and skip ahead here. However, in the midst of this national shouting match are very real kids with very real families facing very real issues in very real time. How can we best lead our teens to have a meaningful conversation in this space?

Increasing numbers of teens identify as gender nonconforming (a general term meaning their behavior or appearance doesn't conform to expected social norms). In 2017, the Gallup organization reported about 4.5 percent of the population identified as gender nonconforming, including about 9 percent of millennials, the fastest-growing generation to do so at the time.[1] A 2022 Gallup poll reported more adults identifying as gender diverse, increasing from 5.6 percent in 2020 to 7.1 percent in 2022. Most notably in this poll, one in six Gen Z adults self-identified as something other than gender-normative or heterosexual.[2] I can tell you from personal experience that in my first fifteen years of pediatric nursing practice, I can recall one teen who vaguely disclosed to me she was *possibly* a lesbian. Rising over the last decade I now see gender nonconforming teens in practice and education *every single day.*

Gender nonconforming teens are at significant risk for poor psychosocial health, including an increased risk of depression, anxiety, psychiatric hospitalizations, and shockingly high numbers of suicidal thoughts or behaviors.[3] There is very little argument over these facts, even among groups and researchers who ardently disagree over the cause. Suicide risk is four times greater than the general population,[4] with estimates of suicide attempts every forty-five seconds.[5] Statistically speaking, the odds are that your teen will not come out to you as gender nonconforming, but the odds are they will know or encounter someone who does identify as such and is experiencing some of these psychosocial stressors. Is your teen adequately equipped to respond comfortably in these encounters?

Parents, your teens are engaging in conversations and experiencing situations in this sphere. They are navigating new situations in the context of some social norms we never had to face. They're making critical decisions in real time about how to respond. Many are not at all confident or comfortable with those decisions. They second-guess themselves and wonder if they did or said the right thing. Look for opportunities to initiate and lead a conversation to equip them to speak and act with grace and confidence. Maybe they casually mention something in passing. Maybe you have a mutual encounter that prompts discussion. Maybe they come to you with a serious concern for a friend or situation they're experiencing. Maybe someone in your family makes a disclosure. Are you being intentional in listening for these conversation cues?

When these moments of opportunity come your way, you'll be faced with a decision as to how you respond. There are three likely scenarios:

- Ignore the question or situation. Shut the conversation down quickly.

- Respond impulsively from a place of emotion, doing most of the talking and little listening.
- Intentionally initiate a meaningful, honest conversation about an incredibly challenging topic in which you listen more than you speak, knowing you'll be asked questions for which you don't have the answers.

Your teens absolutely, 100 percent, for sure are talking to someone about this topic. You have the amazing privilege to choose if that person will be you.

Health Impacts

Rapidly emerging, voluminous vocabulary lists with what seems like new words and norms every day are enough to make even the sincerest efforts at understanding come across as dazed and confused. Words such as *cisgender*, *genderqueer*, *gender dysphoria*, *gender fluidity*, *nonbinary*, and *intersex* are unfamiliar to most of the American public. Unintentional missteps, honest misunderstandings, and well-intentioned disagreement cause offense, argument, pain, and shaming. This is the dynamic your teen is trying to navigate.

When the topic of gender arises, I often hear parents say something like "You know, that LGBTXYZ stuff . . ." with a shrug and an eye roll. One of the reasons I'm able to talk to teens comfortably is because I take time to learn the language they know. During the *Twilight* movies craze, I frequently greeted teens in practice with the question, "Team Edward or Team Jacob?" (Confession: I hadn't seen the movies, but I knew enough to start a conversation.) Guess what? It worked. Learning new words doesn't mean in any way you have to agree or approve. You don't even have to use them regularly in conversation. Learning the new words simply signals to your teen that you've taken the time to invest in preparation for a discussion. That simple gesture means a lot more than you realize.

Let's flip the narrative. Your teen tells you they want to buy a used car from a local dealership. You're curious. Maybe they're serious. You ask how much money they've saved. Answer: "I'm not sure. Maybe like a hundred dollars?" You ask about financing options and interest rates. Blank stare. You ask about Kelley Blue Book value. Answer: "I don't need that. No one cares about that." You ask about the VIN to check the vehicle's history. They're angry and ask why you're not supportive. Your perception? They're not ready for this conversation. And this is what our teens think about us when we aren't ready to have a serious conversation too.

Maybe you're thinking, "I don't really want my teen to know these things yet." The truth is that, unless you're living in an underground bunker, they know. These conversations don't have to produce a lot of fear or anxiety, and they should be developmentally and situationally appropriate. Learning more about how our teens feel empowers us to have influence in that relationship and lets them know they're not alone in figuring this out.

Unless you actively direct this conversation and seek to influence through understanding and relationship building, your teen's views will be shaped by their peers, the media, and outside cultural influences. If you tell them what to think and don't entertain an open conversation, you miss out on your teen's questions and concerns. Let's acquire some knowledge to equip us to start a real conversation. I'm right here with you, learning something new every day.

We'll start with a basic glossary of terms, defined as your teen will encounter them.

AGENDER: identifies as neither male nor female

ALLY: someone who supports the causes of the queer community

ASEXUAL: only experiences romantic, not sexual, attraction

BISEXUAL: physical, romantic, or sexual attraction to same or different genders

CISGENDER: personal identity and gender match one's sex assigned at birth

GAY: attracted to other members of same sex, usually used to refer to men

GENDER DYSPHORIA: distress when sex at birth and gender identity don't align

GENDER FLUID: someone who doesn't identify as having a fixed gender

GENDER IDENTITY: one's internal sense of self

GENDER ROLE: outward expression of gender identity

GENDERQUEER: doesn't accept conventional gender distinctions; identifies with neither, both, or a combination of genders

INTERSEX: physical condition occurring when a baby is born having genitals with ambiguous characteristics (basically it's hard to tell—they look like both male and female) because of chromosomal or hormonal factors (formerly called hermaphrodite, which is now broadly considered offensive); gender is usually selected by parents and assigned through surgery

LESBIAN: a woman physically, romantically, or sexually attracted to other women

PANSEXUAL: attracted to other people regardless of gender

QUEER: an umbrella term for people who are neither heterosexual nor cisgender

QUESTIONING: questioning their gender identity or sexual preference

SEXUAL ORIENTATION: personal identity in terms of to whom they are physically, romantically, or sexually attracted

TRANSGENDER: identifies mentally and emotionally with a gender that doesn't match their biological gender assigned at birth, also an umbrella term generally used for trans people

TRANSSEXUAL: a person who alters themselves physically, either surgically or hormonally, to align their physical body with their gender identity

2S OR 2 SPIRIT: a Native American umbrella term to describe someone who identifies with both masculine and feminine spirits

TERMS CONSIDERED OFFENSIVE: hermaphrodite, homosexual, sexual preference, sex change, transgendered, tranny

What Are the Health Risks Surrounding Gender Identity?

Gender-diverse teens face significantly higher health risks when compared to cisgender teens: assault, bullying (experienced by more than half of transgender teens), disordered eating, forced intercourse, self-harming, dating violence, sexual risk-taking, addiction, and suicide (almost half have considered suicide). They are also more likely to be threatened with a weapon on school property and more likely to be involved in fighting or bringing a weapon to school.[6]

I frequently encounter LGBTQIA+ (lesbian, gay, bisexual, transgender, queer or questioning, intersex, asexual) teens who are engaging in risky sexual behaviors because they are desperately afraid of disclosure and mistakenly don't see the risk. One of my female teen patients disclosed under pressure to her mother that she was having "unprotected sex." The mother gave her condoms and brought her to me. The girl told me she was having "safe sex" because it was with another girl and she couldn't get pregnant. There is a significant lack of understanding of the risks, true for all teens engaging in risky behaviors, but LGBTQIA+ teens are less likely to ask and less likely to have easily accessible resources.

Experiencing homelessness is a significant problem among transgender youth as many teens who come out to their families are either kicked out or feel rejected and unsupported and run away. Homelessness increases the risk of mental health issues and suicide, among other very dark and dangerous things I've seen personally, such as human trafficking. About one-third of teens accessing a transgender crisis hotline reported experiencing homelessness, and the same number of transgender teens reported living in poverty.[7]

What About Hormones and Surgery?

Gender-affirmative care, generally defined as developmentally appropriate care oriented toward understanding a person's gender, is widely discussed in health care and debated in legislative forums with rapidly arising state laws seeking to regulate it. These changing laws and policy regulations have important implications for parents and health-care providers of gender nonconforming teens and should be followed closely as legal action unfolds with judicial interpretation. Some teens seek social affirmation, which means socially transitioning by appearance, hairstyle, clothing, or other outward means without medical intervention. Legal affirmation, or changing gender on legal documents, varies by state. Hormone therapy (sometimes called puberty blockers) has been used for many years to treat children with early onset puberty to prevent short height as an adult. Similar therapy from specialized health-care providers is sometimes selected as an option by families who have a teen identifying as transgender, although rapid developments in state laws may ban this or classify this as abuse, in addition to other treatments. Hormone therapy given before the onset of puberty is generally reversible. The rationale for treatment from some clinicians is that giving teens with gender dysphoria more time gives more space to make life-altering decisions without experiencing the stress of developing what some teens perceive to be undesirable secondary sex characteristics. Laws regulating age requirements for gender-affirming surgery vary by state. Cross-sex hormone therapy (for example, giving testosterone to a biological female or estrogen to a biological male) may be partially reversible, but not after puberty.[8] While hormone therapies may positively influence anxiety and depression, the research on the risks of these treatments, including heart disease, blood clots, bone metabolism, and future fertility, is very limited and should be seriously considered.[9] Studies are ongoing to evaluate the numbers and experiences of teens who detransition[10] or have regrets about permanent medical or surgical interventions.[11] These are the facts framing the situations your teens will encounter.

Parenting Pro Tips

Each teen and each circumstance is unique. Care for gender nonconforming teens occurs on a progressive arc over time, starting with primary care. Preventive health care for gender nonconforming teens should be just as it is for all adolescents, including assessing social and emotional well-being and the individual risk factors with appropriate safety planning.

What Do I Do If My Teen Comes Out to Me as Gender Nonconforming?

If your teen is struggling or you think they're struggling, start with an honest and confidential conversation with your primary health-care provider. Pediatric clinicians are well equipped to help you get started by doing a holistic health evaluation, identifying risk, and addressing mental health concerns. They can facilitate access to health-care services, advocate for safety, give support for encountering stigma, treat mental health concerns, and affirm and promote resilience. Emerging legal implications may impact the response of your pediatric care provider. Seek partnership with a reputable and licensed counselor or therapist who shares your worldview and spiritual beliefs.

What If My Teen's Disclosure Goes Against Our Spiritual Beliefs?

I imagine many of the other teen issues we've talked about in this book go against your spiritual beliefs, but somehow that question seems to hold this singular issue hostage. It's as if simply labeling it will magically resolve the situation. It doesn't. These are deeply personal issues that need to be handled with the utmost care to achieve the best outcomes, which means you'll want to seek spiritual counsel (along with health and mental health professionals) who will walk closely with you on this journey. Guidance from the American Academy of Pediatrics states:

> Some caution has been expressed that unquestioning acceptance per se may not best serve questioning youth or their families. Instead, psychological evidence suggests that the most benefit comes when family members and youth are supported and encouraged to engage in reflective perspective taking and validate their own and the other's thoughts and feelings despite divergent views.[12]

So what does this mean? It means in the middle of this debate are real families with real kids who have real needs in real time.

Continuing to pursue a relationship with your teen is the avenue to influence their health decisions and spiritual beliefs while supporting their physical and emotional health. Family-based therapy is essential to build strong family bonds and navigate complex family dynamics. Family connectiveness and family support are the most significant protective factors for gender nonconforming teens.

For all teens, it's important, wherever they are in their health journey, to emphasize the following support strategies:

- prioritize strength and resilience ("We will get through this" vs. "How could you do this?"),
- reinforce and support spiritual beliefs,
- provide external support through friends, family, health-care providers, and spiritual advisors,
- teach love, respect, and friendship, and
- encourage your teen to express concern about bullying behaviors and empower them for bystander intervention.

BEHIND THE HOME DOOR

Gender stereotypes can be hurtful. There are girls who really enjoy hunting and fishing, and there are boys who appreciate fashion and art. Criticizing these can create distress in teens who may unnecessarily question their gender if they don't have strong support for the unique dimensions of their personalities, gifts, preferences, and interests. With so much conversation surrounding gender, it's important to keep a balanced perspective that gender is only one plane of your teen's identity. It is a big part of who they are, but it's not the only thing.

Conversation Doors

- Affirm other dimensions of your child's identity by choosing your teen's favorite activity or something at which they excel. Schedule a time to intentionally engage. Do they play sports? Ask for a lesson or challenge them to a game. Do they like video games? Pull up a bean bag. Are they into art? Schedule an outing to paint or make pottery. Do they like to hike? Lace up your boots. Find that special thing your teen loves to do the most and come alongside them with genuine interest, affirming the unique aspects of their identity.
- Watch the National Geographic special *Gender Revolution: A Journey with Katie Couric*. Use this as a springboard for discussion.

Conversation Keys

After you complete your activity together, initiate a conversation. Remember to LOVE your teen.

Listen with your face:
- Say, "This is a really complicated, emotional subject."
- Thank them for being willing to share their thoughts and feelings.
- Share with them one thing you learned or observed about their self-image.

Offer open-ended questions:
- "How do you feel when you hear LGBTQ+ people describe their experience?"
- "What part of these conversations do you agree with? When do you disagree?"
- "What part about these conversations makes you most uncomfortable?"

- "What do you wish you knew that you feel like you don't?"
- "What else would you like to share?"

Validate feelings:

- "This is really complicated."
- "There are no easy answers here. I struggle too."
- "It's okay to be (fill in the blank: confused, upset, distressed) about this."
- "No matter what happens, I'll always love you unconditionally."

Explore next steps together:

Answer the following questions together:

- How would my teen safely disclose a struggle? How would I respond?
- How will we respond to a friend or family member who is gender nonconforming?

BEHIND THE HEART DOOR

I want to talk for a moment to the parent whose child is secretly struggling with issues of gender. I see you. Many of you are struggling alone, living in tremendous fear of discovery with your parenting being judged and your teen being ostracized from every social support you trust. You fear they will be supported by people who will influence them further away from you. You fear for their health. You fear for their safety. Friend, you *cannot* walk through this alone. Create a trusted team to support your family. You need a safe place for transparency, encouragement, health care, counseling, spiritual guidance, prayer, and social support. Nothing about this is easy, but there are people who can walk with compassion beside you faithfully in this journey.

The spiritual plane of health and biblical concept of identity cannot be ignored. Conversations of gender uncover deep spiritual questions and can even lead to a crisis of faith. Seek wise spiritual counsel from your pastor, minister, priest, or other leader. These are complex issues. Rather than struggle alone, connect to a community of faith. You can disagree with others but still be kind, loving, and compassionate. Ask God for wisdom and understanding. Scripture tells us He gives generously to those who ask.

I have barely begun to explore the complexities of this topic. I cannot adequately answer every question parents have on this emotionally complex subject, but it's my hope to give you, as parents, encouragement and some tools for the journey to have meaningful conversations with your teens.

Devotional

In a Bible story not often told, we find an Egyptian slave woman named Hagar. She was alone, broken, insignificant, and rejected. In an extraordinary moment in Scripture, an angel encountered Hagar and called her by name, something her mistress had refused to do, and told Hagar the Lord had heard her affliction. In response, she called God by the name *El Roi,* meaning the "God Who Sees Me." God told her to return and submit to her mistress. Her circumstances wouldn't change, but the strength and perspective with which she faced them would be different.

When we feel vulnerable and alone, we can find hope and comfort in the God Who Sees Me. Every character in Hagar's story experienced their own fears, doubts, insecurities, and injustices along a broken road, lost like sheep. The original Hebrew word *Roi'iy* means "shepherd," "seeing," "looking," or "gazing." We see in the New Testament many instances where our Good Shepherd sees people. Are you harassed and helpless, distressed and dispirited, feeling alone in your struggles as if no one sees you? You may feel alone, but God will never leave you or forsake you. Pour out your heart to El Roi, the God Who Sees You. Take comfort in the fact your Good Shepherd is always looking for you, and even when it feels like it, you are never alone.

Reflect

In the conversations you've had with your teen, what are the major points of tension or distress?

How can you see your teen and meet them where they are, just as God saw Hagar?

How can you season your conversation with grace, wisdom, and understanding?

Pray

(From Psalm 6) God, our souls are troubled. We are weary with argument and conversation, and our beds at night swim with the tears of our distress. We worry about our kids. We see their hurt. Our eyes waste away with grief as conflict makes us weary. We know You hear our voices lifted in desperate prayer. Give us faith in times of distress. We ask for mercy in the midst of pain. Bring healing where there is conflict. Pour over us Your unfailing love. We know You accept our prayer. I ask You to walk with _____ daily, putting people in their path who will speak encouragement and the words of life delivered straight from Your heart to theirs, with the confident affirmation they are never alone. Amen.

Act

(Legacy Letter) Make a "Top Ten Things I Love About You" list for your teen, praising ten personality or character traits. You can simply write a list or you can make it artistic, as a poster, to hang in their room, a photo album, or even a video or reel if you've acquired sufficient tech skills along this journey!

EATING DISORDERS

How to Find Healing When Food Is Your Enemy

She was seventeen, and she was not happy with me. She was furious actually. She sat on the exam table, back against the wall, knees tucked under her chin, hands covered with baggy sweatshirt sleeves with the rest of the shirt pulled down around her legs and covering her feet. Lips clenched, jaw tight. Her eyes shot daggers as I pulled my stool to face her. She wanted to fight me. Her mother sat in the corner, business-suit immaculate, hair pulled back revealing pearl stud earrings, briefcase on her lap. She looked annoyed.

The school nurse had called, concerned about a twenty-pound weight loss in the last three months and requested an evaluation, so here they were. Before I could even speak, my patient began to berate me, eyes flashing fire. This was a stupid waste of time. I knew nothing about her. She was fine—no, more than fine. She was proud. She'd finally gotten control of her weight and was the healthiest she'd ever been. Her mother chimed in, saying her daughter had previously been "a little chubby" but now seemed to finally be settled at a healthy weight.

I began a physical exam and my alarm escalated rapidly. Temperature? Low. Blood pressure? Low. Heart rate? Slow. I could see the enamel coming off her teeth. She had scratches on her knuckles.

Her mother began to see my concern, and a quizzical look replaced her previously annoyed expression. I invited her to stand beside me as I asked the girl to stand and touch her toes so I could examine her back. As I lifted her shirt, her vertebrae emerged dramatically like stegosaurus spikes marching through the middle of an impossibly tiny waist. Her mother gasped in shock and began to cry. The girl straightened, pulled down her shirt, and sat back on the table, smirking at me with smug defiance.

BEHIND THE CLINIC DOOR

In your mind's eye, picture the girl in this story. What do you think she looks like? Think about it until you see her face. Pause if you need to. Now imagine someone you know who has an eating disorder. Take your time. Who is that person? Here's the follow-up. In both cases, were you visualizing very thin White females? If you were, you're not alone. Eating disorders affect as many as one in ten girls; however, boys are increasingly impacted. They're usually more severe but more difficult to identify. People of color, and especially those of average weight, more often go unidentified. Stereotypes sometimes prevent us from remembering any teen can be impacted.

Here's another challenge. Do a quick internet search for "cover of Seventeen magazine" and then enter the year you were your teen's age. I did this, and as a hint on my age, I saw a lot of Shannen Doherty. (I wasn't allowed to watch 90210, but I can somehow tell you about the fiasco that was Brenda's and Kelly's matching prom dresses.) Today's magazine covers have had a major glow-up with the advances in digital technology. Dads, you're not immune here. Try checking out *People*'s sexiest man alive the year you were your teen's age (note, it only goes back to 1985). Times have changed, my friends. Media presence today puts pressure on guys too. Male influencers are every bit in the teen consciousness as much as female influencers, from baristas to bodybuilders. This is no longer prepping for a singular photo shoot, but a 24/7 world of social-media image pressure via makeup tutorials, body-morphing photo filters, and fitness influencing. The pressure to look perfect doesn't spare *any* teen today, and we have to accept we didn't experience it and can't fully understand the stress it causes.

Eating disorders are an unhealthy coping response to stress, giving an illusion of control when the rest of life seems out of control. Concern about eating disorders is skyrocketing.[1] Teens face significant stressors in the wake of radically changing social norms. My daughter, a high school senior at the pandemic onset, said, "Mom, every way you prepared me for my senior year is gone. No prom, graduation, SAT, college tours, nothing!" She was right. My teens see peers tearfully disclosing eating disorders in small groups. Your teens need to know eating disorders *cannot* stay secret. When I promise teens confidentiality, I say, "I will keep what you say confidential unless something you tell me can harm you or someone else." This threat is deadly and should always be disclosed to an adult followed by a health-care evaluation. If left untreated, eating disorders lead to serious health conditions such as osteoporosis, heart arrhythmias, kidney disease, infertility, and even death.

Friends, we've walked through some serious topics on this journey together. Many caused you anxiety just by reading the chapter title. This one likely didn't frighten you as much as the others. It will probably surprise you to hear this, but *pay close attention.*

Eating disorders are the deadliest mental health disorder. One in five teens with anorexia nervosa die from electrolyte imbalance, heart failure, malnutrition, or suicide.

Eating disorders cause severe, persistent, harmful eating behaviors related to distorted body image.[2] Body dysmorphic disorder means, when an affected teen looks in the mirror, every minor or even *imaginary* flaw is exaggerated to *obsession.* Although it's not reality, it's *very real.*

Health Impacts

Let's discuss an important nuance in terms before we dive in. Many teens come to me wondering if they have an eating disorder. As with most health issues we've discussed, eating disorders don't happen overnight but progress along a continuum. Seeking early intervention could save your teen's life. The first sign of concern is usually disordered eating.

Disordered Eating

This is really an informal term clinicians use to generally describe abnormal or unhealthy eating habits that are concerning but don't rise to the level of a diagnosable disorder. The primary difference is that disordered eating behaviors are usually sporadic and less severe. Not everyone with disordered eating will develop an eating disorder, but it's important to recognize because it gives an opportunity for early intervention before teens experience significant harm and long-term effects of eating disorders that can impact fertility and even life expectancy.

Disordered eating behaviors include bingeing and purging (overeating followed by self-induced vomiting), skipping meals, restrictive eating, extreme or yo-yo dieting, skipping out on major food groups, eating the same things every day in a ritualistic way, laxative abuse, extreme dieting, and excessive exercise to offset calorie intake. Emotional eating is one of the most common disordered behaviors. Eating sweet, savory, and salty junk food triggers the chemical reward center in our brain and gives us a surge of dopamine to make us feel good. Who hasn't sat with a bag of potato chips in front of the TV or opened a tub of ice cream after an awful day? You'll find me eating Blue Bell ice cream and binge-watching *Call the Midwife* into the wee hours of the morning. We don't need to beat ourselves up about that, but if we find ourselves indulging every night or eating to soothe every emotional pain, that's a warning sign we need better coping skills to avoid a progression to a full-on disorder.

Eating Disorders

These are behavioral conditions with *severe* and *repetitive* abnormal eating behaviors accompanied by distressing thoughts and emotions. The symptoms are severe and specific enough to rise to the level of official medical diagnosis. These serious and life-threatening conditions affect one's physical, emotional, and social ability to function. Although anorexia is most commonly recognized, there is a spectrum of disorders.

Anorexia nervosa (anorexia) is self-starvation with an intense fear of gaining weight. Teens will nonchalantly deny the seriousness of low body weight and wave off any concerns with a casual shrug or indignant denial. One type involves counting and severely restricts calories while the other is binge eating and purging afterward. Both types create extreme thinness and require medical intervention. For severe anorexia, hospitalization is required. *Bulimia nervosa* (bulimia) is eating huge amounts of food in a two-hour period. Usually, teens feel completely out of control during these episodes, followed by guilt and self-induced vomiting, laxatives, excessive exercise, diet pills, or a combination. *Binge eating disorder* is actually the most common problem. It involves habitually eating very large amounts of food in a very short period of time (way beyond being full). It may or may not be followed by vomiting. Weight is typically normal or overweight, and bingeing happens in secret, both of which make it more difficult to detect.

There are other less common but equally serious disorders. *Avoidant restrictive food intake disorder* (ARFID) is severe and similar to anorexia, but the key difference is teens with ARFID aren't concerned about body image, shape, or size. *Pica* involves repeatedly eating things with no nutritional value (paper, paint chips, soap, hair, metal, pebbles, charcoal, or clay) and sometimes requires surgical removal. The bottom line is that any concerning eating behavior should be addressed with your health-care provider.[3]

What Are the Risk Factors?

Participation in sports with weight requirements or expectations for appearance, such as wrestling, running, dance, gymnastics, swimming, and ice-skating, carries risk.[4] Traumas such as divorce, abuse, moving, financial stressors, or family conflict can be triggers.[5] Recently losing weight after previously being overweight can bring a rush of positive feelings and attention (for example, Rebel Wilson). Sometimes this reaction spurs teens to lose more.

What If Eating Disorders Aren't Treated?

These are just a few of the serious, life-threatening health impacts. Eating fewer calories causes your body to eat its own muscle tissue for fuel. The largest muscle is your heart, which can be weakened *irreversibly* to the point of death. Intestine muscles are weakened by malnutrition and laxative abuse and are unable to push digested food, which results in severe constipation. Binge eating can cause your stomach and throat to tear open violently. Your brain only weighs three pounds, but it uses one-fifth of the calories you eat. Lack of energy impacts concentration and academic performance. Lack of fat removes insulation from nerve coverings and causes tingling extremities. Severe dehydration causes seizures and fainting. Lack of hormone production shuts down estrogen and testosterone, impacting one's ability to have babies. Bone density decreases, which increases the risk for fractures. Without enough energy for metabolism, temperature drops and body hair grows for insulation and warmth. There is significant concern for mental health conditions such as anxiety, depression, substance use disorder, obsessive-compulsive disorder, and post-traumatic stress disorder. This is a scary list. You can see why health-care providers are so concerned.

Parenting Pro Tips

Sometimes it's hard to see the signs of concern. Taken in isolation, singular episodes are easy to write off, but as these accumulate, it should alert you to stop and think. *Food behaviors* include a new enthusiasm for vegetarianism, suddenly being a picky eater, food mysteriously disappearing from the pantry, hiding food in unusual places, skipping meals with endless excuses, avoiding social situations with food, cooking for others but refusing to eat, and obsessively reading food labels. The *physical symptoms* include weight fluctuations, sleeping more or less than usual, stomach upset, hair thinning or falling out, dizziness or fainting, and infrequent or absent menstrual periods. The *psychological symptoms* include social isolation, mood changes, rigid schedules, and fear of gaining weight or appearing fat. The *behavioral symptoms* include excessive or intense workouts, substance abuse, self-harming, suicide behaviors, obsessing over body image in photos, visiting pro-anorexia (pro-ana) or pro-bulimia (pro-mia) websites, ritualistic or obsessive behaviors, and wearing baggy or oversized clothes.

Early Intervention

Many parents opt for a wait-and-see approach. They think, "This is just a phase" or "They'll snap out of it." This is a potentially deadly mistake. Teens don't *and won't* see this as a problem. They're proud of their look. They'll hide their behaviors and deny, deny, deny. In the words of a recovered patient: "It was such a severe disease. I remember truly being out of my mind looking for any way possible to manipulate anyone by doing anything to lose another pound." They often appear mature, self-sufficient, and successful, adding fuel to their fire and creating an effective smokescreen. Don't let them make you doubt yourself. You must take the initiative. Their life may depend on it.

If food obsession is affecting your teen's ability to enjoy daily activities and causing frequent family conflict, you should be concerned. Make an appointment with a health-care provider who will use a screening tool to assess the risk of eating disorders. Along with a physical exam, there might be blood work, an EKG to check heart function, and tests to measure bone density.

What Does Treatment Look Like?

Early intervention for mild disorders promotes faster recovery, avoids hospitalization, and doesn't usually result in long-term damage.

Nutritional rehabilitation (eating retraining) helps teens to develop healthy eating habits. Other goals include nurturing a positive self-image and self-esteem. Positive coping skills and strategies help teens respond effectively to triggers. This sounds simple but must be consciously practiced. Sometimes medications for coexisting mental health conditions are helpful in holistic therapy.

Although your primary health-care provider can help to screen for and identify eating disorders, this is one case where you absolutely need referral for specialty care if an eating disorder is diagnosed. Eating disorders are extremely difficult to treat and require complex, high-level interventions, such as medication therapy and cognitive behavioral therapy to influence behavior and emotions. Your primary care provider will provide support along the way. For anorexia, inpatient therapy with scheduled feedings (possibly through a tube for a time), close medical monitoring, and intense psychological therapy are required for successful treatment.

A colleague who specializes in working with teenagers with severe eating disorders gave me a helpful analogy.[6] To most of us, food is pleasurable and nonthreatening. For struggling teens, food is a tiger of which they are deathly afraid. Trying to force them to eat feels like forcing them to spend unguarded playtime with a tiger, activating a physiologic stress response. Their instinct is protective, aversive, and combative. Having a teen with an eating disorder can give parents compassion fatigue. It's understandable to be angry, bitter, frustrated, and just plain exhausted. Cultivate empathy by understanding their mind-set and helping them to learn to be a tiger tamer. They don't need to love food; they just need to feed their body, enjoyable or not. Parents need help to create a safe environment.

I've held the hands of weeping women who were told they should never have children because of their weakened heart status. I've held the dying babies of women who could not see their need for nutrition during pregnancy and were absolutely devastated over their loss. I've seen boys so weak they can't even lift their head off a hospital bed as they lie emaciated beyond recognition. I've seen teens lose their teeth but continue in their pursuit of weight loss. It's beyond sad. These are concerns that need early intervention in order to prevent tragic outcomes.

BEHIND THE HOME DOOR

An eating disorder diagnosis is one of the hardest struggles for parents. Teens deny, deny, deny, and parents start to question themselves and suffer with guilt and self-doubt as teens manipulate them into thinking their concern is actually harmful. Secrets and deception shouldn't be seen as a deliberate choice but a manifestation of illness. Your teen will be defiant, angry, defensive, and in serious denial. *You must act against their will with strength and courage.* The stakes are too high! You need outside help, including support for you.

This is a tough one. I tread gently. Parents who emphasize weight or fitness, expect high achievement, comment on physical appearance, feel difficulty expressing emotions, exhibit overprotectiveness, or struggle with substance abuse are more likely to nurture environments ripe for disordered eating. In a young adult's own words: "My mom said things that have stuck with me forever. I will never look in a mirror without hearing her voice. Encouraging me to eat salad and more fiber or to wear clothes that hide my pear shape. I made a commitment to be present for mealtimes and to show my kids that food is just food." Having said that, we are all imperfect. You can't shoulder the blame and burden. When you see it, move forward with humility, knowing forgiveness and grace await through counseling and spiritual support.

Adopting healthy eating behaviors as a family helps prevent disordered eating behaviors from turning into eating disorders. Avoid fad or crash diets and set healthy limits on exercising. Be mindful of negative body talk. Embrace body positivity with appreciation and respect for different sizes or shapes, whether that be friends, family, people in public or on media. Stop conversations that fat-shame or mock body characteristics. Throw away scales in your house and focus on strength and health rather than numbers displayed on a screen.

Conversation Doors

- Plan a family cooking night with a fun menu theme and new recipes.
- Plan an outing to a fancy or funky restaurant to try something new.
- Watch an episode of *Chopped*, *Top Chef*, or some other competition cooking show, and then host a contest with your teen and their friends. Invite live judging on social media.
- Prepare a meal together for someone in need.
- Volunteer at a food pantry or soup kitchen.
- If food-related activities are triggering, try a spa day (at home or somewhere relaxing), restorative yoga (or goat yoga if you want a fun adventure), meditation, or mindfulness exercises. If pet therapy is your jam, try volunteering at an animal shelter or riding horses.

Conversation Keys

After you complete your activity together, initiate a conversation. Remember to LOVE your teen.

Listen with your face:
- Say to your teen, "Some of these lines between healthy and unhealthy seem confusing."

- Thank them for being willing to share their thoughts and feelings.
- Share with them one new thing you learned or observed about their creative side.

Offer open-ended questions:

- "How do you feel about your eating behaviors?"
- "What have you been wondering about but might be afraid to ask?"
- "When have you experienced feeling worried about a friend or peer with concerning eating behaviors?"
- "What information do you wish you had to help you make decisions?"
- "What do I do or say in this space that hurts you or makes you insecure?"
- "What can I do to better support you?"
- "What else would you like to share?"

Validate feelings:

- "I see you struggling to make the right decision. I know you have the best intentions."
- "I can see how this might make you feel anxious or scared."
- "It's okay to be (fill in the blank: worried, wondering) about this."
- "No matter what happens, I will always love you unconditionally."

Explore next steps together:

Answer the following questions together:

- How can your teen safely disclose to you their concerns about their eating behaviors?
- What would your teen do if they have concern about disordered eating behaviors in a friend?

- Are there any attitudes or behaviors in your home that need to be reexamined or reconsidered to help support healthy eating behaviors?

BEHIND THE HEART DOOR

We live in a toxic environment that shames normal body shapes. What our teens don't know is this doesn't get better as we age. Moms jealously eye other moms dropping off kids at school in body-hugging yoga pants and cropped shirts revealing impossibly flat abs. We obsess over the appearance of any new wrinkle. We talk Botox and fillers. Dads self-consciously suck in their guts when standing on youth sports fields next to guys sporting bulging biceps in impossibly tight T-shirts and drinking muscle milk. Teens are watching all of this and taking detailed notes.

It's time for a difficult heart check. Carefully consider the messages you're sharing at home about body positivity. I'm guilty here. If I'm shopping with my girls and trying on clothes, I'll bemoan being "fluffy" before catching myself. Teens are incredibly sensitive to our self-perceptions. Your teen can likely tell you in a nanosecond your specific physical insecurities. This is no guilt trip either. What I'm saying is that the best way to help your teen embrace body positivity is to love your own body, flaws and all. This is easier said than done. When I was pregnant with my third (and biggest) baby, my four-year-old saw my stomach expanding with older, silvery stretch marks from previous pregnancies and new fiery red lines extending old ones to accommodate my expanding belly for my growing giant. She smiled and blew on my belly and said, "Look! Birthday candles!" Amusing? Yes. Flattering? Not at the time. How do we accept and love our own bodies?

Take some time here for mindfulness and thoughtfully answer these questions. Journal if it's helpful.

- Do you believe the myth you'd be happier if you were thinner or more fit?
- How does your family use food to cope with stress?
- Do you listen to your body and eat only when you're hungry?
- Do you judge other people's bodies and compare them to your own?
- Do you follow social media accounts that make you feel bad about yourself?
- Do you embrace balance and celebrate different foods in moderation?
- Do you label foods as good or bad?
- Do you label yourself as bad for choosing to eat a certain food?
- Do you earn foods by exercising and eating healthy?
- Do your family celebrations revolve around food?

These are tough questions. Be kind to yourself. Choose one thing you'd like to work on and start there.

Devotional

If you have a teen struggling with an eating disorder (or any of the other struggles we've covered in this journey), I know your deepest desire is for your child to be healed. Let's visit Jesus' encounter with a desperate father, Jairus, whose twelve-year-old daughter was seriously ill (Mark 5:21–24, 35–43). Jairus begged Jesus to come and heal her. He agreed, but their journey was derailed, and people came looking for Jairus to give him the terrible news that his daughter had died.

They urged him to stop bothering Jesus. It was too late. Jesus looked at Jairus and said, "Don't be afraid; just believe." They continued on and arrived at Jairus's home, where mourners were outside, wailing and crying at the top of their lungs. Jesus said to them, "Why all this commotion and wailing? The child is not dead but asleep." Here's the interesting part. The Scripture says, "They laughed at him." In response, He sent them all outside, allowing only Jairus, the girl's mother, and his three closest disciples to come in.

He took her by the hand and said to her, "*Talitha koum!*" (which means "Little girl, I say to you, get up!"). Immediately the girl stood up and began to walk around.

What can we learn from this story?

1. Have faith to ask for healing.

    The Greek term for "faith" means "trust" or "firm persuasion." Do you trust God for your teen's healing? Are you firmly persuaded He can do it? The fear and urgency of sickness and death turned a respected and dignified community leader into an imploring father literally on his knees, boldly begging for healing *in faith*. As a nurse, I get chills thinking of parents I've seen in similar crises. We need this boldness of faith to publicly ask for healing when our teens are experiencing health crises. Are you praying for healing from addiction, trauma, depression, or anything else? Ask in faith. Jesus told Jairus, "Don't be afraid; just believe," even when circumstances were both terrifying and unbelievable.

2. Dismiss others who aren't supportive.

When the mourners ridiculed Jesus, He sent them away. Who is the gloomy voice in your struggle? Who whispers doubt in your mind? Who speaks negativity over your teen's journey? Who has given up and tells you to let go, give up, move on, it's too late? Feel free to dismiss them. We rob ourselves of faith in victory when we surround ourselves with mourners who are wailing defeat and ridiculing our faith.

3. Trust Jesus to provide healing in God's timing according to His plan.

To have faith is to let go of trusting yourself and to put your trust in another. Jairus had a specific vision for how his daughter would be healed. Jesus disrupted that plan. In fact, He stopped to heal another woman along the way! Some would say, if Jesus had come sooner, the little girl would not have died. What seemed to Jairus like an unnecessary delay allowed Jesus to powerfully demonstrate it's *never* too late for God to step in and to work more miraculously than we asked or imagined.

As Christians, we believe Jesus Christ was born of a virgin as the Son of God, performed miracles on earth, suffered crucifixion and death on the cross to pay for our sins, and miraculously rose from the dead three days later to conquer sin and the grave forever. We believe He ascended to heaven and is waiting at the right hand of God for all who believe.

If you have faith enough to believe all that, why can't you have faith your teen will be healed in God's timing and plan?

Reflect

How do you feel about your teen's eating behaviors?

What points in this chapter did you find convicting?

What steps can you take to model body positivity and acceptance for your teen?

Pray

(From Psalm 103) God, I bring my prayer with all that is within me. Remind me of the blessings You pour out over us, the sins You've forgiven. Healing is in Your hands. You redeem our lives from destruction. I ask You to crown _____ with steadfast lovingkindness and tender mercies. Satisfy our mouths with good things and renew our strength like the eagle. Help me to be merciful and gracious, slow to anger, and abounding in mercy. Work righteousness and justice for _____ when they feel oppressed. Help me to look past our current struggles and see my teen. Help me to show compassion, just as You show compassion to me. Although our bodies are fragile, Your love is steadfast and everlasting. Bless the Lord, oh, my soul. Amen!

Act

(Legacy Letter)

- Handwrite special recipes for your teen's favorite dishes you make at home. Include anecdotes about memorable family times you've had around these meals.
- Alternatively, as you've been writing letters to your teen, consider writing a thank-you or love letter to your own body that

you can share with your teen. This may be hard to do and feel awkward, but give it some thought. Write down the things you appreciate about what your body has done for you. Maybe it's taken you somewhere or let you do a job that provides for your family. Maybe you're grateful for creating life and giving birth to your child! Set an example for your teen of body positivity.

POSTSCRIPT

How to Heal Generational Hurts

This journey represents a lifelong, eternal investment you intentionally made in your teen that is sure to bless generations to come. This is a significant moment for you, right here, right now, reading this simple sentence.

Congratulations on your decision to intentionally invest in a living legacy for your family by building a healthy relationship with your teen!

Each of the topics we have covered could easily be written into not only books but several volumes. Inevitably, you have unanswered questions. You wish I'd included more of this or less of that. That's okay.

The goal of this journey is not to make you a content expert on teen health, but to make you an expert relationship builder with your teen. The takeaway is not to invest your

time feverishly in studying health issues in an attempt to connect but to study your teen with the intent to connect.

You should feel more confident in talking comfortably about uncomfortable things. The work was hard, the tears were many, and the frustrations were frequent, but hopefully the laughter was sincere, the time together was rich, and the memories you're taking away are priceless. The rewards will be immeasurable as you invest in the generations to come, right down to impacting the reading and transcription of your grandchildren's DNA. I told you this in the introduction and if you've been wondering when I would come back to that, we've finally arrived.

In 1997, researchers Vincent Felitti and Robert Anda from Kaiser Permanente Health published a landmark study on adverse childhood experiences (ACEs), which connected childhood trauma to adult health outcomes.[1] ACEs include abuse, neglect, mental illness, incarcerated relatives, divorce, violence, life-threatening injuries or accidents, loss of or separation from a parent or loved one, natural disasters, wars or terrorist attacks, discrimination, refugee status, or extreme poverty. This is sobering as we consider the current social landscape for our teens.

When we experience trauma, it activates our stress response system. Imagine you're in the woods and you see a bear. Your heart races and adrenaline surges as you get ready to fight or run away from that bear, which is great if you're in the woods and there is a bear. But for teens with adverse childhood experiences, they take the bear home with them. It pops out at any time and activates their stress response.[2] Some stressors you can control; some you absolutely cannot.

Your teen *will* encounter stress, but stress can be positive in small amounts. Tolerable stress is facing serious events when you are buffered by *supportive relationships*. Toxic stress happens when the stress response is activated repeatedly without a support system. This causes physical changes from constantly surging epinephrine, cortisol, and other dysregulated hormone and organ systems. It damages blood vessels and neurological regulation.

The ACE study discovered adults with a score over four had a greater risk of suicide attempt (seventeen times), substance abuse (nine times), alcohol abuse (five times), depression (three times), and heart disease (two times). In fact, nine of the ten leading causes of death are correlated to high ACE scores.[3] (You can actually take a short quiz online to consider your own ACE score.) The bottom line is that childhood trauma and stress are more likely to put you at risk for physical illness as an adult and early death. Very simply speaking, stress and trauma cause DNA changes we pass on to future generations.[4] Whoa!

Before you get too distressed, guess what is the best protective factor to avoid a toxic stress response? It's the presence of a supportive adult in a child's life. And guess what?

Taking the journey in this book helped make that person you.

Your investment in your teen today will pay off in your grandchildren tomorrow as you continue this journey to talk as you walk along the road. Here is your starter set of conversation keys to help you continue to unlock the doors to the heart of your teen. These questions should be printed out and laminated and carried in your wallet, copied into your smartphone, posted on your fridge, or whatever you need to do for access until you have them memorized.

Conversation Keys for the Road

- "How are you feeling about what happened today?"
- "How do you think this impacts you personally?"
- "How can I support you and help you feel safe?"
- "What do you think you can do to be a positive influence?"

I continue to journey alongside you in these days of having four teenagers at once. I thank my grandmother every day for the key she gave me on that fateful day so long ago. It gave me hope to start a new journey. It hasn't been easy, but I've never been so grateful to have had a book thrown at my head. It was a wakeup call that led to fulfilling relationship building with my teens. My favorite memories are having them all hanging out in my office at 1:00 a.m. on the weekend, just chatting and laughing, feeling safe and loved. I truly hope this book has gifted you with a key to a new door for your future, a secret garden full of hope and possibilities.

Friends, I encourage you to keep a prayer journal going forward to continue building relationships and writing future legacy letters. It's a beautiful biblical concept to set physical markers or monuments to remember spiritual encounters as important events during which God showed His faithfulness. After Noah survived the flood, the first thing he did on dry ground was to build an altar. After Jacob's dream of a ladder, he took the stone that was near his head and set it up as a marker and poured oil on top of it. At Mount Sinai, Moses built an altar of stones to remember God's covenant with Israel. Joshua ordered his men to take twelve stones as they crossed the Jordan River for remembrance. There were three purposes for building these monuments: (1) to remember what God had done, (2) to share that testimony with future generations, and (3) to encourage the world.

As we leave this journey, I encourage you to find a way to build a monument or create something special to remember God's faithfulness. Maybe it's a piece of jewelry, a card to carry in your wallet, or a simple artwork with a Scripture or a quote. It could be a special box to hold the letters you've written or the affirmations of gratitude you've started to collect. Put it where you can see it, and each time you pass, give thanks for the gift of time you've had with your teen. I pray these adventures foster cherished memories and meaningful conversations to deepen your relationship with your teens.

> Because of the LORD's great love we are not consumed, for his compassions never fail. They are new every morning; great is your faithfulness. I say to myself, "The LORD is my portion; therefore I will wait for him." The LORD is good to those whose hope is in him. (Lam. 3:22–25)

God loves you, and He gave you your child, uniquely crafted just for you to enter into this stage of parenthood for such a time as this.

I'll be praying for you and your family as you begin the next phase of your journey.

> The LORD bless you and keep you; the LORD make his face shine on you and be gracious to you; the LORD turn his face toward you and give you peace. (Num. 6:24–26)

APPENDIX

CHAPTER 1

*Mental Health: How to Break Free
from Stigma and Silence*

SCRIPTURES: Num. 6:24–26; John 14:27; 16:33; Isa. 9:6–7;
2 Thess. 3:16; Psalm 23

PLAYLIST (PEACE): "The Blessing" (Kari Jobe and Cody Carnes); "Peace Be Still" (Lauren Daigle); "Glory (Let There Be Peace)" (Matt Maher); "Perfect Peace" (Laura Story); "He Will Hold Me Fast" (Keith and Kristyn Getty); "It Is Well" (Kristene DiMarco); "Be Still" (Hillsong Worship); "Prince of Peace" (Hillsong United); "Peace" (We the Kingdom); "Be Still My Soul" (Pat Barrett); "Hold Me Jesus" (Rich Mullins); "I Speak Jesus" (Here Be Lions and Darlene Zschech); "I Will Rise" (Chris Tomlin); "Peace" (Hillsong Young and Free); "Psalm 23" (Shane and Shane)

RESOURCES:
PHQ-9
https://www.mdcalc.com/phq-9-patient-health-questionnaire-9
GAD-7
https://www.mdcalc.com/gad-7-general-anxiety-disorder-7
National Alliance on Mental Illness (NAMI) Helpline

https://nami.org/help
National Alliance on Mental Illness (NAMI) Say It Out Loud Tool Kit
https://www.nami.org/NAMInet/Say-It-Out-Loud
Substance Abuse and Mental Health Services Administration
    (SAMHSA) National Helpline
https://www.samhsa.gov/find-help/national-helpline
Society for Adolescent Health and Medicine Parent Resources
https://www.adolescenthealth.org/Resources/
    Clinical-Care-Resources/Mental-Health/Mental-Health-
    Resources-For-Parents-of-Adolescents.aspx
American Academy of Child and Adolescent Psychiatry Family
    Resource Center
https://www.aacap.org/AACAP/Families_and_Youth/Resource
    _Centers/Depression_Resource_Center/Resources_for
    _Parent_Depression.aspx
Cope2Thrive: Online Cognitive Behavioral Therapy-Based
    Coping Skills for Teens
https://www.cope2thrive.com/order-form-online-program

MOVIES: *A Beautiful Mind, Inside Out, Matchstick Men, It's Kind of a Funny Story, Perks of Being a Wallflower*

CHAPTER 2

*Social Media: How to Be a Tech-Savvy
Parent in an i-Gen World*

SCRIPTURES: 2 Tim. 1:9; 1 Thess. 1:4; 2 Cor. 5:17; Eph. 1:7; Gal. 3:9; John 8:32; Gal. 3:13; Col. 3:12; 2 Cor. 3:18; Ps. 17:8; 23:6; 1 John 3:1; Rom. 8:15; 2 Cor. 2:15; Deut. 31:8; Eph. 2:10; Ps. 139

PLAYLIST (IDENTITY IN CHRIST): "Who You Say I Am" (Hillsong Worship); "Who Am I" (Casting Crowns); "Hello, My Name Is" (Matthew West); "New Name Written Down in Glory/Jesus Is Mine" (People and Songs); "No Longer Slaves" (Jonathan David and Melissa Helser); "You Say" (Lauren Daigle); "Forgiven" (Sanctus Real); "Redeemed" (Big Daddy Weave); "Overcomer" (Mandisa); "I Am Free" (Newsboys); "How He Loves" (David Crowder Band); "Thank You, God, for Saving Me" (Chris Tomlin with Phil Wickham); "Beautifully Broken" (Plumb); "Different" (Micah Tyler)

RESOURCES:

Coby Persin: The Dangers of Social Media

https://www.youtube.com/watch?v=6jMhMVEjEQg

American Academy of Pediatrics Family Media Plan

https://www.healthychildren.org/English/media/Pages/default.aspx

Common Sense Media

https://www.commonsensemedia.org/articles/social-media

Internet Matters

https://www.internetmatters.org/resources/social-media-advice-hub/

CHAPTER 3

Cyberbullying: How to Create a Safe Space in an Unsafe World

SCRIPTURES: Gen. 1:3; 37–50; Heb. 4:12; Luke 1:18–25; Num. 22:21–39; James 3; consider these additional Scriptures in Proverbs offering wisdom to steward our words wisely:

- Evil words destroy one's friends (11:9)
- Gentle words bring life and health (15:4)

- Kind words are like honey: sweet to the soul and healthy for the body (16:24)
- Death and life are in the power of the tongue (18:21)
- Telling lies about others is as harmful as hitting them with an ax, wounding them with a sword, or shooting them with a sharp arrow (25:18)

PLAYLIST (GOD'S POWER): "Oh the Power" (Kari Jobe); "Because He Lives (Amen)" (Matt Maher); "Resurrection Power" (Chris Tomlin); "The Power of the Cross" (Kristyn Getty); "Same Power" (Jeremy Camp); "Your Name Is Power" (Rend Collective); "Lion and the Lamb" (Big Daddy Weave); "Mighty Is the Power of the Cross" (Chris Tomlin); "What a Beautiful Name" (Hillsong Worship); "Promised Land" (Crowder); "Our God" (Chris Tomlin); "Believe for It" (CeCe Winans); "Revelation Song" (Kari Jobe); "Great Things" (Phil Wickham); "Stand in Your Love" (Bethel); "There's Nothing That Our God Can't Do" (Passion); "Power to Redeem" (Lauren Daigle); "All the Poor and Powerless" (All Sons and Daughters); "Breakthrough Miracle Power" (Passion and Kristian Stanfill); "The Power of Your Love" (Hillsong Worship); "All Hail the Power of Jesus' Name" (Shane and Shane)

RESOURCES:

Cyberbullying Research Center

https://cyberbullying.org/resources/parents

Megan Meier Foundation

https://www.meganmeierfoundation.org/

Toby Mac: Speak Life

https://tobymac.com/speaklife

Reporting Cyberbullying on Social Media Platforms

https://cyberbullying.org/report

Stop Bullying
https://www.stopbullying.gov/
Unbound Houston (human trafficking training for parents
and caregivers, students, teachers, school personnel, law
enforcement, health-care professionals, and churches)
https://www.unboundhouston.org/trainings

CHAPTER 4

Suicide: How to Find Hope and
Peace in a Broken World

SCRIPTURES: Gen. 1:27; John 8:44; 10:10; 3:16; Eph. 3:14–21;
Lam. 3:20–23; Rom. 8

PLAYLIST (GOD LOVES YOU): "God So Loved" (We the
Kingdom); "Your Love Never Fails" (Jesus Culture); "How He Loves"
(David Crowder); "At the Cross (Love Ran Red)" (Chris Tomlin); "Jesus
Loves Me" (Chris Tomlin); "Your Love Awakens Me" (Phil Wickham);
"Broken Vessels" (Hillsong); "He Will Hold Me Fast" (Keith and
Kristyn Getty); "Graves into Gardens" (Elevation Worship); "Stand
in Your Love" (Josh Baldwin); "There Was Jesus" (Zach Williams and
Dolly Parton); "Jireh" (Maverick City Music); "Defender" (Francesca
Battistelli); "How Great Is Your Love" (Brett Younker); "If We're
Honest" (Francesca Battistelli)

RESOURCES:

National Suicide Prevention Lifeline
https://suicidepreventionlifeline.org/
Dear Evan Hansen Study Guide
https://dearevanhansen.com/wp-content/uploads/2019/04/Dear
-Evan-Hansen-pages-version.pdf

Suicide Prevention

https://youth.gov/youth-topics/youth-suicide-prevention

Substance Abuse and Mental Health Services Administration
    (SAMHSA) Resources

https://www.samhsa.gov/childrens-awareness-day/past-events
    /2019/resources-suicide-prevention

CHAPTER 5

*Vaping: How to Recognize the Health
Threat You Never Saw Coming*

SCRIPTURES: Gen. 2:7; Mark 15:37; Matt. 27:30; John 20:22; Rom. 1:25; Ps. 150:6; James 1

PLAYLIST (BREATHE): "Breathe on Us" (Kari Jobe); "Every Breath" (Hillsong Worship); "Great Are You Lord" (All Sons and Daughters); "Breathe/What a Friend I've Found" (Hillsong Worship); "Breath of Heaven" (Amy Grant); "This Is the Air I Breathe" (Michael W. Smith); "Holy Spirit Living Breath of God" (Keith and Kristyn Getty); "Awake My Soul" (Chris Tomlin with Lecrae); "Breathe" (Jonny Diaz); "Days of Elijah" (Donnie McClurkin); "Mighty Breath of God" (Jesus Culture); "Rattle!" (Elevation Worship); "Come Alive (Dry Bones)" (Lauren Daigle); "Yet Not I but Through Christ in Me" (CityAlight)

RESOURCES:

Power to the Parent, Hidden in Plain Sight

http://powertotheparent.org/be-aware/hidden-in-plain-sight/

This Is Quitting by the Truth Initiative

https://truthinitiative.org/thisisquitting

FDA Vaping Resources

https://www.fda.gov/tobacco-products/public-health-education
/tobacco-education-resources-parents-and-teachers
CDC Resources
https://www.cdc.gov/tobacco/basic_information/e-cigarettes
/Quick-Facts-on-the-Risks-of-E-cigarettes-for-Kids-Teens
-and-Young-Adults.html

CHAPTER 6

Substance Abuse: How to Accept
Truth with Grace and Courage

SCRIPTURES: Acts 1:3; 1 Cor. 15:57; Gen. 6–9; Josh. 5:6; Matt.
4:1–2, 11; 1 Sam. 17; 1 John 4–5

PLAYLIST (VICTORY): "See a Victory" (Elevation Worship); "My
Victory" (Passion and Crowder); "Victory in Jesus" (Travis Cottrell);
"Champion" (Bryan and Katie Torwalt); "Chain Breaker" (Zach
Williams); "Break Every Chain" (Tasha Cobbs); "No Longer Slaves"
(Voices of Lee or Bethel Music); "Surrounded (Fight My Battles)"
(Tasha Cobbs Leonard); "Victor's Crown" (Darlene Zschech); "Battle
Belongs" (Phil Wickham); "Every Giant Will Fall" (Rend Collective);
"Desert Song" (Hillsong Worship); "Not Today" (Hillsong United);
"Victory Is Yours" (Bethel Music); "Day of Victory" (Rend Collective);
"In Christ Alone/The Solid Rock" (Travis Cottrell); "Crown Him
[Majesty]" (Chris Tomlin); "I Speak Jesus" (Here Be Lions)

RESOURCES:
Substance Abuse and Mental Health Services Administration
(SAMHSA) Treatment Finder
https://www.samhsa.gov/medication-assisted-treatment
/find-treatment/treatment-practitioner-locator

Substance Abuse and Mental Health Services Administration
 (SAMHSA) Recovery and Recovery Support
https://www.samhsa.gov/find-help/recovery
CRAFFT
https://crafft.org/
One Choice: Prevention
https://onechoiceprevention.org/
Substance Abuse and Mental Health Services Administration
 (SAMHSA): Talk They Hear You App
https://www.samhsa.gov/talk-they-hear-you/mobile-application
National Institute on Drug Abuse
https://teens.drugabuse.gov/parents
CDC Resources
https://www.cdc.gov/ncbddd/fasd/features/teen-substance-use.html
Language Surrounding Drug Use
https://www.uabmedicine.org/-/texting-trouble-code-words-that
 -may-hint-at-teen-drug-use

MOVIES: *The Secret Life of Zoey, Perfect High, Home Run*, or *Overcomer*

CHAPTER 7

*Divorce: How to Find Forgiveness
and Raise Resilient Kids*
 SCRIPTURES: Matt. 5:31–32; 6:12; 26:49; Luke 22:44; John 21; Ruth 1:20–21; 4; Rom. 8; 12
 PLAYLIST (FORGIVENESS): "There Will Be a Day" (Jeremy Camp); "Forgiveness" (TobyMac featuring Lecrae); "Losing" (Tenth

Avenue North); "Forgiveness" (Matthew West); "Just Be Held" (Casting Crowns); "Uncomplicated" (Hillsong Young and Free); "Scandal of Grace" (Hillsong United); "Broken Vessels" (Hillsong Worship); "Arms of Grace" (Bryan and Katie Torwalt); "God Is So Good (You Are Worthy)" (Pat Barrett); "Amazing Grace (My Chains Are Gone)" (Chris Tomlin); "By the Grace of God" (Bethel Music); "Forgiven and Loved" (Jimmy Needham); "Broken Together" (Casting Crowns); "How He Loves" (Crowder); "Safe" (Phil Wickham); "Hold My Heart" (Tenth Avenue North)

RESOURCES:

Kenneth Ginsburg

http://www.fosteringresilience.com/about.php

Forgiving What You Can't Forget

https://www.thomasnelson.com/9780718039875/forgiving-what
-you-cant-forget/

CHAPTER 8

Sex and Sexting: How to Be Naked and Unafraid

SCRIPTURES: Gen. 2:25; Song; Prov. 5:18–19; 1 John 4:7–21; John 13:35; 1 Cor. 13

PLAYLIST (CHRISTLIKE LOVE): "Beloved" (Tenth Avenue North); "Fighting for Me" (Riley Clemmons); "Good and Loved" (Travis Greene); "Known" (Tauren Wells); "Love Never Fails" (Brandon Heath); "Together" (Steven Curtis Chapman); "Priceless" (For King and Country); "For My Love" (Bethany Dillon); "Masterpiece" (Steven Curtis Chapman); "Unfailing Love" (Chris Tomlin); "By Your Side" (Tenth Avenue North); "Love Somebody" (Mandisa); "Forever Love" (Francesca Battistelli); "When God Made You" (Natalie Grant and Newsong); "Alone" (Sanctus Real); "Forever Yours" (Michael W. Smith)

RESOURCES:

CDC: Sexually Transmitted Diseases

https://www.cdc.gov/std/life-stages-populations/stdfact-teens.htm

Cyberbullying Parents Resources

https://cyberbullying.org/resources/parents

That's Not Cool: Cool/Not Cool Quiz and Call Out Cards

https://thatsnotcool.com/

Common Sense Sexting Article

https://www.commonsensemedia.org/articles/how-do-i-talk
-to-my-teens-about-sexting

CHAPTER 9

Pornography: How to Find Freedom from Secrets

SCRIPTURES: Eph. 5:9–13; Heb. 4:13; Luke 8:17; Ps. 32; 44:21; 90:8; Rom. 2:16; 1 Sam. 16:12, 23; 17:24–37; 18:20; 2 Sam. 11–12; 22:1; 23

PLAYLIST (FREEDOM AND HOPE): "Freedom" (Zach Williams); "Song of Freedom" (Hillsong Worship); "Living Hope" (Phil Wickham); "Freedom Song" (Christy Nockels); "Freedom Reigns" (Jesus Culture); "Freedom Hymn" (Austin French); "Free to Dance" (Hillsong Worship); "Reckless Love" (Cory Asbury); "My Hope Is in You" (Aaron Shust); "All My Hope" (Hillsong Worship); "Found My Freedom" (I Am They); "Shoulders" (For King and Country); "The Stand" (Michael W. Smith); "I Am Free" (Newsboys); "Set Me Free" (Casting Crowns); "Love Came Down" (Kari Jobe); "You Keep Hope Alive" (Mandisa, featuring Jon Reddick)

RESOURCES:

Brain, Heart, World Documentary

https://brainheartworld.org/

Fight the New Drug

https://fightthenewdrug.org/

Terry Crews

https://fightthenewdrug.org/why-actor-terry-crews-wants-people
    -to-stop-watching-porn/

Love Dare for Parents

https://lovedaretest.bhpublishinggroup.com/parenting-en/test.html

MOVIE: *Fireproof*

CHAPTER 10

Social Justice: How to Talk to Your Teens About Racism

SCRIPTURES: 2 Cor. 5:18–19; Gen. 1:27; Luke 2:8–20; 10:25–37; Matt. 2:12–15; 15:21–28; Rev. 7:9–10; 2 Cor. 13; Phil. 2; 1 Tim. 4:12; Gal. 3:28

PLAYLIST (UNITY): "Make Us One" (Jesus Culture); "With One Voice" (Steven Curtis Chapman); "Build Your Kingdom Here" (Rend Collective); "Love" (Chris Tomlin); "Love Is on the Move" (Leeland); "All for Love" (Hillsong United); "We Are One" (The City Harmonic); "Love Shine Through" (Tim Hughes); "No Greater Love" (Matt Maher); "Undivided Love" (Worship Central); "God of This City" (Chris Tomlin); "Bleed the Same" (Kirk Franklin, TobyMac, Mandisa); "Hold Us Together" (H.E.R. and Tauren Wells); "Heal Our Land" (Kari Jobe); "Good Grace" (Hillsong United); "All to Us" (Chris Tomlin); "1000 Tongues" (Vertical Worship)

RESOURCES:
Neighborliness by David Docusen
https://daviddocusen.com/neighborliness-is-here/
American Academy of Pediatrics: The Traumatic Impact of
 Racism and Discrimination
https://www.adolescenthealth.org/SAHM_Main/media/Anti-Racism
 -Toolkit/Traumatic-Impact-of-Racism-on-Young-People-(1).pdf
American Psychological Association Resources for Parents
https://www.apa.org/res/parent-resources
Harvard Implicit Association Test
https://implicit.harvard.edu/implicit/takeatest.html

MOVIES: *The Perfect Game, Blue Miracle, Black Panther, Crazy
Rich Asians, The Farewell, To Kill a Mockingbird, Te Ata, Remember the
Titans, Million Dollar Arm, The Hate U Give, In the Heights, Hamilton,
Moana, Same Kind of Different as Me, The Help, Hidden Figures, 42, Just
Mercy, Magic of Ordinary Days, The Courageous Heart of Irena Sendler*
 BOOKS: *Just Mercy, Reaching for the Moon, To Kill a Mockingbird,
Claudette Colvin, The Boy in the Striped Pajamas, The Book Thief, My
Family Divided, Same Kind of Different as Me, Warriors Don't Cry, The
Hiding Place, Class Divided*

CHAPTER 11

*Gender Identity: How to Respond
with Compassion and Kindness*
 SCRIPTURES: Gen. 16; Luke 22:61; Matt. 9:36; Eph. 4:32
 PLAYLIST (NEVER ALONE): "Never Alone" (Hillsong Young
and Free); "He Will Hold Me Fast" (Keith and Kristyn Getty); "I

Am Not Alone" (Kari Jobe); "Times" (Tenth Avenue North); "You
Are Faithful" (Kim Walker-Smith and Jesus Culture); "Come Away"
(Chris Quilala and Jesus Culture); "You Carried Me" (Building 429);
"Alive Again" (Matt Maher); "The Words I Would Say" (Sidewalk
Prophets); "Before the Morning" (Josh Wilson); "Another in the Fire"
(Hillsong United); "Rest in You" (All Sons and Daughters); "Together"
(Kirk Franklin, Tori Kelly, and For King and Country); "You're Not
Alone" (Meredith Andrews); "Just Be Held" (Casting Crowns); "In
Christ Alone" (Celtic Worship); "Cornerstone" (Hillsong Worship)

RESOURCES:

American Academy of Pediatrics Policy Statement
https://publications.aap.org/pediatrics/article/142/4/e20182162
    /37381/Ensuring-Comprehensive-Care-and-Support-for
CDC LGBT Youth Resources
https://www.cdc.gov/lgbthealth/youth.htm
National Alliance on Mental Illness (NAMI) Guidance on
    Finding a Mental Healthcare Provider
https://www.nami.org/Your-Journey/Identity-and-Cultural
    -Dimensions/LGBTQI
National Geographic *Gender Revolution* Special
https://www.natgeotv.com/ca/gender-revolution
Find a Christian Therapist
https://www.psychologytoday.com/us/therapists/christian

CHAPTER 12

*Eating Disorders: How to Find Healing
When Food Is Your Enemy*
    SCRIPTURES: Mark 5; Ps. 103

PLAYLIST (HEALING): "Healer" (Hillsong Worship); "Healing Begins" (Tenth Avenue North); "My Hallelujah" (Bryan and Katie Torwalt); "He Will" (Ellie Holcomb); "Healer" (Kari Jobe); "The Name of Jesus" (Chris Tomlin); "Healing Rain" (Michael W. Smith); "Welcome the Healer" (Passion); "Healing Is in Your Hands" (Christy Nockels); "Just One Touch" (Kim Walker-Smith); "Jesus" (Chris Tomlin); "Miracles" (Jesus Culture); "It Is Well" (Bethel Music); "Do It Again" (Elevation Worship); "Oceans" (Hillsong United); "Psalm 23" (Shane and Shane); "Beautiful Things" (Gungor); "Lord I Need You" (Passion); "10,000 Reasons" (Matt Maher)

RESOURCES:

SCOFF Screening Tool

https://www.psychtools.info/scoff/

Eating Disorders Helpline (888) 375-7767

https://anad.org/get-help/eating-disorders-helpline/

National Eating Disorders Association

https://www.nationaleatingdisorders.org/what-are-eating-disorders

POSTSCRIPT

How to Heal Generational Hurts

SCRIPTURES: Gen. 8; 28; Ex. 12; Luke 22

PLAYLIST FOR THE ROAD (MY PARENTING PICK-ME-UP PLAYLIST): "Hills and Valleys" (Tauren Wells); "King of Kings" (Hillsong Worship); "God, You're So Good" (Passion); "Goodness of God" (Jenn Johnson); "King of My Heart" (Steffany Gretzinger and Jeremy Riddle); "Your Glory/Nothing but the Blood" (All Sons and Daughters); "Promises" (Maverick City Music); "Way Maker" (Leeland); "Raise a Hallelujah" (Bethel Music); "10,000 Reasons"

(Matt Maher); "Build Your Kingdom Here" (Rend Collective); "My Lighthouse" (Rend Collective); "You Make Me Brave" (Bethel Music); "Good Good Father" (Chris Tomlin); "Bless the Broken Road" (Selah); "You Raise Me Up" (Josh Groban); "See a Victory" (Bethel Music); "Lord, I Need You" (Matt Maher); "How Great Is Our God" (Chris Tomlin); "O Praise the Name" (Hillsong Worship)

RESOURCES:

ACE Test

https://www.npr.org/sections/health-shots/2015/03/02/387007941
/take-the-ace-quiz-and-learn-what-it-does-and-doesnt-mean

CDC: Adolescent and School Health: Positive Parenting
Practices

https://www.cdc.gov/healthyyouth/protective/positiveparenting.htm

NOTES

Introduction

1. Chun Bun Lam, Susan M. McHale, and Ann C. Crouter, "Parent-Child Shared Time from Middle Childhood to Late Adolescence: Developmental Course and Adjustment Correlates," *Child Development* 83, no. 6 (November–December 2012): 2089–2103, https://doi.org/10.1111/j.1467-8624.2012.01826.x, https://srcd.online library.wiley.com/doi/10.1111/j.1467-8624.2012.01826.x.

Chapter 1

1. Nicole Bartek, Jessica Peck, Dawn Garzon, and Susan VanCleve, "Addressing the Clinical Impact of COVID-19 on Pediatric Mental Health," *Journal of Pediatric Health Care* 35, no. 4 (July 2021): 377–86, https://doi.org/10.1016/j.pedhc.2021.03.006, https://www .jpedhc.org/article/S0891-5245(21)00054-7/fulltext.

2. Carmen Heredia Rodriguez, "Children's Hospitals Grapple with Wave of Mental Illness," Kaiser Health News, January 6, 2021, https://khn.org /news/article/childrens-hospitals-grapple-with-wave-of-mental-illness/.

3. David Finkelhor, Heather Turner, and Deirdre LaSelva, "Receipt of Behavioral Health Services Among US Children and Youth with Adverse Childhood Experiences or Mental Health Symptoms," *JAMA Network Open* 4, no. 3, March 15, 2021, https://doi.org/10.1001 /jamanetworkopen.2021.1435, https://jamanetwork.com/journals /jamanetworkopen/fullarticle/2777440?resultClick=3.

4. U.S. Surgeon General's Advisory, Protecting Youth Mental Health,

2021, https://www.hhs.gov/sites/default/files/surgeon-general-youth -mental-health-advisory.pdf.

5. "Mental Health," HealthyPeople.gov, accessed March 24, 2022, https://www.healthypeople.gov/2020/leading-health-indicators /2020-lhi-topics/Mental-Health.

6. Ali J. Alsaad, Yusra Azhar, and Yasser Al Nasser, "Depression in Children," National Center for Biotechnology Information, U.S. National Library of Medicine, May 4, 2021, https://www.ncbi.nlm .nih.gov/books/NBK534797/.

7. "Major Depression," National Institute of Mental Health, January 2022, https://www.nimh.nih.gov/health/statistics/major-depression.

8. "What Are the Five Major Types of Anxiety Disorders?" U.S. Department of Health and Human Services, accessed March 24, 2022, https://www.hhs.gov/answers/mental-health-and-substance -abuse/what-are-the-five-major-types-of-anxiety-disorders/index.html.

9. Kurt Kroenke, Robert L. Spitzer, and Janet B. W. Williams, "The PHQ-9: Validity of a Brief Depression Severity Measure," *Journal of General Internal Medicine* 16, no. 9 (September 2001): 606–13, https://www.ncbi.nlm.nih.gov/pmc/articles/PMC1495268/.

10. Robert L. Spitzer, Kurt Kroenke, and Janet B. W. Williams, "A Brief Measure for Assessing Generalized Anxiety Disorder: The GAD-7," *JAMA Internal Medicine* 166, no. 10 (2006): 1092–97, https://doi.org /10.1001/archinte.166.10.1092, https://jamanetwork.com/journals /jamainternalmedicine/fullarticle/410326.

11. Manning Marable and Leith Mullings, eds., *Let Nobody Turn Us Around: An African American Anthology* (Lanham, MD: Rowman and Littlefield, 2009).

Chapter 2

1. Monica Anderson and Jingjing Jiang, "Teens, Social Media and Technology 2018," Pew Research Center, May 31, 2018, https://www .pewresearch.org/internet/2018/05/31/teens-social-media-technology -2018/.

2. McAfee, "Technology Fuels Cyberbullying and Cheating in Teens,"

August 30, 2012, https://www.mcafee.com/blogs/family-safety
/technology-fuels-cyberbullying-and-cheating-in-teens/.

3. "Word of the Year," Oxford Languages, n.d., https://languages.oup.com
/word-of-the-year/.

4. Gwenn Schurgin O'Keeffe, Kathleen Clarke-Pearson, and the Council
on Communications and Media, "The Impact of Social Media on
Children, Adolescents, and Families," *Pediatrics* 127, no. 4 (2011):
800–4, https://doi.org/10.1542/peds.2011-0054, https://publications.aap
.org/pediatrics/article/127/4/800/65133/the-impact-of-social-media-on
-children-adolescents.

5. Common Sense Media, "Landmark Report: U.S. Teens Use an Average
of Nine Hours of Media per Day, Tweens Use Six Hours," Common
Sense Media, November 3, 2015, https://www.commonsensemedia.org
/about-us/news/press-releases/landmark-report-us-teens-use-an-average
-of-nine-hours-of-media-per-day-tweens-use-six-hours.

6. Richard Brandt, "Google Divulges Numbers at I/O: 20 Billion Texts,
93 Million Selfies and More," *Silicon Valley Business Journal*, June 25,
2014, https://www.bizjournals.com/sanjose/news/2014/06/25/google
-divulges-numbers-at-i-o-20-billion-texts-93.html.

7. Federal Trade Commission, "Children's Online Privacy Protection Rule
('COPPA')," Federal Trade Commission, accessed March 24, 2022,
https://www.ftc.gov/enforcement/rules/rulemaking-regulatory-reform
-proceedings/childrens-online-privacy-protection-rule.

8. Coby Persin, "The Dangers of Social Media (Child Predator
Experiment)," YouTube, August 10, 2015, https://www.youtube.com
/watch?v=6jMhMVEjEQg.

9. A. M. Williamson and A. M. Feyer, "Moderate Sleep Deprivation
Produces Impairments in Cognitive and Motor Performance Equivalent
to Legally Prescribed Levels of Alcohol Intoxication," *Occupational &
Environmental Medicine* 57, no. 10 (October 2000): 649–55, https://doi.org
/10.1136/oem.57.10.649, https://pubmed.ncbi.nlm.nih.gov/10984335/.

10. Monica E. Hartmann and J. Roxanne Prichard, "Calculating the
Contribution of Sleep Problems to Undergraduates' Academic
Success," *Sleep Health* 4, no. 5 (October 2018): 463–71, https://doi.org

/10.1016/j.sleh.2018.07.002, https://www.sleephealthjournal.org
/article/S2352-7218(18)30119-0/fulltext.

Chapter 3

1. Melvina Brandau and Snehaa Ray, "Caring for the Digital Generation:
   Understanding Electronic Aggression," *Continuing Education* 35, no. 1
   (January 2021): 132–40, https://doi.org/10.1016/j.pedhc.2020.07.010,
   https://www.jpedhc.org/article/S0891-5245(20)30203-0/fulltext.
2. Sameer Hinduja, "The Role of Parents in Preventing Bullying and
   Cyberbullying," Cyberbullying Research Center, accessed March 24, 2022,
   https://cyberbullying.org/parenting-preventing-bullying-cyberbullying.
3. "Tyler Clementi's Story," Tyler Clementi Foundation, accessed
   March 24, 2022, https://tylerclementi.org/tylers-story-tcf/.
4. Jessica L. Peck, Mikki Meadows-Oliver, Stacia M. Hays, and Dawn
   Garzon Maaks, "White Paper: Recognizing Child Trafficking as
   a Critical Emerging Health Threat," *Professional Issues* 35, no. 3
   (May 2021): 260–69, https://doi.org/10.1016/j.pedhc.2020.01.005,
   https://www.jpedhc.org/article/S0891-5245(19)30669-8/fulltext.
5. "Report: Core Competencies for Human Trafficking Response in
   Health Care and Behavioral Health Systems," National Human
   Trafficking Training and Technical Assistance Center, February 2021,
   https://nhttac.acf.hhs.gov/resource/report-core-competencies-human
   -trafficking-response-health-care-and-behavioral-health.
6. "Human Trafficking: Online Safety," National Center on Safe
   Supportive Learning Environments, June 17, 2020, https://safesupportive
   learning.ed.gov/events/webinar/human-trafficking-online-safety.

Chapter 4

1. "Suicide," National Institute of Mental Health, accessed March 24,
   2022, https://www.nimh.nih.gov/health/statistics/suicide.
2. Sally C. Curtin, "State Suicide Rates Among Adolescents and Young
   Adults Aged 10–24: United States, 2000–2018," *National Vital Statistics
   Reports* 69, no. 11 (September 11, 2020), https://www.cdc.gov/nchs
   /data/nvsr/nvsr69/nvsr-69-11-508.pdf.

3. Asha Z. Ivey-Stephenson, Zewditu Demissie, Alexander E. Crosby, Deborah M. Stone, Elizabeth Gaylor, Natalie Wilkins, Richard Lowry, and Margaret Brown, "Suicidal Ideation and Behaviors Among High School Students—Youth Risk Behavior Survey, United States, 2019," *Morbidity and Mortality Weekly Report* (Supplements) 69, no. 1 (August 21, 2020): 47–55, https://doi.org/10.15585/mmwr.su6901a6, https://www.cdc.gov/mmwr/volumes/69/su/su6901a6.htm.

4. Deborah M. Stone and Alex E. Crosby, "Suicide Prevention: State of the Art Review," *American Journal of Lifestyle Medicine* 8, no. 6 (2014): 404–20, https://doi.org/10.1177/1559827614551130, https://www.ncbi .nlm.nih.gov/pmc/articles/PMC6112615/.

5. Ester di Giacomo, Micheal Krausz, and Fabrizia Colmegna, "Estimating the Risk of Attempted Suicide Among Sexual Minority Youths: A Systematic Review and Meta-analysis," *JAMA Pediatrics* 172, no. 12 (2018): 1145–52, https://doi.org/10.1001/jamapediatrics.2018.2731, https://jamanetwork.com/journals/jamapediatrics/fullarticle/2704490.

6. Holly Hedegaard and Margaret Warner, "Evaluating the Cause-of-Death Information Needed for Estimating the Burden of Injury Mortality: United States, 2019," National Vital Statistics Reports 70, no. 13 (December 7, 2021), https://www.cdc.gov/nchs/data/nvsr/nvsr70/NVSR70-13.pdf.

7. Sarah M. Coyne, Jeffrey L. Hurst, W. Justin Dyer, Quintin Hunt, Emily Schvaneveldt, Sara Brown, and Gavin Jones, "Suicide Risk in Emerging Adulthood: Associations with Screen Time over 10 Years," *Journal of Youth and Adolescence* 50 (December 2021): 2324–38, https:// doi.org/10.1007/s10964-020-01389-6, https://link.springer.com/article /10.1007/s10964-020-01389-6.

8. Brian K. Ahmedani, Christine Stewart, Gregory E. Simon, Frances Lynch, Christine Y. Lu, Beth E. Waitzfelder, Leif I. Solberg, "Racial/ Ethnic Differences in Health Care Visits Made Before Suicide Attempt Across the United States," *Medical Care* 53, no. 5 (May 2015): 430–35, https://doi.org/10.1097/MLR.0000000000000335, https://pubmed .ncbi.nlm.nih.gov/25872151/.

9. Oxford Reference, s.v. "stigma," https://www.oxfordreference.com /view/10.1093/oi/authority.20110007171501221.

10. Bernardo Carpiniello and Federica Pinna, "The Reciprocal Relationship Between Suicidality and Stigma," *Frontiers in Psychiatry*, March 8, 2017, https://doi.org/10.3389/fpsyt.2017.00035, https://www.frontiersin.org/articles/10.3389/fpsyt.2017.00035/full.

11. Thomas R. Simon, Alan C. Swann, Kenneth E. Powell, Lloyd B. Potter, Marcie-jo Kresnow, and Patrick W. O'Carroll, "Characteristics of Impulsive Suicide Attempts and Attempters," *Suicide and Life-Threatening Behavior* 32, no. 1 (January 2011): 49–59, https://doi.org/10.1521/suli.32.1.5.49.24212, https://onlinelibrary.wiley.com/doi/abs/10.1521/suli.32.1.5.49.24212.

Chapter 5

1. U.S. Department of Health, Education, and Welfare, Public Health Service, Surgeon General's Advisory Committee on Smoking and Health, *Smoking and Health: Report of the Advisory Committee to the Surgeon General of the Public Health Service* (Washington, DC: U.S. Government Printing Office, 1964), https://profiles.nlm.nih.gov/101584932X814; Kayla Ruble, "Read the Surgeon General's 1964 Report on Smoking and Health," PBS News Weekend, January 12, 2014, https://www.pbs.org/newshour/health/first-surgeon-general-report-on-smokings-health-effects-marks-50-year-anniversary.

2. U.S. Food and Drug Administration, "Family Smoking Prevention and Tobacco Control Act—An Overview," U.S. Food and Drug Administration, accessed March 24, 2022, https://www.fda.gov/tobacco-products/rules-regulations-and-guidance/family-smoking-prevention-and-tobacco-control-act-overview.

3. Tobacco Media Campaign, "Tips from Former Smokers," Centers for Disease Control and Prevention, March 1, 2021, https://www.cdc.gov/tobacco/campaign/tips/about/impact/campaign-year.html.

4. World Health Organization, "Tobacco," World Health Organization, https://www.who.int/news-room/fact-sheets/detail/tobacco.

5. Office on Smoking and Health, National Center for Chronic Disease Prevention and Health Promotion, "Smoking and Tobacco Use: Youth and Tobacco Use," Centers for Disease Control and Prevention,

accessed March 24, 2022, https://www.cdc.gov/tobacco/data_statistics /fact_sheets/youth_data/tobacco_use/index.htm.

6. News Release, "National Survey Reveals One in Five Young Adults Regularly Uses E-Cigarettes and Believes They Are Harmless, Not Addictive," ASCO, September 24, 2019, https://www.asco.org/about -asco/press-center/news-releases/national-survey-reveals-one-five -young-adults-regularly-uses-e.

7. Teresa W. Wang, Linda J. Neff, Eunice Park-Lee, Chunfeng Ren, Karen A. Cullen, and Brian A. King, "E-cigarette Use Among Middle and High School Students—United States, 2020," *Morbidity and Mortality Weekly Report* 69, no. 37 (September 18, 2020): 1310–12, https://dx.doi.org/10.15585/mmwr.mm6937e1, https://www.cdc.gov /mmwr/volumes/69/wr/mm6937e1.htm.

8. News Release, "FDA Finalizes Enforcement Policy on Unauthorized Flavored Cartridge-Based E-cigarettes That Appeal to Children, Including Fruit and Mint," U.S. Food and Drug Administration, January 2, 2020, https://www.fda.gov/news-events/press-announcements /fda-finalizes-enforcement-policy-unauthorized-flavored-cartridge-based -e-cigarettes-appeal-children.

9. "Where Are Kids Getting JUUL?," Truth Initiative, May 29, 2018, https://truthinitiative.org/research-resources/emerging-tobacco-products /where-are-kids-getting-juul.

10. Richard A. Miech, Megan E. Patrick, Patrick M. O'Malley, Lloyd D. Johnston, and Jerald G. Bachman, "Trends in Reported Marijuana Vaping Among US Adolescents, 2017–2019," *Journal of the American Medical Association* 323, no. 5 (December 17, 2019): 475–76, https://doi .org/10.1001/jama.2019.20185, https://jamanetwork.com/journals/jama /fullarticle/2757960.

11. Office on Smoking and Health, National Center for Chronic Disease Prevention and Health Promotion, "Smoking and Tobacco Use: Outbreak of Lung Injury Associated with the Use of E-cigarette, or Vaping Products," Centers for Disease Control and Prevention, accessed March 24, 2022, https://www.cdc.gov/tobacco/basic_information/e-cigarettes/severe -lung-disease.html.

12. Joanne T. Chang, Baoguang Wang, Cindy M. Chang, and Bridget K. Ambrose, "National Estimates of Poisoning Events Related to Liquid Nicotine in Young Children Treated in US Hospital Emergency Departments, 2013–2017," *Injury Epidemiology* 6, no. 10 (2019), https://doi.org/10.1186/s40621-019-0188-9, https://injepijournal.biomedcentral.com/articles/10.1186/s40621-019-0188-9.

Chapter 6

1. CDC Healthy Schools, "The Buzz on Energy Drinks," Centers for Disease Control and Prevention, May 29, 2019, https://www.cdc.gov/healthyschools/nutrition/energy.htm.
2. National Institute on Alcohol Abuse and Alcoholism, "College Drinking," National Institutes of Health, accessed March 24, 2022, https://www.niaaa.nih.gov/publications/brochures-and-fact-sheets/college-drinking.
3. Kate B. Carey, Alyssa L. Norris, Sarah E. Durney, Robyn L. Shepardson, and Michael P. Carey, "Mental Health Consequences of Sexual Assault Among First-Year College Women," *Journal of American College Health* 66, no. 6 (August–September 2018): 480–86, https://doi.org/10.1080/07448481.2018.1431915, https://www.ncbi.nlm.nih.gov/pmc/articles/PMC6311089/.
4. Alejandro Azofeifa, Bárbara D. Rexach-Guzmán, Abby N. Hagemeyer, Rose A. Rudd, and Erin K. Sauber-Schatz, "Driving Under the Influence of Marijuana and Illicit Drugs Among Persons Aged ≥16 Years—United States, 2018," *Morbidity and Mortality Weekly Report* 68, no. 50 (2019): 1153–57, https://www.cdc.gov/mmwr/volumes/68/wr/mm6850a1.htm?s_cid=mm6850a1_w.
5. Nicholas Rice, "OWN Host Dr. Laura Berman and Her Husband Detail How Their Family Is Doing After Son's Fatal Overdose," *People*, March 20, 2021, https://people.com/tv/laura-berman-husband-detail-how-their-family-is-doing-after-sons-fatal-overdose/.
6. U.S. Department of Health and Human Services, "Recovery and Recovery Support," Substance Abuse and Mental Health Services Administration, April 23, 2020, https://www.samhsa.gov/find-help/recovery#:~:text=SAMHSA%20established%20recovery%20

support%20systems%20to%20promote%20partnering,secure%20
necessary%20social%20supports%20in%20their%20chosen%20
community.

7. Boston Children's Hospital and Harvard Medical School Teaching
   Hospital, "About the CRAFFT," CRAFFT, accessed March 24, 2022,
   https://crafft.org/.

Chapter 7

1. "Kenneth Ginsburg," Fostering Resilience, accessed March 24, 2022,
   http://www.fosteringresilience.com/about.php.

2. Linda Dillow, *Calm My Anxious Heart: A Woman's Guide to Finding
   Contentment* (Colorado Springs: NavPress, 1998).

3. Lysa TerKheurst, *Forgiving What You Can't Forget: Discover How to
   Move On, Make Peace with Painful Memories, and Create a Life That's
   Beautiful Again* (Nashville, TN: Thomas Nelson, 2020).

Chapter 8

1. Committee on Adolescent Health Care, "The Initial Reproductive Health
   Visit," American College of Obstetricians and Gynecologists, accessed
   March 24, 2022, https://www.acog.org/clinical/clinical-guidance
   /committee-opinion/articles/2020/10/the-initial-reproductive-health-visit.

2. "Helping Teens Resist Sexual Pressure," American Academy of
   Pediatrics, November 2, 2009, https://www.healthychildren.org
   /english/ages-stages/teen/dating-sex/pages/helping-teens-resist-sexual
   -pressure.aspx.

3. National Center for Health Statistics, "Over Half of U.S. Teens Have
   Had Sexual Intercourse by Age 18, New Report Shows," Centers for
   Disease Control and Prevention, June 22, 2017, https://www.cdc.gov
   /nchs/pressroom/nchs_press_releases/2017/201706_nsfg.htm.

4. Adolescent and School Health, "Talking with Your Teens About
   Sex: Going Beyond 'The Talk,'" Centers for Disease Control and
   Prevention, November 21, 2019, https://www.cdc.gov/healthyyouth
   /protective/factsheets/talking_teens.htm.

5. Texas School Safety Center, "'Before You Text': Bullying and Sexting

Course," Texas State University, accessed March 24, 2022, https://txssc
.txstate.edu/tools/courses/before-you-text/module-3-2.

6. Larry Kim, "The Snappening: Over 200,000 Snapchat Photos Leaked
Online," Social Media Today, October 20, 2014, https://www
.socialmediatoday.com/content/snappening-over-200000-snapchat
-photos-leaked-online.

7. Aina M. Gassó, Bianca Klettke, José R. Agustina, and Irene Montiel,
"Sexting, Mental Health, and Victimization Among Adolescents: A
Literature Review," *International Journal of Environmental Research
and Public Health* 16, no. 13 (July 3, 2019): 2364, https://doi.org
/10.3390/ijerph16132364, https://www.ncbi.nlm.nih.gov/pmc/articles
/PMC6650829/.

8. "Amanda's Legacy," Amanda Todd Legacy Society, accessed March 24,
2022, https://www.amandatoddlegacy.org/.

Chapter 9

1. Antonia Quadara, Alissar El-Murr, and Joe Latham, "The Effects
of Pornography on Children and Young People: An Evidence Scan,"
Australian Institute of Family Studies, December 2017, https://aifs
.gov.au/publications/effects-pornography-children-and-young-people.

2. Oxford Reference, s.v. "pornography," https://www.oxfordreference.com
/view/10.1093/oi/authority.20110803100337901.

3. Mary Mycio, "Archeology Isn't for Prudes: Some of the Oldest Porn
in the World Is at Least 3,000 Years Old, and Bi-Curious," *Slate*,
February 14, 2013, https://slate.com/technology/2013/02/prehistoric
-pornography-chinese-carvings-show-explicit-copulation.html.

4. Marta Falconi, "Pompeii's Most Popular Brothel Goes on Display," NBC
News, October 26, 2006, https://www.nbcnews.com/id/wbna15434770.

5. Patricia Stuthridge, "Internet and the Youth, Statistics You Should Be
Aware Of," Lucid View, February 6, 2020, https://www.lucidview.net
/internet-and-the-youth-statistics-you-should-be-aware-of/.

6. "Pornhub's Annual Report: Can You Guess the Most Popular Porn
Categories in 2019?" Fight the New Drug, December 17, 2019,
https://fightthenewdrug.org/2019-pornhub-annual-report/.

7. Paul J. Wright, Bryant Paul, and Debby Herbenick, "Preliminary Insights from a U.S. Probability Sample on Adolescents' Pornography Exposure, Media Psychology, and Sexual Aggression," *Journal of Health Communication* 26, no. 1 (February 24, 2021): 39–46, https://doi.org /10.1080/10810730.2021.1887980, https://www.tandfonline.com/doi /abs/10.1080/10810730.2021.1887980?journalCode=uhcm20.

8. Răzvan Mureşan, "One in 10 Visitors of Porn Sites Is Under 10 Years Old," Bitdefender, September 20, 2016, https://www.bitdefender.com /blog/hotforsecurity/one-in-10-visitors-of-porn-sites-is-under-10-years-old.

9. Jochen Peter and Patti M. Valkenburg, "Adolescents and Pornography: A Review of 20 Years of Research," *The Journal of Sex Research* 53, no. 4–5: Annual Review of Sex Research (2016): 509–31, https://doi.org /10.1080/00224499.2016.1143441, https://www.tandfonline.com/doi /full/10.1080/00224499.2016.1143441.

10. "Statistics: Youth & Porn," Enough Is Enough, accessed March 24, 2022, https://enough.org/stats-youth-and-porn.

11. Hashir Ali Awan, Alifiya Aamir, Mufaddal Najmuddin Diwan, Irfan Ullah, Victor Pereira-Sanchez, Rodrigo Ramalho, "Internet and Pornography Use During the COVID-19 Pandemic: Presumed Impact and What Can Be Done," *Frontiers in Psychiatry*, March 16, 2021, https://doi.org/10.3389/fpsyt.2021.623508, https://www.frontiersin.org /articles/10.3389/fpsyt.2021.623508/full.

12. Gianna M. Galindo, "The Effects of Violent Video Games, Websites, and Internet Pornography on Adolescents' Attitudes About Dating and Sexual Violence" (PhD diss., Alliant International University, 2020), https://www.proquest.com/openview/224b02042460b6afc07fa a5364124136/1?pq-origsite=gscholar&cbl=18750&diss=y.

13. Jason S. Carroll, Dean M. Busby, Brian J. Willoughby, and Cameron C. Brown, "The Porn Gap: Differences in Men's and Women's Pornography Patterns in Couple Relationships," *Journal of Couple and Relationship Therapy* 16, no. 2 (2017): 146–63, https://doi.org/10.1080 /15332691.2016.1238796, https://www.tandfonline.com/doi/abs/10.10 80/15332691.2016.1238796.

14. Elena Martellozzo, Andy Monaghan, Joanna R. Adler, Julia Davidson,

Rodolfo Leyva, and Miranda A.H. Horvath, "'I Wasn't Sure It Was Normal to Watch It,'" NSPCC Learning, May 2017, https://learning.nspcc.org.uk /research-resources/2016/i-wasn-t-sure-it-was-normal-to-watch-it.

15. Rebecca L. Collins, Victor C. Strasburger, Jane D. Brown, Edward Donnerstein, Amanda Lenhart, and L. Monique Ward, "Sexual Media and Childhood Well-Being and Health," *Pediatrics* 140 (Supplement 2): S162–S166, https://doi.org/peds.2016–1758X, https://publications.aap.org/pediatrics/article/140/supplement_2 /s162/34185/sexual-media-and-childhood-well-being-and-health.

16. Christian Laier and Matthias Brand, "Mood Changes After Watching Pornography on the Internet Are Linked to Tendencies Towards Internet-Pornography-Viewing Disorder," *Addictive Behaviors Reports* 5 (June 2017): 9–13, https://doi.org/10.1016/j.abrep.2016.11.003, https://www.sciencedirect.com/science/article/pii/S2352853216300499.

17. Jennifer Riemersma and Michael Sytsma, "A New Generation of Sexual Addiction," *Sexual Addiction & Compulsivity* 20, no. 4 (2013): 306–22, https://doi.org/10.1080/10720162.2013.843067, https://www .tandfonline.com/doi/abs/10.1080/10720162.2013.843067.

18. "Press Release: The Nobel Prize in Physiology or Medicine 1973," The Nobel Prize, accessed March 24, 2022, https://www.nobelprize.org /prizes/medicine/1973/press-release/.

19. Daniel Sher, "Porn-Induced Erectile Dysfunction–Can Porn Cause ED?" Between Us Clinic, accessed March 24, 2022, https://www .betweenusclinic.com/erectile-dysfunction/excessive-porn-consumption -can-cause-erectile-dysfunction/.

20. Jerel P. Calzo, S. Bryn Austin, Brittany M. Charlton, Stacey A. Missmer, Martin Kathrins, Audrey J. Gaskins, and Jorge E. Chavarro, "Erectile Dysfunction in a Sample of Sexually Active Young Adult Men from a U.S. Cohort: Demographic, Metabolic and Mental Health Correlates," *The Journal of Urology* 205, no. 2 (February 2021): 539–44, https://doi.org/10.1097/JU.0000000000001367, https://www .auajournals.org/doi/abs/10.1097/JU.0000000000001367.

21. Michele L. Ybarra and Richard E. Thompson, "Predicting the Emergence of Sexual Violence in Adolescence," *Prevention Science* 19,

no. 4 (2018): 403–15, https://doi.org/10.1007/s11121-017-0810-4, https://jhu.pure.elsevier.com/en/publications/predicting-the-emergence -of-sexual-violence-in-adolescence.

22. Willy Pedersen, Anders Bakken, Kari Stefansen, and Tilmann von Soest, "Sexual Victimization in the Digital Age: A Population-Based Study of Physical and Image-Based Sexual Abuse Among Adolescents," *Archives of Sexual Behavior* (January 2022), https://doi.org/10.1007/s10508-021 -02200-8, https://link.springer.com/article/10.1007/s10508-021-02200-8.

23. Glenn R. Mesman, Shannon L. Harper, Nicola A. Edge, Tiffany W. Brandt, and Joy L. Pemberton, "Problematic Sexual Behavior in Children," *Journal of Pediatric Health Care* 33, no. 3 (May 2019): 323–31, https://doi.org/10.1016/j.pedhc.2018.11.002, https://www .jpedhc.org/article/S0891-5245(18)30500-5/fulltext.

24. Stephen Kendrick and Alex Kendrick, *The Love Dare* (Nashville, TN: B&H Publishing Group, 2008).

25. Stephen Kendrick and Alex Kendrick, *The Love Dare for Parents* (Nashville, TN: B&H Books, 2013).

Chapter 10

1. Beata Mostafavi, "National Poll: More Teens Participating in Protests Against Racism," Michigan Medicine, October 26, 2020, https:// healthblog.uofmhealth.org/childrens-health/national-poll-more-teens -participating-protests-against-racism.

2. National 4-H Council, "New Survey Finds That 83 Percent of Teens Acknowledge That Systemic Racism Is an Issue and They Want to Be Included in the National Conversation Around Social Justice," 4-H, August 13, 2020, https://4-h.org/about/blog/new-survey-finds-that -83-percent-of-teens-acknowledge-that-systemic-racism-is-an-issue -and-they-want-to-be-included-in-the-national-conversation-around -social-justice/.

3. Dennis P. Carmody and Michael Lewis, "Brain Activation When Hearing One's Own and Others' Names," *Brain Research* 1116, no. 1 (October 2006): 153–58, https://doi.org/10.1016/j.brainres.2006 .07.121, https://www.ncbi.nlm.nih.gov/pmc/articles/PMC1647299/#R5.

4. Theresa Louise-Bender Pape, Joshua M. Rosenow, Monica Steiner, Todd Parrish, Ann Guernon, Brett Harton, and Vijaya Patil, "Placebo-Controlled Trial of Familiar Auditory Sensory Training for Acute Severe Traumatic Brain Injury: A Preliminary Report," *Neurorehabilitation and Neural Repair* 29, no. 6 (July 2015): 537–47, https://doi.org/10.1177/1545968314554626, https://pubmed.ncbi.nlm.nih.gov/25613986/.

5. "Genetics vs. Genomics Fact Sheet," National Human Genome Research Institute, September 7, 2018, https://www.genome.gov/about-genomics /fact-sheets/Genetics-vs-Genomics.

6. Maria Trent, Danielle G. Dooley, Jacqueline Dougé, Robert M. Cavanaugh, Jr, Amy E. Lacroix, Jonathon Fanburg, and Maria Rahmandar, "The Impact of Racism on Child and Adolescent Health," *Pediatrics* 144, no. 2 (August 2019): e20191765, https://doi.org/10.1542 /peds.2019-1765, https://publications.aap.org/pediatrics/article/144/2 /e20191765/38466/The-Impact-of-Racism-on-Child-and-Adolescent.

7. Nia Heard-Garris, Patricia O. Ekwueme, Shawnese Gilpin, Kaitlyn Ann Sacotte, Leishla Perez-Cardona, Megan Wong, and Alyssa Cohen, "Adolescents' Experiences, Emotions, and Coping Strategies Associated with Exposure to Media-Based Vicarious Racism," *JAMA Network Open* 4, no. 6 (June 2021): e2113522, http://doi.org/10.1001 /jamanetworkopen.2021.13522, https://jamanetwork.com/journals /jamanetworkopen/fullarticle/2780958.

8. David J. Kelly, Paul C. Quinn, Alan M. Slater, Kang Lee, Alan Gibson, Michael Smith, Liezhong Ge, and Oliver Pascalis, "Three-Month-Olds, but Not Newborns, Prefer Own-Race Faces," *Developmental Science* 8, no. 6 (November 2005): F31–F36, https://doi.org/10.1111/j.1467-7687 .2005.0434a.x, https://www.ncbi.nlm.nih.gov/pmc/articles/PMC 2566511/.

Chapter 11

1. Jeffrey M. Jones, "LGBT Identification Rises to 5.6% in Latest U.S. Estimate," Gallup, February 24, 2021, https://news.gallup.com /poll/329708/lgbt-identification-rises-latest-estimate.aspx.

2. Jeffrey M. Jones, "LGBT Identification in U.S. Ticks Up to 7.1%,"

Gallup, February 17, 2022, https://news.gallup.com/poll/389792/lgbt
-identification-ticks-up.aspx.

3. "Differences in Suicide Risk Among Subgroups of Sexual and Gender
Minority College Students," National Institute of Mental Health,
September 8, 2020, https://www.nimh.nih.gov/news/research
-highlights/2020/differences-in-suicide-risk-among-subgroups-of
-sexual-and-gender-minority-college-students.

4. Michelle M. Johns, RIchard Lowry, Laura T. Haderxhanaj, Catherine
N. Rasberry, Leah Robin, Lamont Scales, Deborah Stone, and Nicolas
A. Suarez, "Trends in Violence Victimization and Suicide Risk by Sexual
Identity Among High School Students—Youth Risk Behavior Survey,
United States, 2015–2019, *Morbidity and Mortality Weekly Report,
Supplements*, 69 (August 2020) (Supplement 1):19–27, https://www.cdc
.gov/mmwr/volumes/69/su/su6901a3.htm.

5. "Estimate of How Often LGBTQ Youth Attempt Suicide in the U.S.,"
The Trevor Project, March 11, 2021, https://www.thetrevorproject.org
/research-briefs/estimate-of-how-often-lgbtq-youth-attempt-suicide
-in-the-u-s/.

6. Adolescent and School Health, "Results," Centers for Disease Control
and Prevention, accessed March 24, 2022, https://www.cdc.gov
/healthyyouth/data/yrbs/results.htm.

7. "Homelessness and Housing Instability Among LGBTQ Youth," The
Trevor Project, February 3, 2022, https://www.thetrevorproject.org
/research-briefs/homelessness-and-housing-instability-among-lgbtq
-youth-feb-2022/.

8. Jason Rafferty, Michael Yogman, Rebecca Baum, Thresia B. Gambon,
Arthur Lavin, Gerri Mattson, Lawrence Sagin Wissow, "Ensuring
Comprehensive Care and Support for Transgender and Gender-Diverse
Children and Adolescents," *Pediatrics* 142, no. 4 (October 2018):
e20182162, https://doi.org/10.1542/peds.2018-2162, https://publications
.aap.org/pediatrics/article/142/4/e20182162/37381/Ensuring-Comprehensive
-Care-and-Support-for.

9. Consult QD, "Gender-Affirming Hormone Therapy Improves Body
Dissatisfaction in Youth," Cleveland Clinic, May 29, 2020, https://

consultqd.clevelandclinic.org/gender-affirming-hormone-therapy
-improves-body-dissatisfaction-in-youth/.

10. Lisa Littman, "Individuals Treated for Gender Dysphoria with Medical and/or Surgical Transition Who Subsequently Detransitioned: A Survey of 100 Detransitioners," *Archives of Sexual Behavior* 50 (2021): 3353–69, https://doi.org/10.1007/s10508-021-02163-w, https://link.springer.com/article/10.1007/s10508-021-02163-w.

11. Sasha Karan Narayan, Rayisa Hontscharuk, Sara Danker, Jess Guerriero, Angela Carter, Gaines Blasdel, Rachel Bluebond-Langner, "Guiding the Conversation—Types of Regret After Gender-Affirming Surgery and Their Associated Etiologies," *Annals of Translational Medicine* 9, no. 7 (April 2021): 605, https://doi.org/10.21037/atm-20-6204, https://www.ncbi.nlm.nih.gov/pmc/articles/PMC8105823/.

12. Rafferty et al., "Ensuring Comprehensive Care and Support."

Chapter 12

1. "Eating Disorders in Teens Skyrocketing During Pandemic," Harvard School of Public Health, 2021, https://www.hsph.harvard.edu/news/hsph-in-the-news/eating-disorders-in-teens-skyrocketing-during-pandemic/.

2. Jon Arcelus, Alex J. Mitchell, Jackie Wales, and Søren Nielsen, "Mortality Rates in Patients with Anorexia Nervosa and Other Eating Disorders: A Meta-Analysis of 36 Studies," *Archives of General Psychiatry* 68, no. 7 (July 2011): 724–31, https://doi.org/10.1001/archgenpsychiatry.2011.74, https://pubmed.ncbi.nlm.nih.gov/21727255/.

3. Laurie L. Hornberger, Margo A. Lane, Cora C. Breuner, Elizabeth M. Alderman, Laura K. Grubb, Makia Powers, Krishna Kumari Upadhya, "Identification and Management of Eating Disorders in Children and Adolescents," *Pediatrics* 147, no. 1 (January 2021): e2020040279, https://doi.org/10.1542/peds.2020-040279, https://publications.aap.org/pediatrics/article/147/1/e2020040279/33504/identification-and-management-of-eating-disorders.

4. Vivienne M. Hazzard, Lauren M. Schaefer, Allison Mankowski, Traci L. Carson, Sarah M. Lipson, Claire Fendrick, Ross D. Crosby, and Kendrin R. Sonneville, "Development and Validation of the Eating Disorders

Screen for Athletes (EDSA): A Brief Screening Tool for Male and Female Athletes," *Psychology of Sport and Exercise* 50 (September 2020): 101745, https://doi.org/10.1016/j.psychsport.2020.101745, https://www.sciencedirect.com/science/article/abs/pii/S1469029219307204.

5. "Risk Factors," National Eating Disorders Association, accessed March 24, 2022, https://www.nationaleatingdisorders.org/risk-factors.

6. National Association of Pediatric Nurse Practitioners, "TeamPeds Talk," Spotify, accessed March 24, 2022, https://anchor.fm/teampeds-talks/episodes/Effective-Strategies-for-Managing-Severe-Eating-Disorders-etsm7j.

Postscript

1. Vincent J. Felitti, Robert F. Anda, Dale Nordenberg, David F. Williamson, Alison M. Spitz, Valerie Edwards, Mary P. Koss, and James S. Marks, "Relationship of Childhood Abuse and Household Dysfunction to Many of the Leading Causes of Death in Adults: The Adverse Childhood Experiences (ACE) Study," *American Journal of Preventive Medicine* 14, no. 4 (1998): 245–58, https://doi.org/10.1016/S0749-3797(98)00017-8.

2. Nadine Burke Harris, "How Childhood Trauma Affects Health Across a Lifetime," TedMed, September 2014, https://www.ted.com/talks/nadine_burke_harris_how_childhood_trauma_affects_health_across_a_lifetime?language=en.

3. Violence Prevention, "CDC-Kaiser ACE Study," Centers for Disease Control and Prevention, accessed March 24, 2022, https://www.cdc.gov/violenceprevention/aces/about.html.

4. Maria Clara de Magalhães-Barbosa, Arnaldo Prata-Barbosa, and Antonio José Ledo Alves da Cunha, "Toxic Stress, Epigenetics and Child Development," *Jornal de Pediatria*, 98 (November 16, 2021): S13–S18, https://doi.org/10.1016/j.jped.2021.09.007, https://www.sciencedirect.com/science/article/pii/S0021755721001431.

ACKNOWLEDGMENTS

"But God . . ." That's my favorite phrase in the history of ever. (I used it in each chapter; see if you can find it.) I'm so grateful for God's redemptive story in my life. He who started a good work is faithful to complete it. This book was born unexpectedly in the peaceful solitude of my backyard one day during the early weeks of the COVID-19 pandemic. As I was praying, reading my Bible, and journaling after receiving an invitation to submit a book proposal on a topic yet to be determined, within one hour the complete vision for this book was born. It was a sacred and divine moment of God calling me on a journey to a destination unknown. I have no greater joy than walking with God.

Without my husband, the love of my life, none of this would be possible. He gave me the extraordinary gift of believing in me before I was able to believe in myself. His patience, sacrifice, and servant leadership as the silent partner in this team is indescribable. He deserves every ounce of credit for every bit of success with which I've ever been blessed.

I'm grateful for my husband's parents and my sisters-in-law, who adopted me and treated me as their own. Without their support and love, especially in my early years of parenting, I never would have been able to take this nursing journey that has now led to this book. My father-in-law is truly a shining example of someone whose life has been radically changed by Christ, and my children have had the gift of a front-row seat. Their legacy of faith for my children is a beautiful gift.

To my granny, what could I ever say to repay her for her kindness? Her strength and heritage of faith have shaped me immeasurably. She is a woman who simply lives to love her family and to serve others faithfully and generously.

To the Apple Dumpling Gang, my siblings, my ride-or-dies. I thank you from the bottom of my heart for easing the ache of loneliness and walking through this journey together. I love each and every one of you and cherish our new memories. Thank you for giving me the courage to share authentically and for your ever-present support. Thank you especially to my sisters, my most faithful and true reviewers, who never left me alone in this journey. I adore every one of my bajillion nieces and nephews. Know that I am *always* here for each of you.

I'm so grateful for my pediatrician, Dr. George E. S. Reynolds, who changed my life one day by asking me to work for him, which started a twenty-year primary care partnership and deep friendship. He helped shape me into a competent expert. His encouragement and confidence in me spurred me on to higher education and a career in teaching.

To the National Association of Pediatric Nurse Practitioners, thank you for giving me a professional home and the extraordinary honor of leading colleagues whom I esteem most highly as experts in pediatrics and advocates for children.

To Kerri Taylor, Nancy Stewart, and everyone at Unbound Houston, thank you for your anti-trafficking work that led to a dramatic left turn in my professional life that ignited my passion for teen health promotion.

To all my nursing colleagues, fellow guardians of the most trusted profession, I've never found anyone more inspiring and tenacious than you. It's a joy and an honor to stand shoulder to shoulder with you. I've had many colleagues who graciously spent time reviewing my health advice sections, generously sharing their expertise and perspective to make this a stronger book. Thank you Robyn Driskell, Dawn Garzon, Bridgett Hodridge, Sahr Mbwira, Amee Moreno, Laura Searcy, and Susan VanCleve.

I'm also incredibly grateful to my fantastic focus group of parents and teens, who I won't name to protect confidentiality of sharing their experiences, but you know who you are, and I am so *very* grateful to each one of you!

The people in my church family are so precious to me. There are so many in my cloud of witnesses, I couldn't possibly thank them all here. I'm especially grateful to those in the worship ministry and children's and youth ministry, alongside whom I've served and walked through the lowest valleys and the highest mountaintops. You know who you are, but I'd like to especially call out my former worship pastor Bill, who has been a most faithful encourager and prayer warrior. He was the first one to give me a microphone to speak, and I haven't stopped speaking since. I'm grateful for all our ministerial staff, my dear friends and co-laborers. Thank you to my pastor, who spent many hours reading and reviewing manuscript drafts. His guidance and suggestions, along with those of other pastors in my community, helped shape the spiritual aspect of this book to be much stronger and clearer.

I'd like to thank the people in the writing process whose dedication to their ministry helped create a pathway for me to use my voice. First, a heartfelt thank-you to Lysa TerKeurst, whose She Speaks conference served as the unexpected but delightful catalyst in this book-writing journey. It's amazing to me that her commitment to the

Lord to amplify other voices created this opportunity that brought me here. I'd like to thank Robin Jones Gunn, whose books have nourished my faith since my teen years and who was kind enough to correspond words of encouragement with me. She also connected me to hope*writers, an important support and learning community throughout this process. I'd like to thank my agent, Teresa Evenson, who believed in me from the first video encounter and has been a skilled, faithful, and wise adviser and advocate. I could have never done this without her. I'd also like to thank Kyle Olund with W Publishing, who has welcomed me onto an excellent team who makes me feel uplifted and supported every day of this journey.

I'd like to give a special acknowledgment to Linda Livingstone, president of Baylor University, and Linda Plank, dean of the Louise Herrington School of Nursing, along with all my Baylor colleagues. Having the support of the Baylor community in stepping out in my academic role on this faith-based platform to integrate science and faith, calling and vocation, and service and leadership would not have been possible anywhere else. Dr. Livingstone often says, "The world needs a Baylor," and for me, Baylor has completely transformed my world.

ABOUT THE AUTHOR

Jessica L. Peck, DNP, APRN, CPNP-
PC, CNE, CNL, FAANP, FAAN

Dr. Jessica L. Peck has been a pediatric nurse practitioner for twenty years. A native Texan, she is a clinical professor at the Baylor University Louise Herrington School of Nursing as well as president of the National Association of Pediatric Nurse Practitioners. Most importantly, she has been happily married to a rocket scientist for nearly twenty-five years and is a mom of four teens.

A passionate advocate for underserved children and anti-trafficking, Dr. Peck equips families to promote physical, mental, emotional, relational, and spiritual health. She especially loves encouraging parents in her clinical practice and equipping them to build healthy relationships with their children. She speaks to nurses all over the world while also reaching out to more parents so they feel engaged, equipped, encouraged, and empowered to raise resilient, holistically healthy kids.

Dr. Peck is an accomplished author of dozens of clinical articles for peer-reviewed journals, is a regular contributor for parenting magazines, and is a frequent guest on radio and television shows to promote the health of children. She is a regular guest on *The Nurse Practitioner Show* on Sirius XM's Doctor Radio and has also appeared on syndicates for CBS, NBC, ABC, and Fox.